Advanced Scientific Methods for Environmental Safety and Economic Development

Advanced Scientific Methods for Environmental Safety and Economic Development

Dr. A. Raja Sekhar

SERIALS PUBLICATIONS
NEW DELHI (INDIA)

First Published – 2011

ISBN: 978-81-8387-437-3

Published by

SERIALS PUBLICATIONS
4830/24, 1st Floor, Ansari Road
Darya Ganj, New Delhi-110002 (India)
Phone : 23245225. Fax : 91-11-23272135
E-mail : serials@sify.com
serialspublications.india@gmail.com
Website : www.serialspublications.com

CONTENTS

SECTION – III
Urbanisation and Environment

SECTION – IV

Law & Government Policy and Environment

ACKNOWLEDGEMENTS

It is my pleasant duty to place on record my gratitude to a number of individuals and institutions. I would like to express my grateful acknowledgements to the authors who contributed their articles.

I deem it a distinct pleasure to express my indebtedness and deep sense of gratitude to the Management of Hindu College, Guntur in general and Sri SVS Somayaji, President, Hindu College Committee and to Sri MVRK Muthyalu, Secretary & Correspondent, Hindu College Committee in particular for their constant encouragement and cooperation. I am also thankful to Dr. T. Nageswara Rao, Principal, Hindu College; and to Sri S. Ravi Babu, Vice-Principal, Hindu College, Guntur.

My chief debt of gratitude in preparation of this book goes undoubtedly to *late* Prof. G, Raghava Reddy, Tirupathi, who is my Guide, Mentor, Philosopher and every thing.

My sincere thanks are due to Sri. A. Leelamohan Rao, Sr. Lecturer in Economics (Retd.), Government College for Women, Guntur and to Dr. P. Venu Gopal, Lecturer in Economics, Hindu College, Guntur.

I am also very much thankful to other collogues in my department Dr. P. Vasudeva Rao, Reader in Economics; Smt. K. Vydehi, Sr. Lecturer in Economics and Dr. LSN Prasad, Reader in Economics for their continued support and encouragement.

I express my heartful thanks to my wife Smt. Neela Krishna Veni, Lecturer in Commerce, Hindu College; my son Mr. AVS Rahul Chandra (USA) my daughter Chy. Sahithi Sravanthi and to my parents who had much to contend with during the preparation of this work.

I extend my sincere thanks to Mr. T. Nagaraja and Smt Ch. Rama Lakshmi, Computer Operators who helped me in bringing out the final prints.

Finally, I wish to express my sincere thanks to the Serials Publishers, New Delhi for their kind support and interest in publishing the volume.

INTRODUCTION

Economic development is often intricately intertwined with agriculture modernization and commercialization on the one hand and the growth of modern industry, transport and energy sectors and services on the other and there is a direct relationship between commercial energy consumption and the level of economic development and the extent of environmental pollution. Pollution costs are being computed and deducted from the GNP to arrive at the Net Economic Welfare of any Nation. Therefore, the preservation of the natural environment and rational use of non-renewable resources is a pre condition for sustainable development.

The Environmental Problems of a country vary with its stage of development, structure of its economy, production, technologies in use and its environmental policies. Some problems may be associated with the lack of economic development. Enormous economic activity, compounds further environmental imbalance.

The time may be ripe for using 'sci-tech' tools to solve the most pressing needs of the world's poorest countries in food, water natural resource management, environment pollution, climate change and health. New challenges such as the choice between major energy sources, mining, agricultural strategies, industrial development, urbanization, growing concerns about global climate need to be examined as they are related to environment.

All these issues connected with environmental degradation in the context of development in an increasingly market oriented economy need to be examined by an enlightened group with a view to evolving a consensus on some of these matters of vital importance to development policy. In this context, the present book aims to deal with various aspects of Environmental Safety and Economic Development.

The contents of the volume have been divided into four major chapters namely Scientific Methods and Environmental Safety, Environment and Economic Development, Urbanization and Environment and Law and Government Policy and Environment.

Chapter I concentrates on the Scientific Methods to Safeguard the Environment. 12 research papers by different scholars are included in this chapter. Dr. Sk. Chirala, in his article, highlighted the role of Necular Technology in Environmental Safety and in Economic Development in a developing country like India. Dr. I. Satya Sundaram, Dr. B.Venkateswara Rao and Dr. Sudarshana Rao, Dr. G.Vijaya Lakshmi, Smt. V.Jaya have examined the methods to control pollution in agricultural sector. A new approach for sustainable development in India was highlighted by Prof. Dulasi Brundha. Issues relating to Solar Energy were touched by Dr. T. Suselendra Sarma and Dr. B. Syamala in their papers. Prof. G. Prasad and Dr. T. Srinivas, Prof. M.V. Narasimha Sharma and others have examined the health aspects of the problem at micro level.

Chapter II examined the relationship between Environment and Economic Development. This chapter contains 17 research papers. This chapter starts with the article written by Prof. G. Raghava Reddy on the issues concerning of environmental development. Prof. K. Nageswara Rao examined the impact of environmental concerns on agriculture at micro level. Another micro level study of Dr. Prajana Mishra on Environmental Externalities, with special emphasis on Mining in IB Valley Coal Field of Orissa is also included. The remaining articles mainly focussed on the impact of environment on agriculture, industry and concluded with suitable conclusions and offered some acceptable solutions to overcome the obstacles.

Chapter III throws a light on the issues relating to Urbanisation and its Impact on Environment. 11 Eco-environmentalist's papers are included in this chapter. Prof.

K.B. Reddy in his article examined the problems of urban solid waste scientifically. The issues relating to the sanitation were theoretically explained by Prof. K. Narasimhulu. Dr. Sivalingam, M. Sekhar, Mrs. S. Jameelunnissa Begam, T. Jaya Kumar, along with some suggestions. Dr. P. Venu Gopal, in his article, opinioned that improper town planning in India leads to negative effects on environment and they used various census figures to explain the concept. Issues relating to Urban poverty and migration were presented by Dr. M. Tirupalaiah and Dr. H. Sadasiva Rao and Abhishikh Sandeep respectively in their papers. Sri B. Srinivasa Rao in his article highlighted the effects of Stone Crushing on Environment.

The role of Law and Government Policy on the Environmental issues were analysed in Chapter IV. This chapter includes 9 papers by eminent researchers in this field. The first paper in this chapter is on Global Environmental Problems by Prof. Sudhakar Panda. In his paper he offered some solutions at micro level to overcome of the problems relating to the environment. Role of Government in maintaining the Environmental ethics was analysed by Dr. S. Vijaya Kumar. Dr. N. Namasivaham presented treats to environmental safety and highlighted the responsibility of the countries. Dr.C.Basavaiah concentrated on sustainable development and examined the role of Environmental Policies in achieving the goal of sustainable development. The laws relating to the environment were examines indetail by Dr. D. Nageswara Rao and Dr. M.R.S. Babu in their research papers. Smt. K. Vydehi's article depicts the measures taken by the government of India during 10th plan for the protection of environment. Problems relating to Global Environmental Pollution were attempted by Dr. I. Annapurna. She concluded with the concept to sectorial planning. Similarly Dr. B. Saranga Paani examined the issues relating to environment and development in his article.

DR. A. RAJASEKHAR

SECTION - I

Scientific Methods and Environmental Safety

1

A NOTE ON ENVIRONMENTAL ISSUES

Dr. A. Raja Sekhar

"No longer is Economics merely a science of production and distribution; it has to take into account the ecological repercussions of economic activities that could affect both production and distribution"

– *Arun Balasubramaniam*

INTRODUCTION

Environment has an important role to play in affecting the life of a man. The term Environment means the surrounding conditions. The elements of Environment are broadly subdivided into two categories namely Natural Elements and Cultural Elements. The major Natural Elements are Lithosphere, Hydrosphere, Atmosphere and Biosphere. The Cultural Elements are the products of human activities and include buildings, industries, roads, fields etc., The Environment is an integrated system in which all its elements act and react in such a way that a balance is always maintained.

With the advancement of Science and Technology man has become the master of the Environment. Though Environment influences man, man in turn also changes his Environment. The relation between Man and Environment has changed over a period of time owing to changing needs and aspirations of the people. Man is a user of the Environment for his developmental activities and always disrupt the natural system and creates a background for Environmental degradation. When this degradation is lesser, nature recovers it by its own system of recovery, but whenever its quantity is more it creates an imbalance in nature.

Environmental degradation has emerged as a major global challenge for human survival in the recent past. Modernization is steadily transforming the nature into products. The resource squeeze has led to an ever-intensification of ecological damage. The strains of the ecological crisis are so apparent that the task to preserve and protect the Environment has become the primary requisite of the economics of development. Therefore, Man has to live in perfect adjustment with the Environment by understanding the delicate ecological balance in the Environment. Environment protection is a concern of great importance to mankind. Conservation and planned development of resources would enable the earth to sustain future generations. Otherwise, there is the danger of man becoming extinct in a few centuries owing to degradation of environment.

The challenge we face today is to reconcile the demands of population growth, the desire for continued industrial development and the need to preserve our environment. We must find new approaches to industrial development both in developed and developing countries, that will allow us to preserve the ability of our environment to sustain us. In short, we must achieve ecologically sustainable industrial development. The only way to do this is to reduce the pollution intensity of industrial activities. The term sustainable development was brought into common use by the world commission on environment and development in its seminal report called Our Common Future. Despite a wide acceptance of sustainable development no single definition is yet available which every effort today accepts. Most of the definitions are built upon the view expressed by the Brundtland commission which defines sustainable development as development that meets the needs of the present generation without compromising the ability of the future generations to meet their own needs. According to Mutofa K Tolba of UNEP the concept of sustainable development implies-development should not degrade environmental quality, nor should it reduce productivity in the long run. Sustainable Industrial Development should be the objective of us and to reach this goal economics of environment is a tool that helps us with costs, benefits computation and analysis. Industry is a major contributor to the environmental concerns. It includes activities such as manufacturing, mining, utilities and construction.

LINK BETWEEN ECONOMICS AND ENVIRONMENT:

The economic activities of humanity have a profound impact on the natural environment in the form of rapid depletion of natural resource stock as well as through pollution. It is only with the transformation of environmental goods into economic goods that economists started applying economic principles and theories to environmental issues. The demand for environment quality is highly income-elastic and environmental quality is a luxury item for many.

Hence there is a trade off between environmental quality and other goods and services i.e., the provision of environmental quality involves opportunity cost. The presence of opportunity cost in the provision of environment quality makes environmental problem an economic problem and calls for the integration of economic mechanism and environmental issues for the efficient management of environmental resources.

Prof.Larry Ruff says that we are going to make little real progress in solving the problem of pollution until we recognize it for what primarily it is an economic problem. The conflict arises as a result of the incompatibility of the basic ecological principle of stability as a pre condition for the sustainability of ecological system and the economic principles of business profitability, economic growth. To restore harmony to reconcile the interests of human beings and nature an ecological reorientation of the Economic Policy is required.

Failure to recognize the prices of the economic functions of the environment on account of the absence of market for environmental goods and services have resulted in misallocation and mismanagement of resources. The economy is clearly a part of the environment as much as the environment could be seen as part of the economy. Hence a meaningful solution of environmental problems calls for an interdisciplinary integrated approach.

The theoretical basis of environmental economics centers on the issues of deviations from optimum efficiency conditions and the solutions for these deviations involve equity considerations. Hence it may be rightly said environmental economics is a branch of Welfare Economics. The adverse effects of our actions on the quality of environment are explained by Economics of Pollution. The word environment consists of physical, social, economic, aesthetic environments.

The firm actually has an economic incentive to pollute. It is cheaper to pollute the air than it is to make needy arrangements to reduce pollution before discharging wastes into air. So long as the firm is not legally prevented from doing so, a rational firm will pollute and not treat its emissions.

ENVIRONMENT AND SUSTAINABLE DEVELOPMENT

The UN Conference on Environment at Stockholm in june,1972 heralded the first serious effort to take note of the environmental issues at the global level. Ever since then concepts like environmental sustainability and carrying capacity of earth have become central themes for policy making around the world. The UNCED in 1992 in Rio, known as the Earth Summit provided further momentum for change. The implementation of national strategies for sustainable development in all countries by 2005 so as to ensure that current trends in the loss of environmental resources are effectively reversed at both global and national levels by 2015.

Integrating environmental concerns with developmental issues has become sine qua non of policy planning. There is widespread agreement that development is critically linked with the state of environment and vice versa. Environmental degradation, in most of the developing countries, is becoming a major constraint on future growth and development. The real costs of environmental degradation are increasingly felt in terms of health costs, declining productivities of natural resources like land, water, grass lands, etc. the impacts are widespread and conspicuous in land hunger agrarian economies like India. Though the impacts, in terms of loss of production, are not discernible at the macro level, the problem is of very serious concern at the regional level.

The two way relationship of natural and economy gave the concept of environmental sustainability of the development process by pointing out the biophysical limits to use of nature as a source of resources and sink for waste disposal. Few argue that resource substitution would correspond to technology substitution and would result in change in waste composition with their attendant differential impact on the eco system. The problem becomes particularly acute if the wastes flow into sink and affect nature's life support function and bio-diversity. (solow,1974, Pearce et al 1989).

The conflict between economic and ecological principles is an issue of ethics relating to how the natural world is valued in which human beings evolved and reached the present stage of civilization. The main issue of contention has whether the well-being index or the stocks of natural resources would be required to be non-declining over time for characteristics of sustainability.(ehrlich,1988)

Sustainable development, the concept of enhancing the living conditions while ensuring the stream of future consumption rates to be at least the same as of now can be taken as the most acceptable guiding principle. The different approaches to operationalise and implement sustainable development are Hartwrik's Approach, London School Approach, Safe Minimum Approach And Daly's Approach.

The most objective and potentiality measurable criterion for sustainable development is the preservation of the productivity and full functioning of natural resource base. Sustainable development necessarily involves the pursuit of economic efficiency social equity and environmental protection. It requires policies and projects to be designed and implemented in such a way that environmental degradation is anticipated and minimized rather than first reacted to alter the damage has occurred.

ENVIRONMENT AND INTERNATIONAL TRADE

Globalization and environment have the issues at debate ever since the developed countries became industrialized. In the process of rapid industrialization, the developed countries had prospered at the cost of exploitation of natural resources of underdeveloped nations. The rapid industrialization and construction activities, globalization process in the underdeveloped nations too caused many environmental problems. In the Uruguay Round, a relationship between trade and sustainable development was emphasized.

AIR POLLUTION

The atmosphere is an insulating blanket around the earth. It is source of essential gases,maintains a narrow difference of day and night temperatures and provides a medium for long distance radio communication. It also acts as shield around the earth against lethal UV radiations. With out atmosphere, there will be no lightening, no wind, no clouds, no rains, no snow and no fire. But now clean air no longer be taken for granted. Today, the air in most parts of the world is severely polluted and this pollution has a tremendous impact on the environment as well as human beings.

WHO'S DEFINITION

Air pollution is defined by WHO as "the presence in the air of substances put thereby acts of man in concentrations sufficient to interfere with the comfort, safety, or health of man or with the full use or enjoyment of his property. The presence of contaminants in the atmosphere is considered to be in sufficient quantities and duration, to cause them to be injurious to human health, animal and plant life, and reduce welfare in general.

SOURCES AND POLLUTANTS

Air pollution results mainly from gaseous emissions of industry, thermal power stations, automobiles, domestic combustions, smoke from the fire etc. From the different sources of air pollution, a variety of pollutants are released in to atmosphere.

Particulate matter . PM (one of the main pollutants): These are fly ash, dust, grit and other suspended particulate matter released from power plants and industries (stone crushers) The smoke of automobiles and thermal power and hot mix plants, stone crushers etc also contribute to CO. level in air. The smoke, fog, mist, dust, soot etc in the smog reduce the visibility, damage crop, and cause corrosion of metals, stones, building materials, painted surfaces, paper, leather etc.

Particle pollution is the term for particles found in the air, including dust, dirt, soot, smoke, and liquid droplets. They come from a variety of sources such as cars, trucks, buses, factories, construction sites, tilled fields, unpaved roads, stone crushing, and burning of wood. They are also indirectly formed when gases from burning fuels react with sunlight and water vapor. These can result from fuel combustion in motor vehicles, at power plants, and in other industrial processes. Particles come in a wide range of sizes. Those less than 10 micrometers in diameter pose the greatest health concern because they can be inhaled and accumulate in the respiratory system.

What are the Effects of Particle Pollution? (EPA Definition)

When exposed to particle pollution, people with existing heart or lung diseases, such as asthma, chronic obstructive pulmonary disease, congestive heart disease, or ischemic heart disease, are at increased risk of premature death or admission to hospitals or emergency rooms. The elderly also are sensitive to particle pollution exposure. When exposed to particle pollution, children and people with existing lung disease may not be able to breathe as deeply or vigorously as they normally would, and may experience symptoms such as coughing and shortness of breath.

"Particulate matter," also known as particle pollution or PM, is a complex mixture of extremely small particles and liquid droplets. Particle pollution is made up of a number of components, including acids (such as nitrates and sulfates), organic chemicals, metals, and soil or dust particles.

The size of particles is directly linked to their potential for causing health problems. Environmental Protection Agency (EPA) is concerned about particles that are 10 micrometers in diameter or smaller because those are the particles that generally pass through the throat and nose and enter the lungs. Once inhaled, these particles can affect the heart and lungs and cause serious health effects. EPA groups particle pollution into two categories:

- "Inhalable coarse particles," such as those found near roadways and dusty industries, are larger than 2.5 micrometers and smaller than 10 micrometers in diameter.
- "Fine particles," such as those found in smoke and haze, are 2.5 micrometers in diameter and smaller. These particles can be directly emitted from sources such as forest fires, or they can form when gases emitted from power plants, industries and automobiles react in the air.

Health and Environment

The size of particles is directly linked to their potential for causing health problems. Small particles less than10 micrometers in diameter pose the greatest problems, because they can get deep into your lungs, and some may even get into your bloodstream.

Exposure to such particles can affect both your lungs and your heart. Small particles of concern include "inhalable coarse particles" (such as those found near roadways and dusty industries), which are larger than 2.5 micrometers and smaller than 10 micrometers in diameter; and "fine particles" (such as those found in smoke and haze), which are 2.5 micrometers in diameter and smaller.

The Clean Air Act requires EPA to set air quality standards to protect both public health and the public welfare (e.g. crops and vegetation). Particle pollution affects both.

Health Effects

Particle pollution-especially fine particles-contains microscopic solids or liquid droplets that are so small that they can get deep into the lungs and cause serious health problems. Numerous scientific studies have linked particle pollution exposure to a variety of problems, including:

- increased respiratory symptoms, such as irritation of the airways, coughing, or difficulty breathing, for example;
- decreased lung function;
- aggravated asthma; silicosis
- development of chronic bronchitis;
- irregular heartbeat;
- nonfatal heart attacks; and
- premature death in people with heart or lung disease.

People with heart or lung diseases, children and older adults are the most likely to be affected by particle pollution exposure. However, even if you are healthy, you may experience temporary symptoms from exposure to elevated levels of particle pollution.

Environmental Effects

Visibility reductionFine particles ($PM_{2.5}$) are the major cause of reduced *visibility (haze)* in parts of the United States, including many of our treasured national parks and wilderness areas.

Environmental Damage

Particles can be carried over long distances by wind and then settle on ground or water. The effects of this settling include: making lakes and streams acidic; changing the nutrient balance in coastal waters and large river basins; depleting the nutrients in soil; damaging sensitive forests and farm crops; and affecting the diversity of ecosystems..

Aesthetic Damage

Particle pollution can stain and damage stone and other materials, including culturally important objects such as statues and monuments.

"Env.Impact Assessment (Govt. Of India) For Stone Crushing Industry" Definition: Particulate Matter:

Effect on Visibility: Due to absorption and scattering of light by airborne particulates, the visibility gets reduced. The sky frequently appears gray, and in severe cases, the tops of nearby buildings are obscured.

Effect on Materials, Vegetation and Animals: Particles will soil painted surfaces, clothing, and curtains merely by settling on them. The cost of repainting interior and exterior surfaces of homes and buildings and of cleaning or replacing textiles is estimated at hundreds of millions of dollars annually.

Particulate matter can cause direct chemical damage by corrosion.

Little is known of the effects of particulate matter in general on vegetation. However, several specific substances have been observed to cause some damage. Cement-kiln dust in combination with mist or light rain has been observed to form a crust on the leaves of plants, resulting in plant damage. Particles containing fluorides appear to cause some plant damage, and magnesium oxide falling on agricultural soils has resulted in poor plant growth.

An animal's health may suffer when the animal feeds on plants covered by toxic particulate. Fluorosis in animals has been attributed to their ingestion of vegetation covered with a fluoride-containing particulate matter. Cattle and sheep that have ingested vegetation on which arsenic containing particles have settled have been victims of arsenic poisoning.

Effects of Atmospheric Particulate Matter on Human Health: It is extremely difficult to obtain a direct relationship between exposure to various concentrations of particulate matter and the resulting effects on human health. However, statistical analysis of data indicate a relationship between increases in particulate concentration and rises in the number of clinic and hospital visits for upper respiratory infections, cardiac diseases, bronchitis, asthma, pneumonia, emphysema, and the like. Deaths of elderly persons afflicted with respiratory diseases and cardiac conditions also show an increase during periods when the concentration of particulate matter is unusually high for several days. A growing volume of evidence indicates that much of the particulate matter in the atmosphere is carcinogenic in nature.

In some cases it has been observed that exposure to particulate in combination with other pollutants such as SO_2 produces more severe health deterioration than does exposure to each pollutant separately

There is one to one correspondence between industrial growth and environmental degradation. Experience suggests that industrial growth results in adverse effect on Ecological balance. The industrial policies do not take environmental aspects into account. Although environmentalists measure the costs of pollution, there are no effective policy instruments to guarantee compliance. The main reasons for industrial pollution are weak institutions, lack of cost effective technologies, political interference, nexus between industry, bureaucracy and politicians absence of awareness and weak bargaining power of the victims. The expected spurt in the industrialization in the coming years is bound to aggravate the problems related to environment. The thrust sectors are among the worst polluters and hence extra caution is needed. Strengthening the institutional structure is a precondition for proper implementation of the existing pollution controls and ensuring compliance. Equal priority should be given to clear the present mess. The sufferings of the people continue unabated despite numerous protests and the appointment of a judicial committees nothing much is expected from these enquiries unless there is a change in the attitude of the state, implementing agencies and the industry.

REFERENCES

Bijendra Ahlawat (2002), "Govt. Developing Stone Crusher Zones to Augment Revenue", Tribune News Service.

Sachchidananda (1997), "Voluntary Action and Alternative Developmnet in Tribal Areas", DK Print World Pvt Ltd., New Delhi.

Centre for Resources and Environment, Hyderabad (2001), "Rock Mining in Hyderabad: Assessment of the Industry and its Impact on Environment."

CPCB, New Delhi, "Data on Air Quality Trends."

Department of the Environment and Heritage (2005), Australia, "Air Quality Fact Sheet."

Environmental Protection Agency, USA, data, Website.

EPTRI, Hyderabad, Andhra Pradesh (2004), "State of the Environment."

http://minerals.usgs.gov/minerals

L. Renganathan (December 17th, 2006), "Stone Crushers Belch misery on Villages in Tamil Nadu", The Hindu.

Naik D.P., Ushamalini, Somashekar R.K. (2005), Jnana Bharathi, Bangalore University, Bangalore) "Reduction of Protein and Chlorophyll Contents in Some Plant Species due to Some Stone Quarrying Activity" Environ Polln Contl J, 8 (2) (2005),42-44.

National Institute of Occupational Health (NIOH), "Generation of Database on Occupational Diseases."

Quetta, Pakistan, "Quantitative Estimation of Dust Fall and Smoke Particles in Quetta Valley" Sami. et.al./J Zhejiang Univ Science B 2006 7(7):542-547

Tribune News Network Website.

V.B. Ghotkar, B.R. Maldhure, S.P. Zodpey (1995), "Involvement of Lung and Lung Function Tests in Stone Quarry Workers", Indian J. Tub.,42, 155.

2

NUCLEAR TECHNOLOGY IN ENVIRONMENTAL SAFETY AND ECONOMIC GROWTH

S.K. Chirala

Human knowledge and human progress go hand in hand. As knowledge expands the potential for development grows. Over the last century, nuclear science and technology have played an increasingly important role in improving human well-being and the world around us. **Nuclear age :** Nuclear energy was harnessed to produce electricity, preserve food, eradicate insect pests, grow better crops and combat cancer. **Nuclear technology for sustainable economic development :** The time may be ripe for using "sci-tech" tools, particularly nuclear-related ones to solve the most pressing needs of the world's poorest countries in food, water, natural resources management, environmental pollution, climatic change and health. New challenges such as the choice between major energy sources, growing concerns about global climate are being addressed by nuclear technology Eradication of the tsetse fly, isotope hydrology in saving the people of Bangladesh from arsenic poisoning, nuclear medicine for early detection and cure of cancer are few examples of nuclear technologies are work.

AGRICULTURE

Strong radiation has been successfully used in developing over 1500 new strains of food crops and plants that give better yield and more resistant to heavy rain, frosts or pests than the original species.

Biofertilizers: More economical use of fertilizers while avoiding environmental pollution is made possible by nuclear methods which assess crop residues and locally available wastes, including radiation sterilized sewage sludge as ecologically sound nutrient sources. Biofertiliser- biologically fixed nitrogen-more than doubled grain yields on farms across Zimbabwe.

Sterile Insect Technique (SIT) : Radiation has been used to control the Tseste fly in Zanzibar, the Mediterrainean fruit-fly in Mexico and the New world screw worm in southern USA and North Africa.

MEAT AND MILK OUTPUT

Better feed from local resources: Urea-molasses block : Isotopes provide unique information about the nutrition of farm animals thereby increasing the animal productivity and improved nutrition and health of consumers..

Food Preservation : 20% of food stuffs spoils before reaching the consumer. Irradiated food keeps or several months. Eliminates parasites like trichinae and pathological bacteria like salmonella.

Improved Water Use : Application of the modern irrigation technologies using sprinklers, mini sprayers and drippers is enhanced with the use of neutron moisture gauzes, nuclear-based instruments that accurately measure soil moisture content and optimise water usage and prevent wastage.

FOOD FOR ALL

- More than 800 million people, mainly in africa and asia suffer from hunger
- Most depend on agriculture and many on imported food or relief aid

- Food and Agriculture Organisation (FAO) of the united nations : food for all
- In 1997 : world summit : 180 countries participated and resolved to reduce the number of malnourishd people by half by 2015
- Determination, resources, technologies and effcetive startegies are the cornerstones to achieve food for all.

TAKING THE LEAD FROM NATURE

- Drought, insects and disease : affect plant growth and crop qulaity and are beyond farmer's control
- Difficult to create ideal growing conditions
- By plant genetics and radiation technology it is possible to produce plants 'tailored' to thrive in imperfect conditions

SCIENCE IMITATING NATURE

- Mutations occur naturally, extremely rarely, due to mistakes in dna replication
- Contolled use of ionising radiation : increases the natural diversity 10,000 fold
- Development of new varieties is accelerated
- Identify and select strains with desired characteristics
- Develop cultivars for direct use or further cross breeding

IN VITRO CULTURE

- Invitro culture of irradiated plant tissue
- Plants that do not produce seeds
- Improve staple crops: banana, cassava, sweet potato

MUTANT VARIETIES

- 2 million hectares of cotton are cultivated in the punjab province of pakistan with new mutant strain

- Raw cotton, edible oil and animal seed cake : 800 million us$
- Rice, wheat, maize : 2/3 rds of world's carbohydrate supply
- Rice: 300 varieties Chinese "zhefu 802" cultivar : 11 million hectares :1986-94
- Mutant of naked barley: "una-la molina 95" : early maturity and high yield : peru

BOOSTING PRODUCTIVITY FROM GROUND UP

- Study of soil-plant interactions : isotope methods
- More rational use of mineral fertilizers
- Organic fertilizers to reduce the need for mineral fertilizers

BIOFERTILIZER

- Biofertiliser- biologically fixed nitrogen- more than doubled grain yields on farms across zimbabwe.
- More economical use of fertilizers while avoiding environmental pollution
- Nuclear methods assess crop residues and locally available wastes, including radiation sterilized sewage sludge as ecologically sound nutrient sources.

BETTER FEEDS FROM LOCAL RESOURCES

- Isotope methods helped develop animal fodder: umb (urea-molasses block)
- Fosters growth, milk production, reproduction and work
- Umb increases milk production by 10 to 25 % and cattle growth rates by upto 200 %

BREEDING EFFICIENCY

- Radioimmunoassay ria to measure hormones monitors reproductive processes

- Determine when animals are ready for breeding
- Diagnose pregnancy earlier
- Correct health disorders
- Improve artificial insemination
- Mexico
- Few offspring : poor nutrition and inadequate reproduction management
- Low beef and milk production
- Better feed and ria directed improved reproduction
- Doubled the number of cows per hectare
- Reduced the interval from calving to conception by 40 days
- Milk output : from 4.5 litres to 7.2 litres per cow per day
- 10 million litres of milk per year in the country

INSECT BIRTH CONTROL

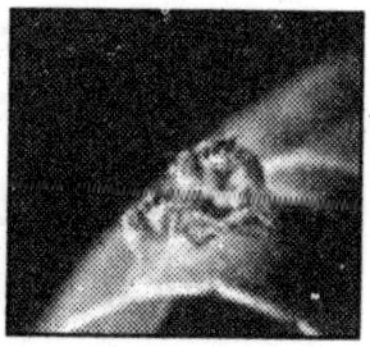

- Sterile insect technique : environmentally sound pest-control method
- Mass rearing of insects
- Gamma irradiation sterilisation of males
- Release in target areas
- No offspring
- Fly factories

FOOD QUALITY & SAFETY

- 20 % of foodstuff spoils before reaching the consumer
- Irradiated food keeps for months
- Eliminates parasites like trichnae and pathological bacteriae like salmonella
- Complete disinfestation of grain, spices, vegetable seasonings and dried fruit
- Long term storage

- Inhibits sprouting
- Extends shelf-life
- Destroy bacteria associated with food-borne diseases

FRESH WATER RESOURCES

- Global demand for water is doubling every 20 years
- Renewable water resources available per person are half what they were in 1960 and are expected to drop by half again by 2025
- Growing scarcity is compounded pollution
- Is water resources are not better managed and protected, shortages and contamination will present major dangers to health and environment
- Application of the modern irrigation technologies using sprinklers, mini sprayers and drippers is enhanced with the use of neutron moisture gauzes, nuclear-based instruments that accurately measure soil moisture content and optimise water usage and prevent wastage

RATIONAL WATER USE

- Isotope hydrology is used for better management and protection of precious water resources
- Groundwater recharge rate could be calculated by measuring tritium levels in the soil
- Sustainable new wells could be identified
- Damascus, syria ; caracas, venezuela
- Radioisotope gold-198 could be used to locate leaks in dams and reservoirs
- Isotope hydrology is saving the people of bangladesh from arsenic poisoning

ENERGY ALTERNATIVES GEOTHERMAL POWER

- Geothermal energy : uses steam from deep inside the earth to drive turbines to produce electricity
- Cleanest way to generate power

- Initial capital investment is high
- Energy costs are 1/3 rd of price of oil
- Sophisticated technolgy is required : waste water containing harsh chemicals must be reinjected into the reservoir and the wells must be drilled where they will not reduce the energy resource
- Isotope techniques provide an understanding of the water and heat flows within the reservoir so that geothermal plant operate profitably

ELECTRICITY : ENVIRONMENTALLY SAFE SOLUTIONS

Argentina

- Like any other form of energy production the nuclear generation of electricity also creates waste.
- Nuclear industry is one of few industries that take complete care of all their waste Nuclear power plant

MEDICINE

Diagnostic Radiation: In many countries women in middle age are checked by mammography for breast cancer. X-rays are used for osteoporosis and fractures.

Healing Radiation: Radiation is used to treat diseases and cancer or as a compliment to surgery or drugs. Telecobalt unit or Linear Acceleartor are used in radiotherapy. In nuclear medicine the radioactive material is ingested and finds its way to the tumour tissue.

Early Diagnosis : is possible at a curable stage.

Sterilisation : Very strong radiation can be used to sterilise equipment such as surgical instruments and gloves and certain drugs that are unable to withstand temperatures of heat sterilisation.

STERILISATION

- Very strong radiation
- That can not stand heat sterilisation

- Surgical instruments and gloves
- Drugs

RADON

- *Protecting the Environment : Radon Gas :* radon is a natural radioactive gas created when radium-226 decays. it comes from the breakdown of uranium found in rocks and soils. indoors it builds up to high concentrations and poses health risks.

  Global Warming : isotopic measurements help assess global warming : grrenhouse effect caused by co_2 from coal and other fossil fuel burning.

  Guarding the Oceans and Seas : isotope techniques monitor marine pollution.

  Cleaning Up Wastes : radiation technology turns dangerous wastes into harmless or even useful material.

- Natural radioactive gas
- From uranium in all rocks and soils
- Outdoor :disperses
- Trapped inside home, office, school : builds up to high conc.

ENVIRONMENTAL SUSTAINABILITY

- Nuclear science and technology can help to understand and mitigate a number of pressing problems
- Global climatic change
- Pollution of fresh water resources
- Contamination of the atmosphere, ocean and seas

CLIMATIC CHANGE

- Isotopic methods help assess global warming
- Rapid rise in atmospheric carbon dixide resulting from burning of coal and fossil fuels
- Greenhouse effect

- Isotopic measurements help assess global warming: greenhouse effect caused by CO_2 from coal and other fossil fuel burning.

AIR POLLUTION

- Asia-pacific region
- Healthy, non-smoking residents
- Showed signs of injury to lung membrane by nuclear techniques

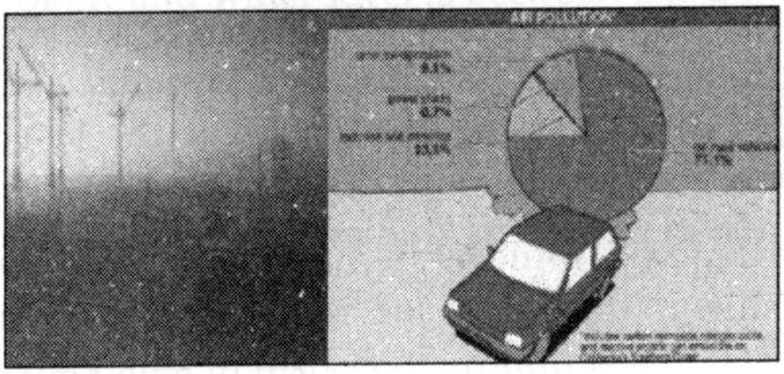

- Severity of urban population problems
- Increase in childhood respiratory problems and cardiovascular problems in the elderly

ACID RAIN

- Emissions containing high concentrations of sulphur dioxide and nitrogen oxides are the main causes of acid rain
- Damages forests, lakes and farm lands
- Electron beam irradiation facility cleanses flant-flue gases
- Gases blended with ammonia and subjected to electron beam irradiation produce high-grade fertilizer

CLEANING UP WASTES

- Radiation technology turns dangerous wastes into harmless or even useful material

- Tucuman, argentina: cobalt-60 gamma ray irradiation plant for decontamination of urban sludge and usage as fertilizer on commercial scale

As the world becomes more reliant on scientific advance, society appears less and less aware of, or perhaps indifferent to, its achievements. If wise use of science in the future is to be assured, key applications for everyday use need to be better understood, not only by decision-makers but by people whose lives they touch. Human knowledge and human progress go hand in hand. As knowledge expands the potential for development grows. Over the last century, nuclear science and technology have played an increasingly important role in improving human well-being and the world around us.

REFERENCES

Building Better Future : IAEA Booklet : Wagramer Strasse 5, A-1400 , Vienna.

Radiation, Health and Soceity : Dr.Bjorn Wahlstrom, IAEA Booklet, Austria.

3

SUSTAINABLE DEVELOPMENT IN INDIA – AN ENVIRONMENTAL SAFETY APPROACH

Dhulasi Briundha Varadarajan, Arockia Raj. K.

INTRODUCTION

Sustainable development as defined by the world commission on Environment and Development (WCED, 1987) requires a boundary condition to be satisfied so as to take care of the considerations of intergenerational equity in resource use. Sustainable development is the total development of the society, economic changes, social and cultural transformation taking into consideration the social well-being and security of the sections (Barbier 1987).

Sustainability condition has emphasized conservation, which requires that stock of all individual resources should not be declining over time. For exhaustible resources, the sustainability condition is to be interpreted as the discovery of new sources of the resource or that of an alternative resource.

Since Rachel Carson wrote the book on " Silent Spring" in the early 1960's, the club of Rome published " the limits to growth (Meadows et al, 1972), The Ecologist magazine published " Blue print for survival and Barbara ward and Rena Bubos published "only one earth for UN conference on human environment against the back ground of nuclear Holocaust predicting "Darkness at Noon", environment and sustainable development have attracted attention of the policy makers and people (Nayer, M.P.).

The two-way relationship of nature and economy gave the concept of environmental sustainability of the development process by pointing out the biophysical limits to use of nature as a source of resources and sink for waste disposal. Few argue that resource substitution would correspond to technology substitution and would result in change in waste composition with their attendant differential impact on the eco-system. The problem becomes particularly acute if the wastes flow into sink and affect nature's life support function and bio-diversity (Solow, 1974, Pearce et al 1989).

The conflict between economic and ecological principles is an issue of ethics relating to how the natural world is valued in which human beings evolved and reached the present stage of civilization (Ehrlich, 1988). The main issue of contention has whether the well-being index or the stocks of natural resources would be required to be non-declining over time for characteristics of sustainability.

Sustainable development, the concept of enhancing the living conditions while ensuring the stream of future consumption rates to be atleast the same as of now can be taken as the most acceptable guiding principle. the different approaches to operationalise and implement sustainable development are: Hartwrik's approach, London school approach, safe minimum approach and Daly's approach.

Hartwick's Approach: The starting point here is maintaining the consumption levels over generations, if not allowing to improve. Then a balance between the use of renewable, non-renewable and man made capital in production process has to be worked. In a seminal article Hartwick (1977) shows that 'as lone as all the profits (rents) from the use of extracted non-renewable resources are re-invested on either man made capital formation or on regenerating renewable resources, the stream of consumption flows remains constant over generations. Then such a development process is sustainable.

London School Approach (David Pearce, Gulies Atkinson and Kerry Turner): They argue that societies should identify all such critical non-substitutable natural resources and must resolve to preserve them. Examples are endangered species, several environmental services such as security, spiritual values, aesthetic values and nutrient cycle. This is commonly known as holding natural capital in fact as a concept but as a rule to be applied for critical natural resources.

The capital theory approach can take account of the role of regeneration of resources and life support in the formulation of the problem. While relating the utility maximization as the objective (Das Gupta, et al., 1997, 1999).

Safe Minimum Approach (Ciriacy Wantrup and Bishop): Closely linked to the non-declining natural capital stock approach is the safe minimum standards approach. The rule is to prevent reductions in the natural capital stock below a safe minimum standard identified for each component of this stock, unless the social opportunity cost of doing so is "unassailably large". It is advocated here that safe minimum standard to be applied to account for inter-generational fairness, resource constraints and effects on human quality of life.

Daly's Operational Principles: Herman Daly sets out four basic rules. First the main principle is to limit the human scale to a level which is not optimal is atleast within carrying capacity and therefore sustainable. Second technological progress for sustainable development should be efficiency increasing rather than through put increasing. Third harvesting rates should not exceed regeneration rates and waste emissions should not exceed the renewable assimilative capacity of the environment. Fourth non-renewable resources should be exploited at best at a rate equal to the creation of renewable substitutes. Daly, while proposing these operational rules hints at population control directed by the carrying capacity of the earth and implementing Hartwick's rule simultaneously. Additionally, he suggests efficiency in using renewable resources while managing the waste systematically. Daly's rules in a way to bridge the gap between efficiency in production processes and externality.

DEVELOPMENT ENVIRONMENT INTER-RELATIONSHIP

Development has always involved mankind to continuously establish a Utilitarian relationship with the environment (Hay, 1978). The issue of development bears accordingly an inescapable dual commitment of geographic as well as ecological quality. The geographical environment acts to control and encourage man to carry development at different area scales of region. This alone cannot cause it to be determining "initialing force" for development (Taltam, 1951).

The Environment–Economy nexus has been the concern of all societies. Along with economic development the nature content and quality of environment are also changing. Kuznets in 1955 hypothesized the newly coined hypothesis briefly referred as "Environment Kuznet's Hypothesis" on the most likely relation between environment and economic development. The Environmental Kuznet's Curve (EKC) states that during the initial phase of economic development, degradation of environmental quality and quantity can take place but subsequently it improves for the better. The increasing degradation in the initial phase is attributed to economic and institutional conditions. Heavy emphasis on economic growth as viewed from capital formation addressed to enhance production and consumption neglect by people on environmental matters, high poverty levels and high income inequality and lack of community level institutions are cited as the main factors.

Thus sustainability refers to both ecological and economic attributes. The most objective and potentiality measurable criterion for sustainable development is the preservation of the productivity and full functioning of natural resource base (Raymond, 1992) one may define sustainable development as the preservation of the production possibilities of an economy to provide the same goods and services including services obtained from the state of nature (K. Parikh, 1989). Sustainable development necessarily involves the pursuit of economic efficiency social equity and environmental protection (Karl Goran Maler, 1996). It requires policies and projects to be designed and implemented in such a way that environmental degradation is anticipated and minimized rather than first reacted to alter the damage has occurred.

Having recognized that the process of development has accelerated the progressive degradation in the states of the world and human conclusion, this paper focuses on problems of environmental degradation caused by India's economic development and an analysis of sustainability commitment component of India's developmental policies.

ENVIRONMENTAL DEGRADATION IN INDIA

Population Growth

One of the major factors behind India's environmental degradation has been identified to be India's population growth and pattern of human settlement. India has approximately 18 per cent of world population and 2 per cent of the geographical area. India's population increased from 238 million in March 1901 to 361.09 million in 1951 and 846.90 million in 1991. The annual average growth rate of population increased from 0.56 per cent in the first decade of 20th century to 1.96 per cent in the 1950's and reached the peak of 2.22 per cent in the decade of 1970's. The 1991 census shows a decline of the rate to 2.16 per cent for the 1980's. By 2001 the size of population in India reached to 102.7 millions. Table 1 gives the dynamics of India's population growth and shows slower phase of decline of the birth rate per 1000 population than the death rate. The almost constant decadal natural growth rate of population since 1970's has however marked the underlying demographic transition experienced by the country.

The achievement of demographic transaction in India has been very unevenly distributed regionally. The states of UP, Bihar M.P. Rajasthan account for about 40 per cent of India's population. The total fertility rate in their states is as high as 6 live births per woman during her reproductive life while the national average is 4 (World Resource Institute, UNDP and UNEP, 1994). This is explained by the prevalence of poverty, high female literacy, low life expectancy and high infant mortality rate of this region (Table 2).

Table 1
Dynamics of India's Population Growth

Period	*Population in Million at the End of the Term*	*Rates per 1000 Population* *Birth*	*Death*	*Natural Growth*	*Per Capita Availability of Farmland ha*
1911	252.09	49.20	42.60	6.60	-
1921	251.32	48.10	48.60	-0.50	-
1931	278.98	46.10	36.30	10.10	-
1941	318.66	45.20	31.20	14.00	-
1951	361.09	39.90	27.40	12.50	0.91
1961	439.23	41.70	24.80	18.90	0.75
1971	548.15	41.20	19.00	22.20	0.60
1981	683.33	37.20	15.00	22.20	0.48
1991	846.30	32.50	11.40	21.01	0.39
2001	102.70	25.4	8.4	13.3	0.35

Source: Pachauri et al.,

Table 2
Poverty Female Literacy Infant Mortality and Life Expectancy at Birth Rate in India

States	*Poverty Ratio 2003-04* *Rural*	*Urban*	*Overall*	*Female Literacy (2001)*	*Infant Mortality (2007)*	*Life Expectancy at Birth 2002-06*
Bihar	58.21	34.5	54.96	22.89	58	61.6
IP	42.68	35.39	40.85	25.31	54	64.4
MP	40.64	48.38	42.52	28.85	72	58
Rajasthan	26.46	30.49	27.41	20.44	65	62
Kerala	25.76	24.55	25.43	86.17	13	74
Tamil Nadu	32.48	39.77	35.03	51.33	35	66.2
Overall	28.3	27.5	27.5	54.16	55	63.5

Source: Various issues of Economic Survey.

Poverty

Poverty being an important attribute of the quality of human life and a factor associated with the state of environment and poverty index is considered as one of the important proxies of environmental indicators of a society. While poverty is the consequence of over population relative to the availability of man made and natural capital endowments, the removal of poverty is a result of partly of the process of growth and partly the policy initials that shape the strategy of development and of distribution of benefits of economic growth.

Table 3
Poverty Measurement

NSS Round	*Survey Period*	*Regional Coverage*	*Head Count Index*	*Poverty Gap Index*	*Squared Poverty Gap Index*
3	August 1951 - Nov 1992	R	43.37	16.05	7.53
		U	35.46	11.14	4.82
		N	45.31	15.20	7.06
24	June 1966 - June 1970	R	57.61	18.24	7.73
		U	47.16	14.32	5.86
		N	55.57	17.47	7.32
45	July 1989 June 1990	R	34.30	7.80	2.58
		U	33.40	8.51	3.04
		N	34.07	7.98	2.69
50	July 1993 June 1994	R	36.66	8.39	2.79
		U	30.51	7.41	2.42
		N	35.04	8.13	2.69
54	July 1999 June 2000	R	35.8		2.18
		U	30.0		2.17
		N	**32.9**		**2.18**

Source: Gaurav Datt.

In India poverty has been measured in terms of the alternative indices of Head Count (H) poverty gap (PG) and squared poverty gap (SPG) indicating respectively the incidence, the depth and severity of poverty with reference to a poverty line of Rs. 49 / per capita per month at October 1973–June 1974 all India rural prices. The head count poverty ratio of India fell from 45:31 per cent in 1951-52 as per NSS round 3 to 35:04 per cent in 1993-94 as per NSS round 50. Even during 54th and 55th rounds of NSSO reveals the same picture. Table 3 gives the rural-urban poverty indices for all the three measures showing that poverty declined also in terms of indices for depth and severity over the same period. Most of the decline in poverty has, however, taken place since 1970 seems to have occurred by 2004-05.

Land Availability

The growth of population pressure with worsening of the distribution problem thus reduces further the resource to man ratio though not only rise in the denominator but also fall in the value of the numerator. The decline in ratio reduces carrying capacity of nature and biological limits to growth and aggravates the problem of sustainable development. Although percapita availability of land and farm land have declined from the level of 0.91 hectares and 0.64 hectares respectively in 1991, the percapita availability of food grain improved from 141 kg in 1950-51 to 193 kg in 1995. Technology has played an important role in augmenting the carrying capacity of the Indian resource base. In agriculture the new technology along with extension of irrigation facilities enhanced the gross cropped area, output and yield at an annual rate of 0.5 per cent, 3 per cent and 2.4 per cent respectively, for food grains between 1950-51 and 1994-95. (Ram prasad Sengupta, 2001:125).

Deforestation

India has recorded forest area of 76.52 million hectares while the actual forest area as per satellite imagery data have been found to be 63-96 million hectares that is 83.6 per cent of total recorded area. The land use of 16.5 per cent of recorded forest area has changed. Diversion of forest land to other uses accounting for 4.696 million hectares between 1951 and 1995 accounting for 6.1 per cent of recorded area.

The presence of population and poverty has made rural households increasingly dependent on forest for their needs. The total fuel wood consumption in India has been 260 million m^3 in 1997 while the sustainable production for the same year was estimated to be 52.6 million m^3. As the survey of NCAER (1985) rural households of most of the populous states had more than 90 per cent dependence of non-commercial energy including fuel wood.

As far as the industrial wood requirement is concerned, it increased from 2.5 million m^3 in 1947 to 34 million m3 in 1997, while the production increased from 2.5 million m^3 in 1947 to

34 million m^3 in 1997, while the production increased from 2.5 million m^3 in 1947 to 14 million m^3 in 1997 meeting only 41 per cent of the requirement (Pachauri et al, 1998).

Soil Erosion

In India the total degraded land area has been 191.8 million hectares due to soil erosion or salinity often involves irreversible as on 1994. Out of which 80 million hectares have been degraded between 1947 and 1994. Out of the degraded 162.4 MH of land were degraded due to soil erosion, 11.6 million hectares due to water logging and 10.1 million hectares due to salinity. The degradation of land due to soil erosion or salinity often involves irreversible damages in the human time scale of planning (Parikh et al., 1992).

The total area affected by wind erosion in India is about 15.5 million hectares with most of these affected area in Rajasthan, Gujarat, Haryana and Punjab. The loss of top soil accounts for almost half of soil degradation while terrain deformation has a share of 30 per cent in the total degradation due to wind erosion of the soil.

In India nearly 3.7 million hectares have been degraded due to nutrient loss located due to wrong choices of agricultural practices and cropping pattern. The total area affected by salinity and alkalinity has been estimated to be 10.1 million hectare out of which the share of salt affected area has been estimated to be 7.8 million hectares. The cannel command area accounts for a share of 45 per cent of such affected area.

Bio Diversity

The ecological balance of flora, fauna has been seriously disturbed by the rapid growth of population, urbanization and industrialization in the present century all over the world. In respect of bio-diversity India which is tropical country has a share of 6 per cent of the world species and has a rich heritage of species and genetic forms. India is the tenth plant rich country of the world, eleventh in terms of endemic species of higher vertebrates and sixth in terms of centers of bio-diversity and origin of agro diversity. The total number of living species identified in India till so far is 1,50,000. Out of the 12 hot spots of bio-diversity two are located in India one in the North Eastern region and the other in the Western Ghats of Southern India (Government of India, CSO 1997, Khoshoo 1995).

Urbanisation

Urbanisation is an important dimension of demographic process of an industrializing country like India. India's share of urban population has grown from 10.84 per cent in 1901, 23.34 per cent in 1981 to 25.72 per cent in 1991. This has resulted in the development of property right violated unauthorized colonies called slums in the developing countries. The slum population of India as on 1991 was of the order of 46.3 million constituting nearly 21 per cent of urban population. The class I cities had 68.8 per cent of total slum population in 1991. The share of slum population in the metropolitan cities has been about 26.6 per cent in 1991. In spite of efforts to control the growth of slums the number of slum dwellers has been growing fast and is projected to increase to 61.8 million in 2001 (Ramprasad Sengupta, 2001:132).

Water Availability

Due to a large and increasing population, the amount of utilizable water available per person per year is only 1250 cubic metres and is likely to decrease further. The average consumption per person is only 680 cubic meters per person per year for all uses. In 1993 only 78 per cent of rural and 85 per cent of urban inhabitants had access to drinking water. About 1,43,000 villages still have acute water problems and many more have unreliable water supply.

Over exploitation of ground water is a very serious problem and the water table has steadily been falling in many parts of the country. There are more than 4.79 million electric and 3.7 million diesel pumps withdrawing ground water across the country. Of the ground water extracted some 90 per cent is used for irrigation and only 6 per cent of the total volume pumped is used for domestic purposes.

Sanitation

The coverage of population by sanitation has been as manfully low as 3.15 per cent in March 1991 in rural areas. In urban areas the coverage has been 47.9 per cent which has also public health implication in view of density and congestion factor of living in the urban areas. Only 3.15 per cent of the rural population had access to sanitation services in 1993. According to CSO in 1993, about 75.7 million people in cities and 563.6 million people living in rural areas do not have access to toilets of any type.

Housing

About 45 per cent of Indian population lives in one roomed housing units with 2.7 persons living per room. The number of home less households and that of population have been 522,000 and 2.007 million respectively in 1991. The share of rural homeless in the total homeless population of India was 74 per cent in 1981 which later decline to 64 per cent in 1991. The estimate of shortage of housing would be 2.147 million in metropolitan cities only after taking account of the congestion factor. The piped water supply and toilets installed in India in India is shown in Table 4.

Table 4
Piped Water Supply and Toilets Installed in India Percentage covered

Year	*Region*	*Total*	*Instated*	*Outside*	*Toilet Installation of Any Type*
1981	RUOverall	10.363.323.0	2.836.110.8	7.527.112.2	NA58.1NA
1991	RUOverall	20.665.132.3	6.042.315.5	14.622.816.8	9.563.923.7

Source: Government of India, CSO .

POLLUTION LOAD IN INDIA

Air Pollution

Clean air no longer be taken for granted. Today, the air in most large Indian cities is severely polluted and this pollution has a tremendous impact on the health of the population. Industrialisation, the growth in the number of vehicles in urban areas and the burning of bio-fuels in rural households has lead to a rapid deterioration of indoor and outdoor air quality. Air emissions in Delhi (Table 2) has an impact on health and property and cutting down this pollution would cost about Rs. 170 crore a year. Investments of Rs. 14 crore would be necessary in the industrial sector, Rs. 8 crore in the power sector, and Rs. 80 crore in transportation sector, while people would have to spend some Rs. 67 crore to clean up at home. This is easily justifiable as at the moment the health costs of pollution are as much as Rs. 117 crore per year and some Rs. 32 crore is lost due to vegetation production losses in the region. The study also revealed that people are willing to make a one time payment of as much as Rs. 509 crore for clean air in Delhi (IGIDR, 1999)

Table 5
Air Emissions Account for National Capital Territory, Delhi (1995) Tonnes/year

Sector	*SPM*	*Sox*	*NOx*	*CO*	*HG*
Industrial	46289	35173	7685	-	-
Power	88743	46030	15221	5602	2776
Transport	9846	3900	54063	135362	55320
Domestic	3462	0	891	27297	-
Total	148340	85103	77860	16861	58096

Source: TGIDR, 1999, p.5.

Transportation Pollution

In urban areas the transport sector causes the most pollution, producing 74 per cent of the Carbon monoxide and all the lead emitted. In the last 25 years the number of registered vehicles increased over ten times from a mere 2.1 million in 1973 to 25.2 million in 1993. In the next 5 to 7 years the number of vehicles is expected to double. The vehicular emission load in 1994 was estimated at 3596.8 tonnes per day in 12 major Indian cities which was a significant part of total air pollution in these cities. Table 6 explains the emissions of pollutants fro vehicles in metropolitan cities of India as on 1994.

Table 6
Emission of Pollutants from Vehicles in Metropolitan Cities–1994
Amount of Pollutants (Tonnes per day)

Cities	*Suspended Particles*	*Sulphur Dioxide*	*Oxides of Nitrogen*	*Hydro Carbons*	*Carbon Monoxide*
Delhi	10.3	9.0	126.5	249.6	651.0
Mumbai	5.6	4.0	70.8	108.2	469.9
Bangalore	2.6	1.8	26.2	78.5	195.4
Calcutta	3.3	3.7	54.7	43.9	188.2
Chennai	2.3	2.0	28.2	50.5	143.2
Hyderabad	1.9	1.6	16.8	56.3	126.2
Ahmedabad	3.0	2.9	40.0	67.8	179.1

Source: Central pollution control Board Air Pollution and its control–1995.

Solid Waste

Solid wastes are unwanted materials disposed off by man which can neither flow into streams nor escape immediately to the atmosphere. As urbanization increases so also does the extent and dimensions of the solid waste problem. For a country as a whole per capita waste generation varies, between 0.1 bio-grams and 0.6 kilograms per day an average of 0.33 kilograms. The composition of solid wastes from cities is shown in Table 7.

Table 7
Composition of Solid Wastes from Cities (in Percentage)

Cities	*Paper*	*Plastics*	*Metal*	*Glass*	*Ash*	*Others Degradable*
Calcutta	3.18	0.65	0.66	0.38	34.00	47.00
Delhi	6.29	0.85	1.21	0.57	36.00	35.00
Nagpur	1.88	1.35	1.33	1.34	41.42	34.81
Bangalore	4.00	2.00	0.00	1.00	15.00	78.00
Mumbai	10.00	2.00	3.60	0.20	44.20	40.00

Source: India's Development Report 1997.

Industrial Pollution

Industry, power plants and the burning of solid waste also add to the pollution load. Some 1551 medium and large industrial units in the country in 17 highly polluting industrial sectors have been identified as polluting by the Central Pollution Control Board (CPCB). Of these about 77 per cent are predominantly water polluting and 15 per cent are predominantly air polluting and 8 per cent are both air and water polluting industries.

Indoor Pollution

Burning of unprocessed cooking fuels (bio-fuels) in homes causes, most of the air pollution in India, Bio-fuels in India consist of wood, crop residue and dung -cakes and in 1989, accounted for roughly 50 per cent of the energy consumption. The major user of bio fuels is household sector. In 1991, 113 million households in rural areas or 75 per cent of rural households used bio-fuels. In 1989-90 some 82 per cent of sulphur dioxide omission, 20 per cent of carbon monoxide omission, 88 per cent of volatile organic compound omissions and about 96 per cent of the particulate matter omissions in the country came from household sector. According to 1998 estimate 0.4 to 0.5 million premature death per year might be due to indoor are pollution (Smith, 1998).

Water Pollution

About 200 million people in India do not have access to safe drinking water. Most of our water sources are polluted with untreated, partially treated wastes from industry, domestic sewage and fertilizer and pesticide run off from agricultural fields. Fertilizer and pesticide use in agricultural sector has considerably increased in the last 2 decades. While fertilizer use increased from 7.7 to 13.9 million tonnes between 1984 and 95-96, pesticide use has increased more than there folds from 24305 tonnes in 1971 to 85030 tonnes in 1994-95.

According to ministry of Rural Development about, 1.5 million children under 5 years die in the each year due to water related diseases. Studies show that better water supply and sanitation facilities can considerably reduce illness and death due to water related diseases. Death due to diarrhea can be reduced by 65 percent while overall child mortality can be reduced by 55 percent. According to Murray and lopes, (1996)

India, loses about 30.5 million Disability Adjusted Life Years (DALYS) due to water and sanitation related diseases.

The main source of water pollution are domestic sewage industrial effluent 75 percent of the wastewater produced is from domestic sector but the sewage treatment facilities are inadequate in most cities and almost absent in rural India. Only 25 percent of class I cities (population more than 1,00,000) have waste water collection treatment and disposal facilities and less than 10 percent of the 241 smaller some 20 percent of all the waste water generated in class I cities and only 2 percent of all waste water generated in class II towns is treated.

According to estimates more than Rs. 46000 crores would be required to construct toilets in the 115 million homes that are presently with out toilets. Under Cranga Action plan sewerage provision in marzipan, a city with a population of one million. Cost Rs. 10.87 crores with appropriate water conservation strategies as much as 63 cubic KM of water can be saved in the agriculture sector, 2 cubic KM in the industrial sector by 2025. The Government has planned to provide drinking water to these villages in the 9th five year plan at a cost of Rs. 40,000 crores.

Soil Pollution

As per the estimate of food and Agriculture organisation (Brandon et al 1995) the loss of production of major crops imputable to soil erosion only is about 7.23 million tones of major crops in 1993. The total annual loss of 5.3 billion tones of soil erosion in India has led to a nutrient depletion of 73.93 million tones, that is, 1.4 percent of total soil loss which has been responsible for such loss of agricultural crops (Pachauri et al, 1998 Brandon et al, 199%). Of this total amount of soil lost, 29 percent is permanently lost to ocean, about 10 percent of soil is deposited in the reservoirs causing loss of storage capacity due to siltage by 1 percent to 2 percent every year. The remaining 61 percent of the soil is merely displaced.

ENVIRONMENTAL COSTS

As Environmental resources are used, there is an obvious depreciation in their value. The costs of environmental

Table 8
Rough Estimates of Economic Value of Environmental Degradation in India

Aspects	*Loss in Billion Rupees*
Human health damages due to water pollution and poor sanitation	360
Loss of crop due to soil degradation	89-232
Loss of wood due to forest degradation	57
Human health damage due to air pollution	885-4250
Total	1391-4899

Source: IGRDI, 1999, p.14.

Table 9
Economy Environment Nexus

States	*Per Capita Income in Rupees 99-2000*	*Sen's Poverty Index*	*Deforestation 87-97 in Percentage*	*Total Waste Land as Percentage of Total Area in 1988-90*
Punjab	13390	0.15	81.07	7.51
Hariyana	14331	0.11	-6.21	8.46
Kerala	10712	0.13	-0.65	4.25
Maharastra	15172	0.13	4.77	25.78
Gujarat	12975	0.19	-7.31	23.36
Tamil Nadu	12779	0.16	-7.16	17.67
Assam	6157	0.12	-9.71	20.29
Andhra Pradesh	9982	0.8	-13.75	21.63
Karnataka	11910	0.18	-0.43	14.14
Rajasthan	7937	0.20	7.01	32.19
Uttara Pradesh	5770	0.22	8.11	22.27
Madhya Pradesh	7003	0.15	2.69	20.71
Bihar	3345	0.21	-7.36	14.85
West Bangal	9778	0.24	-5.24	5.69
Orissa	5187	0.30	-110.70	13.31

Source: Draft version, Environment and Development, 2000.

degradation manifest in forms like reduced agricultural yields, health damages loss of human productivity and material and property damage etc. Conventional national income accounts do not include depreciation of Environmental resource. Rough estimate of economic value of environmental degradation in

India amounts to 1391 billion rupees to 4899 billion rupees (Table 8) (IGIDR 1999). The Economy environment interlink age between the variables for fifteen states in India has been shown in Table 9. The higher percapita income of the six states show that their ranking in poverty index and environmental indicators variables are varied in nature.

CONCLUSION

Sustainable development is the total development of the society economic changes, social and cultural transformation taking into consideration the social well being and security of the poorer sectors. The possible strategies to achieve sustainable development are:

1. Existing industries must be encourage to create environmental and safety cells in their organizations.
2. Resource and environmental considerations must be a part of over all industrial planning and be a part of the feasible reports of every public and private sector project.
3. Incentives for environmentally cleaner technologies recycling and re-use of wastes and conservation of natural resources fiscal incentives to small scale Industries for pollution control and for reduction of wastes.
4. Evolving of institution so as to respond to a deteriorating rural environment by increasing the level of co-operation over common resources. Chopra and Camlet (1996) have shown that property rights have evolved in such a way so as to reduce out migration and improve the management of common resources. Similarly Chopra and Kadekodi (1988) show how the transference of property rights from the state to village communities and from individual to pooled community management has generated benefits in terms of the management of the resource base in selected Indian cases.

5. While the appropriate property rights of landless women and families and user rights of rural community to village commons and forests are crucial to creating a sustainable Development. This state of bureaucracy has to accept and adopt the participatory approach to resource management.
6. Various subsidies on fertilizer, power, irrigation, diesel should be removed. These subsidies encourage their excessive and uneconomical use and further degrade the environment. Even the forest based industries are eligible for a large number of incentives. These incentives prove to be counter productive for deforestation.

So a national policy on sustainable economic development which should include.

- Acceptance of the concept of sustainable development.
- Integration of environmental consideration into economic development objectives.
- Synthesis of environmental dimension in all sectors of development and
- Sustainable utilization of national resources.

Thus we need a dynamic and holistic approach to have a healthy environment for every one for today and tomorrow.

REFERENCES

Barbier, E.B. (1987), "The Concept of Sustainable Economic Development, 'Environmental Conservation 14 (2) : 101-110.

Bishop R.C. (1993), "Economic Efficiency, Sustainability and Bio diversity Ambio 22(2-3), 69, 73.

Brandon et. al. (1995), "The Cost of Inaction : Valuing the Economy-Wide Cost of Environmental Degradation in India, Washington De World Bank.

Ciracy Wantrup S. (1952), "Resource Conservation Economics and Policy, Berkeley, University of California Press.

Chopra K and G. Kadekodi (1988), "Participation Institutions, The Context of Common and Private Property Resources, Environmental and Resource Economics 1, 353-372.

Chopra K and S.L. Gulati (1996), "Environmental Degradation and Population Movements: The Role of Property Rights' Environmental and Resource Economics 9(4) 383-403.

Daly, H. (1990), "Toward Some Operational Principles of Sustainable Development, Ecological Economics, 2, 1-7.

Dasguplaet al (1997), "The Environment and Emerging Development Issues, Vol. 1 and 2, Oxford: Clarondon Press".

Dasgupta, P. (et.al) (1999), "Net National Product and Social well being", Mimeo.

Ehrlrch (1988), "The Loss of Bio Diversity in E.O. Wilson (ed) Bio Diversity, Washington DC : National Academy Press USA.

Gaurav Datt (1988), Poverty in India and Indian States-and update FCND" Discussion paper No. 47, Washington DC : International Food Policy Research Institute.

Government of India, CSO (1998), "Compendium of Environmental Statistics", 1998, New Delhi, (CSO).

Harwcol (1977), "Intergeneration Equity and the Investing of Rents from Exhaustible Resources ", American Economic Review, 67 (5), 972-4).

Hay, D.R. (1978), "Geography and Development", Macmillan Pub. Co. Inc, New York, p.20.

IGIDR (1999) "Clean Air, Environmental Governance ", Indira Gandhi Institute of Development research publication.

IGIDR (1999) "Environment, Economics and Development, Environmental Governance), Indira Gandhi Institute of Development Research Publication.

Khoshoo, T.N. (1995), "Census of India's Bio Diversity : Tasks Ahead", Current Science, Vol. 69, No : 1, p.14-17.

Kuznets, S. (1995) "Economic Growth and Income Inequality', American Economic Review 49, 1-28.

Nayar, M.P. (1996) , "Conceptual Issues of Sustainable Development" in Shukla (et. al) (1996) sustainable Development Stratey, Mittal Pub., 1996.

Pachauri (et. al) (1998), Looking back to Think Ahead : Green India", 2047, New Delhi; Tata Energy Research Institute.

Parik (1989), "An Operational and Measurable Definition of Sustainable Development", Indira Gandhi Institute of Development Research, Bombay.

Parik (et.al) (1992), "National Resource Accounting-A Framework for India", Bombay Indira Gandhi Institute of Development Research.

Pearce, D.W., EB. Barbier and A. Markandya (1989), "Sustainable Development : Economics and Environment in the Third World", Aldershot, England : Edward Elgar.

Pearce D.W., and R.K. Turner (1990), "Economics of Natural Resources and the Environment", Hemel-Hampstead, Harvester-wheat sheaf.

Pearce, D. and G. Atkinson (1993), "Capital Theory and The Measurement of Weak Sustainability", Ecological Economics, 8, 103-108.

Raymond F. Mikasell (1992), "Environmental Assessment and Sustainability of the Project and Programme Level", World Bank Conference on Environment and Sustainable Development, Washington DC.

Smith (1998), "Indoor Air Pollution India", Report prepared for capacity 21 project of India.

Solow (1974), "The Economics of Resources and Resources of Economics", reprinted in R. Dorfman and N. Dorfman (eds.) 1977 Economics of the Environmental : selected Readings, New York: Norton.

Tatham (1951), "Environmentalism versus Possibilism " in G. Taylor (ed.) Geography in the 20th century Philosophical library, New York, p.96.

World Research Institute, UNDP, UNEP (1994), World Resource 1994-95, New York, Oxford University Press.

WCED (1987), Selected Reference "World Commission on Environment and Development, Our Common Future, Oxford, New York.

4

IMPORTANCE OF ORGANIC FARMING

I. Satya Sundaram

The Green Revolution in India has no doubt contributed to the present comfortable food grain situation in the country. However, the food grain production which was 199.4 million tonnes in 1996-97, fell to 192.3 million tonnes in 1997-98. However, it rose to 203.6 million tonnes in 1998-99, and to 209.8 million tonnes in 1999-2000. It again fell to 196.07 million tonnes in 2000-01.

The yields are also low. For total food grains, it was 1636 kg per hectare in 2000-01 for cereals 2622 kg and for pulses 533 kg only. For rice, it was placed at 1913 kg and for wheat 2743 kg.

- Economics say that only the commencement of the second phase of green revolution can improve the situation. In future, we have to concentrate on better use of agricultural inputs, particularly water resources. It is further agreed that agricultural growth in the coming years should be sustainable and eco-friendly. There are serious limitations to seed-fertilizer technology.
- Organic Farming: Organic farming differs from conventional farming mainly in crop rotation, fertilizer applications and pest control methods.

To work in close cooperation with nature is to accept the law of diminishing return and the relationship between in density of input and capacity of the production system.

- Bio-technology offers possibilities for breaking the barriers, especially in the unfavorable agricultural regions. Environment-friendly bio-technologies can reduce pressure on natural resources and can minimise the pollution from the excessive use of chemicals.
- Organic farming depends on compost in the form of a mixture of leaves, manure and plant waste. Organic farming is a system in which the maintenance of soil fertility and the control of pests and diseases are achieved through the enhancement of biological processes and ecological interaction. Also, organic residue from biogas plants is an excellent source of organic matter for soils.
- In organic farming system crop rotation has a pivotal role. Different crops obtain nutrients from different depths of soil and as such soil nutrients are utilised in a balanced way. Also recycling of crop residue may be done by burying the farm waste (leaves, stem etc., left after harvesting) in the field itself.
- Farm forestry needs to be encouraged. Soil erosion is one of the major reasons for the rapid reduction in soil fertility. Farm forestry can reduce soil erosion and also maintain water table. It also offers nutritious fodder.
- For weeling out pests, insecticides made from herbs and trees are used. For example, neem based pesticides have been found to be effective.

VERMICOMPOSTING

Vermicomposting is the process of growing earth-worms in various kinds of waste material and using the excretion of the earthworms as manure which contains NPK.

The earthworms are useful in land reclamation, soil improvement and organic waste management. The worms can accumulate certain heavy metals, industrial effluents, various bio-pesticides and other agricultural chemicals and their residues. They are also used as protein-rich sources of animal feed. They thus act as waste controllers, compost manufacturers, and protein producers. They incorporate organic matter turn over large amounts of soil by burrowing, feeding and castings.

- The earthworms take up into their tissues a number of unwanted organic and inorganic chemicals. They enrich the soil with oxygen and encourage aerobic micro organisms. They enhance the water-holding capacity of soil.
- Research work must continue on the selection and development of appropriate species and technology for Vermiculture, Vermi composting and vermin feed industries as a part of the National Biotechnology Programmes.

INTEGRATED NUTRIENT MANAGEMENT

There is an erroneous impression that higher fertilizer use leads to higher yields. With less fertilizer per hectare, highest productivity is possible. For instance, the per hectare consumption of NPK (US) in 42 kg, but the cereal yield is around 5.5 tonnes. Likewise, cotton yields in India are less than 20 per cent of the yields achieved elsewhere. However, Indian farmer uses 25 times as much water to produce a tone of cotton as compared to California.

We should give importance to Integrated Nutrient Management (INM). INM is a flexible approach to minimise the use of chemicals, but maximise use efficiency and farmer's profit. Over-use and abuse harms the biological property of soil.

INM is based on three principles :

(i) assessment of the basic soil fertility and climate;

(ii) nature of the crop, not in isolation, but as a part of the cropping system and yield target; and

(iii) at least 30 per cent of the total nutrient levels of NPK to be in organic form. 'Precision agriculture' is gaining popularity. It is that form of agriculture where site-specific management practices are adopted giving due considerations to the spatial variability of land in order to maximise crop production and minimise the environmental damage.

Land is heterogeneous, Ignoring this, under conventional farming fertilisers, herbicides and fungicides are applied at a uniform rate throughout the crop field. On the other hand, precision agriculture lays emphasis on judicious crop management at the micro level wherein only required amounts of inputs are applied.

ADVANTAGES

The advantages of organic farming are many, but the following deserve mention:

- Organic fertilisers provide readily available plant nutrient in a concentrated form and generally they do not have any significant effect on the physical properties of soil.
- Organic manures are low in nutrients but play a vital role in the improvement of physical, physio-chemical and biological soil properties; and
- Use of organic manure's alone will result in a soil with improved physical and micro biological properties, use of mineral fertilizers alone will increase the quantity of available plant nutrient and the use of both together will give a soil rich nutrients with physical and micro logical properties.

MEASURES NEEDED

The use of chemical fertilisers and pesticides will have to continue, as it is not easy to revert to the old system of no inputs. These inputs are required to obtain high, sustainable yields, but they need to be used judiciously. A combination of organic manures and fertilisers should ensure increased yields as well as long-term sustainability.

An amount of Rs.100 crore had been allocated in the Tenth Plan (2002-07) to promote organic agriculture. The Task force set up by the agriculture ministry to study the various aspects of organic farming has submitted its report on November 29, 2001. It recommended the establishment of a permanent national board to promote environment friendly chemical-free agriculture. The task force suggested that all state governments should be advised to introduce organic farming on half of the government's farmland. The task force also recommended that all ventures engaged in the production of compost, vermin compost and other forms of substances meant to replace fertilisers and pesticides should be exempted from taxes. There is no doubt that organic farming, in the Indian context, would not only raise farm yields, but also protect the environment.

REFERENCES

Ministry of Finance, Govt. of India (2001-02), "Economic Survey". p.s.-18.

Sankaram Alaya (2001), "Sustainable Pathways for Agricultural Productivity", The Hindu, July 26.

Ch. Hanumantha Rao and Ashok Gulati (1994), India Agriculture: "Emerging Perspectives and Policy Issues", Economic and Political Weekly, Dec, 31.

Ch. Hanumantha Rao (1998), "Sustainable Development in Agricultural", The Economic Times, Nov 16.

Y.L. Neme (1999), "Sustainable Agriculture: Only way out", The Indian Express (Science Express) May 4.

M. Anadam (1998), "Organic Farming for Eco-Friendly Agriculture", Employment News, Sep., 19-25.

S. Rajesh at S1 (1999), "Farm Forestry for better Yield", The Indian Express (Science Express) June 22.

Janardhan Singh and S.N. Rai (1998), "Potential of Earthworm in Sustainable Agriculture", Yojana Nov., p-10.

Radha Krishna Rao: "Earth Warm: Nature's Bio-Reactors", The Indian Express (Science Express).

Sk. Santra and K.L. Bhowmik (2001), "Vermiculture and Development of Agriculture", Yojana, March, p-45.

5

ENVIRONMENTAL IMPACT OF NEW TECHNOLOGY COTTON IN WARANGAL DISTRICT–IMPLICATIONS FOR SUSTAINABLE DEVELOPMENT

B. Venkateswara Rao, A. Sudarshan Reddy

INTRODUCTION

The interface between agriculture and environment is complex in view of its role both as a source and receptor of environmental externalities and non-point sources of pollution. Agricultural externalities, although influenced by scale, location and methods of agricultural production were at most a secondary consideration. On the other, point sources in manufacturing, which could be identified and regulated has become the logical choice for first generation of environmental programmes. Although, new inputs like HYV seeds fertilisers, pesticides etc. and specialization have made social economic gains possible in agriculture, have also created a range of new environmental hazards. The indiscriminate use of these inputs not only escalates cost of production but also causes several ecological problems. The resultant externalities are resource depletion, contamination of water and soil by chemicals, pest resistance, loss of wild foods, restricted seed varieties, mono-culture displacement of traditional varieties etc.

REGIONAL, CROP DIMENSIONS IN RESOURCE USE

The green revolution technology rice which favoured areas already endowed with irrigation facilities in late 60's entered into semi-arid regions like Telangana in the later period with the development of well irrigation. But, soon it has resulted in depletion of ground water in the absence of measures for replenishment and conservation. As a result, irrigation has become major constraint for agriculture in these regions. In the case of fertilizer and pesticide use though India consumers less in average terms compared to developed countries, there are regional and crop wise variations. Tamilnadu, Punjab, Haryana, Andhra Pradesh claim highest share. Among the crops, pesticide consumption is highly uneven, cotton with only 5 percent of cultivated area consumes more than half. Rice and Vegetables are the other crops receiving higher coverage. (32 percent of area consumes 84 percent of pesticides). Added to this, the rate of increase in the use of agro chemicals is considerably higher in the developing countries and the potency of new chemicals is much higher.

In fact, countries like U.S.A. have reduced the consumption of pesticides from 7 to 1 kg/ha and Japan from 15 to 1.5 kg/ha. Though in India, the average pesticide consumption is only 500g/ha, the use was a high as 10-20 kg/ha in certain intensive cotton producing zones like Andhra Pradesh (Reddy and Rosaiah, 1986). These are exceptionally high when compared to even developed countries. Though overall state of knowledge about chronic human health effects is quite limited, the concern has been raised about the consequences of low exposures over long period of time which might cause genetic mutations and reproductive disorders in addition to cancer. (Council of Scientific Affairs, 1988). It is found that pesticide residues in pulses milk products, vegetables are high in the samples collected from different states of India (Balwinder Singh and G.S. Dhaliwal, 1994). The externalities that are arising out of new crop technologies in Indian agriculture deserve immediate attention for their environmental and economic impacts in view of large section of people draw their livelihood and food requirements from this sector. Since resource use has regional and crop variation, there is a need to examine the agricultural externalities in the context of regions and crops. The present note confines to Warangal district in Andhra Pradesh, which has witnessed the serious crisis in ground water depletion and cotton cultivation and has drawn the attention of the government, agricultural scientists as well as social scientists.

The Case of Warangal District

Ground Water Sources: The Warangal district in Telangana region of Andhra Pradesh falls in the semi-arid zone. The geographical area being 12.8 lakh ha, the net area sown is 4.45 lakh ha and accounts for 36 per cent . It has 32.31 lakh population (2001) census) with 80.8 percent rural base. Cultivators numbering 4.73 lakhs account for 14.64 percent. The normal annual rainfall of the district is 1055.7 mm. One sensitive aspect is dwindling rainfall where during the last 20 years, ten are falling short of normal and are occurring in a cyclical fashion. For a long period, the main source of irrigation was rain fed tanks. The Techno-Economic Survey of NCAER 1962 mentions that the scope for large scale exploitation of ground water is absent as the substrata are trap or granite, in capable of yielding prolific ground water supplies, barring few eastern areas in the district. Even then, severe drought in mid-sixties, introduction of new technology rice and the government assistance to promote minor irrigation contributed to the growth of well irrigation in the district.

Tanks have been the major source of irrigation in 1960s, 1970s. In 1980s and 1990s the relative share of tanks has gone down considerably in spite of the fact that the number of tanks have increased. At present there are 5068 tanks in the district. Lack of adequate investments on tanks, poor maintenance, breaches, siltation, occupations have reduced the irrigation capacity of tanks. Against this, the number of wells which were about 30,000 in 1963-64 increased to 2 lakhs in 1994-95. Besides, the mode of water drafting has also undergone a metamorphosis, commencing with oil engines in 1970s to electric pump sets in 1980s to 1990s. Such a change has reflected in a shift from tanks to that of well irrigation. Well Irrigation now accounts for four-fifths of gross irrigated area in the district. In a semi-arid area like Warangal, large scale exploitation of ground water against scientific opinion has led to depletion in the ground water table. Between 1983-84 and 1994-95 there is a net fall in the ground water level to the extent of 1.04 meters.

The departmental estimates for 1994-97 show that general depletion of ground water level is between 1 to 2 meters. The depth ranges of wells in some parts, ranges from 10 to 15 mts. And depth of water levels 9 to 14 mts. Hither to, atleast normal years used to contribute for an increase in the gross water level in the wells but 1994-97 being normal rainfall years, peculiarly water levels have gone down Ground Water Department Survey (1989) has classified not less than 469 villages in the district as dark area in respect of ground water. Deepening of open wells has been almost a continuous activity. The process of in-well bores has been taken up effectively since early eighties and has become intensive in the 1990s, and the rate of success is hardly less than one-third yielding little water and drying up very soon is common. Owing to increased fast of digging wells and failure to yield enough water there is growing reliance on bore wells at the depths of 150 to 200 feet on an average. The failure of wells and in-well bores and bore wells has raised the investment needs and thrown the farming community into the debt trap more particularly, the small and marginal farmers.

Over drafting of ground water in a semi-arid region for a water intensive crop like rice has made the ground water availability a severe constraint to the agriculture and greater irrigation costs to the farming community. Gross negligence of tanks which acts as a complementary resource to recharge ground water further aggravated the problem. Erosion of traditional institutions for maintenance of tanks, declining public support are the other reasons.

Input Use in Cotton Cultivation

During sixties, Jowar (41 percent) followed by rice (23) were the two major food grain crops. Groundnut, Greengram, Castor and Seasamum were the other crops in the district agriculture. Rice was grown mostly under tank irrigation. With the introduction of improved varieties in rice followed by development of well irrigation through farm electrification, rice crop got an impetus particularly in mid-seventies. By mid-eighties, as mentioned earlier, declining ground water tables, periodic occurrence of droughts, coupled with acute power shortages made the rice cultivation more difficult. In search for less water intensive crops, they found an alternative in cotton and chilli. Besides, Andhra settler farmers' cultivation of chillies and cotton on the black soil patches in this area acted as a demonstration to the local farmers. The area under cotton that was hardly 3,548 ha in 1982-83 has been continuously rising and it has reached an all time high of 1.23 lakhs hand emerged as the principal crop in district agriculture both in terms of area and product value. However, during the last couple of years, it noticed slight decline owing to the constant failure in yields on account of several adverse conditions.

Traditionally, the farmers do not have any knowledge about the cultivation practices in cotton. Indigenous varieties were used in the beginning but soon hybrids have become popular and are restricted to two or three varieties like RCH_{2}- Brahma, Bunny etc. Heavy demand for one or two varieties, led to higher prices (Rs.1200 – 1500 per bag) for seed and seed auction system at the village level whenever scarcities occurred for popular brands. These being long duration varieties, cannot withstand dry spells, hence require assured irrigation. It is estimated that each dry spell causes at least 10 percent yield loss. But-only about 40 percent of the area is grown under assured irrigation. By the very nature, these varieties require better irrigation, larger investment and better crop and insecticide management on scientific lines.

As the very nature of hybrids demand more chemical fertilizers and pesticides, by mid-1990s their use has gone up considerably. The average consumption of fertilizers per acre is 400 kgs under irrigated cotton and 250 kgs for unirrigated cotton. Cotton hybrids under conditions of irrigation and fertilizers use are highly pest prone and require pest management. In the early period pesticide use was less, but subsequently in order to control the increasing pest eminence farmers are accustomed fro dusting and spraying once in five to six days without regard to whether pest is there or not. Between July 10 December not less than 20 to 25 sprayings will be done. The average consumption of pesticides in irrigated cotton is between 4 to 5 liters per acre and strong doses like synthetic pyrethroids at early stages of the crop. Today it stands first in the country in terms of per acre use of pesticides. Such a growing demand has increased the number of fertilizer dealers from 500 to 1200 and pesticide dealers and sub-dealers from 300 to 1300 during 1980 to 1998. In the absence of effective extension services, pesticide dealer himself assumed the role of extension agency. Guided by profit, these dealers recommended unwanted high priced pesticides and adulterated pesticides. As farmers in large number could not possess enough cash, were tied to a dealer for obtaining pesticides on credit, at higher prices. The indiscriminate use of pesticides particularly synthetic pyrethroids, mono culture practices has resulted in greater resistance among the pests like Helicoverpa armigera and spodoptera litura. Thus, monoculture of cotton crop retained the pest cycle and indiscriminate pesticide use has raised the pest resistance by at least 600 times in the recent past leading to greater costs to the farmers on one side and fall in the yields on the other.

The externalities of persisting pest cycle and pest resistance have not only reduced the yields of cotton crop but also raised the costs to the farmers. The share of fertilizer and pesticide costs for cotton is about 50 percent in the total paid costs and about one-third in the total operational costs. According to the agricultural scientists at Research Station, Warangal, the use of these inputs is far above the norms suggested for cotton (Chart I). In view of the serious crisis in cotton cultivation in the district from 1997-98 onwards in the form of adverse return cost ratios 0.49 and 0.55 for irrigated and un-irrigated cotton as well as farmers' suicides, agricultural scientists have come up with measures like, Integrated Pest Management (IPM) and other alternatives which will not only reduce the use of these inputs as well as costs to the farmers and make the cotton cultivation. Sustainable. Though few of these measures have entered into the present cotton cultivation, they have not become popular due to the mean reduced use of inputs, they involve substitution of management, skills, knowledge and labour for previously used external inputs which are labour intensive. In the Indian context, such alternative are more appropriate keeping in view the labour abundance, specially for effective utilization of family labour on small farms.

Soil Degradation

Resource inventory of Telangana clearly mentions that the soils in the region are not suitable for cotton, more in view of hard soil incapable of moisture retention and periodic dry spells which occur in this region. The increasing mechanical ploughing and more number of ploughings and inter-cultural practices have become sources of soil erosion. The mono culture practice and utmost care in preventing breeds to grow and burning of the crop residue is not permitting organic matter fixation in the soil. In fact, soil organic matter is a basic resource of agricultural land serving as an important reservoir of nutrients. Moreover the excessive and indiscriminate use of chemical fertilizers and pesticides has been resulting in pest resistance and loss of productivity.

Thus, there is a need to identify the areas in agriculture that have become sensitive from the point of view of resource depletion and unsustainable cultivation practices. The policy design should be to contain agricultural externalities in order to have food security, supply of quality food and to protect the large section of people depending on agriculture. No doubt, the interface between agriculture and environment being complex and is rich with economic and policy ambiguities. Standard economic prescriptions involving emission based policy instruments are difficult owing to large number of agricultural pollution sources. Public persuasion with technical assistance to encourage and facilitate adoption of environmental friendly technologies has been extensively used to address agricultural non-point pollution in developed countries. The direction of policy should be towards encouraging the supply of positive externalities and reducing negative externalities.

Some of the experiences in sustainable agriculture world over offer much scope for adoption to mitigate the challenges of present day agriculture. The herbicide-based zero-tillage first adopted in few crops like maize, soybean is being gradually evolved into a much broader and ecologically sound approach known as "Conservation Agriculture" (CA). It is popular in U.S.A., Australia and Latin America. The three technical principles, which are crucial in CA are I) no mechanical soil disturbance ii) permanent soil cover with the use of crop residues and cover crops iii) judicious choice of crop rotation. It is no doubt that CA is a challenge to the farmers to produce in a more integrated ecological way by following a) Integrated Pest Management (IPM), b) Integrated Weed Management (IWM), c) Integrated Soil Fertility Management (ISFM) and Organic Farming.

Most cotton farmers in Warangal district appreciate that the current reliance on input vendors for expensive industrial inputs, skill and credit is unsustainable, indeed in urgent need of change. Two different directions of change are on the horizon. One is to depend on new categories of industrial input such as Bt Cotton, while other is development of more sustainable practices such as Integrated Pest Management (IPM). As elsewhere, IPM programme which is in under way in Warangal show some promises of success in the future. The programme run by CROPS Jangaon, Modern Architects for Rural India in Parvathagiri CEC in Gavicherla, RDF in Kalleda as also several cotton cultivation practices with zero-pesticides consumption appear to be promising. The success of these programmes hinges on them doing more than simply directing new information at farmers: they must be exercises in reskilling. Self learning is vital for sustainable agriculture as

Pretty and Ward (2001) point out; farmers need to experiment not only to learn what works agronomically but how to coordinate with each other in the performance of agriculture. Integrated nutrient management in cotton experiment (P.Munirathnam (2001 and 2002)) demonstrate significantly higher seed cotton yield as compare to other treatments. The field experiment conducted 1996-97 in Adilabad (G.Srinivas) clearly reveals higher response of American Cotton to micro-nutrients under rain fed conditions, in respect of higher yield and higher additional net returns per rupee spent on micro nutrients Several experiments also report favourable response from green manuring integrated nutrient management, conservative tillage as low cost technology for other crops like rice (K.Surender Reddy and A.Krishna in Warangal and S.P.Singh et. al in Hyderabad and R.M.Kumar et. al Hyderabad) However, this knowledge need to be carried to the farmer fields extensively in the future.

Water being the crucial input, the mining of ground water without reference to recharge has emerged as a serious constraint. Much headway is needed in conservation of limited water through restoration of existing tanks, water shed management, moisture retention methods, choice of crops and modern water management techniques. In view long gestation for benefits to occur, heavy investments on war footing is required which mostly has to come from public sources with local participation. It should be kept in view that the systems available outside should be adapted to the local situations. It is also pertinent to learn from local insights and combine indigenous knowledge with new technologies. No doubt, that such an approach has several constraints and challenges. The practice of Conservation Agriculture or for that matter, water conservation technologies call for a drastic change in the mindset on the part of actors like government, researchers, technocrats and the farmers.

REFERENCES

Balwinder Singh Pollution Hazards of Insecticides in Agriculture in G.S. Dhaliwal (1994): G.S. Dhaliwal, B.D. Kansal (ed) Management of Agricultural Pollution In India, Commonwealth Publisher, New Delhi.

Council of Scientific, Cancer Risk of Pesticides in Agricultural Workers, Affairs (1998), Journal of the American Medical Association, 260.

Reddy, A.S. and Rosaiah B. (1998), Recent Outbreak of Heliothis Amigera is Common in Andhra Pradesh, National Seminar on Changing Pest Situation in the Current Agricultural Scenario of India, Indian Agricultural Research Institute, New Delhi.

Govt. of A.P. Planning and Corporation Dept. (1972), Perspective Plan for Telangana Resources Inventory Volume-I.

Society of Agronomies ANGRAU and ANGRAU Hyderabad (2000), Proceedings of Symposium on Challenges in Agronomic in Early 21st Century.

Society of Agronomies ANGRAU and ANGRAU Hyderabad (2002), Symposium on Low Cost Production Technologies to Meet Global Challenges.

Jose Benites et.al. LEISA Volume 18 No. 3 (2002), Conservation Agriculture: Planting Concepts and Harvesting Good Results.

John Ashburner et.al. LEISA Vol. 18 No.3 (2002), Opportunities and Constraints for Conservation Agriculture in Africa.

Sudarshan Reddy A. and Venkateswara Rao B. Report on Gathering Agrarian Crisis and Farmers Suicide in Warangal District (1998) can be visited at : http://artsci.wustl.edu~stone/suicide.html

University of California Agriculture & Natural Resources, Davis (2002), Conservation Tillage (2002) Research and Farmer Innovation Conferences-Proceedings.

Chart – I : Cotton Cultivation Norms – Practices

Norms/Suggestions from Agricultural Dept. Current Practices

Short duration varieties Long duration varieties

Irrigation essential during dry spells More than 50% of area is un-irrigated cotton

Crop rotation and intercropping Mono Culture

Cattle and green manure 20 percent

Identification of pests, application of pesticides at Right time and dosage, 10-15 sprays Indiscriminate and excessive use, 30 sprays and above 4-5 lit/per acre (Synthetic Pyrethrodis)

Fertilizers around 100 kgs per acre along with cattle and green manure 400 kgs per acre

Measures to mitigate the Crisis by Agricultural Department

Reduction of area under cotton Increased first and then declined slightly

Seed regulation and suggestion of suitable varieties, Not followed properly

Integrated Nutritional Management (INM) Mostly in experimental stage About 5% use micro nutrients

Integrated Pest Management (IPM), 10 percent

Use of biological pesticides, Negligible

Restrictions on the use of synthetic pyrethoroids, Not adhered to

Crop rotation and inter cropping, Not followed

Use of suction traps, 5 - 10 percent

Trap crops to divert the pests, Nil

Erection of bird perches, 10 - 15 percent

Handpicking of egg masses, larvae etc., 5 percent

Proper disposal of crop residue, Burning

Note: The information on irrigation, cotton cultivation used in this presentation is drawn from the Report "Gathering Agrarian Crisis and Farmers' Suicides in Warangal District, 1998" by Dr.A.Sudarshan Reddy and Dr.B.Venkateswara Rao and interviews with agricultural scientists and field observations and farmers' interactions.

6

INTEGRATED PEST MANAGEMENT: A REMEDY TO PESTICIDE POLLUTION

G. Vijayalakshmi

India has been suffering a loss of million tonnes of food every year by pests where climatic conditions are more favourable to rapid multiplication. Pests constitute an important limiting factor in agricultural production.

Pests are a special category of animals and Plants those destroy our economic crops, biological products and transmit pathogens. Pests like several insects, nematodes, molluses, rodents, bitds and weeds threaten human health, comfort or welfare. Pest control is a continuous war fare ranging from those of the house wife, farmer to the global efforts of the FAO and the WHO.

The principal methods of pest control are :

1. *Mechanical and Physical Methods:* Include manual devices like hand Picking of large sized animals, use of hand nets, flame throwers and mechanical traps, heating of stored grains and refrigeration of fruits, vegetables etc.
2. *Cultural Methods:* Include post harvest field sanitation like burning of debris, removal of weeds, Inter cropping, rotation of cropping pattern shifting the

harvesting date and use of genetically engineered pest resistant varieties.

3. ***Biological Control:*** Destruction of pests by the introduction of their natural enemies (parasites, predators and pathogens) by rearing and releasing. Many insects, birds and other animals are parasites and Predators of Pests. Eg. Indian myna Jungle crow, king fisher, spider, bat etc.
4. *Legislative Control:* Some times the exotic species accidentally enter the country through seed transport and other ways. It is necessary to prevent their entry.
5. *Chemical Control:* Pesticides are biologically active chemicals which are used for killing pests. Presently on a world wide basis more than 10,000 chemicals are in commercial use as pesticides and it is estimated that the total number of formulations may exceed 1,00,000 in the coming years.

ADVANTAGES OF PESTICIDES

Pesticides have been useful world wide in controlling such deadly diseases like malaria, yellow fever and encephalitis, which spread mainly by insect vectors. The destruction of weeds and safe guard of agricultural products have been achieved by the use of insecticides, rodenticides, nematicides, fungicides, herbicides etc. India is still loosing annually crores worth of agricultural production due to pests though the consumption of pesticides has been increased from 150 tonnes in 1953 to more than one lakh tonnes with the current estimates.

DISADVANTAGES OF PESTICIDES

The use of Pesticides became most common and automatic to the man. He rarely bothered to see if the pests were actually there in significant numbers or not, but simply sprayed according to a time schedule. The indiscriminate use of Pesticides leads to environmental contamination or Pesticide Pollution resulted in serious hazards to man, wild life, natural enemies of Pests and important industries such as fishing and bee keeping.

PESTICIDE POLLUTION

Post world war II period is the Pesticide revolution age. Major environmental consequences of Pesticides are :

Accumulation of Pesticide Residues

The Persistence of these Pesticides is very high (Toxaphene - 6 years, DDT-10 years, B H C-11 years, Chlordae - 12 years). Pesticide residue disperses from its area of application and drifted towards non-target surfaces, air and a portion build up in soil. A portion of soil residue is absorbed by micro organisms and a part leaked into the ground water creating the problem as ground pollution. Finally the pesticide residue tend to concentrate in food chains (bio magnification) and affecting the ultimate consumer. A significant portion of pesticides comes in runoff water and ultimately reaches the rivers, lakes and oceans, settle to the bottom of water and the bodies of aquatic organisms. The problem of food contamination is most acute with chlorinated hydro carbons, because they are soluble in oils and are concentrated in the fatty tissue of animals. The systemic insecticides which form toxic residues with in plant tissues and may persist until decomposed by enzymatic action or hydrolysis.

All pesticides are highly toxic to animals. Chlorinated hydrocarbons affect mainly the nervous system, parathion on the other hand has a higher dermal and respiratory toxicity. Pesticides reach human being through contaminated food, water and air and cause cancer, birth defects, leukemia, hypertension, sterility and kidney damage.

Aquatic animals like oysters and fishes can pickup and store high amount pesticide residues from their environment and accumulate in their body causing decline of fish eating birds. In 1976 both the Commercial and sport fishing industries were shut down in the ches a peak Bay due to Industrial pollution from a company manufacturing the insecticide.

Pest Resistance

Another problem associated with the continuous use of pesticides is the development of resistance in the pests with time. The resistant population of pests grow faster and damage the Crop with more viour that necessitate the invention of more and more new pesticides. Several resistant fish species like Mosquito fish, Blue gills, Golden shiners have evolved by the heavy use of pesticides. These specides may be beneficial with regard to their survival but cause mortality when a non resistant Predator eats them. The insecticidal resistance is observed in A nopheles gambiae to dieldrin, California red scale to hydrogen cyanide, Housefly to DDT. With in 20 years some 224 species of insects had been recorded as resistant to insecticides.

Affect on Non-target Organisms

Pesticides also diminish the non-target beneficial organisms, phyto and zooplankton.

Our environment has been bombarded with pesticides during the last four decades. There is heated debate on use and disuse of pesticides. Morally it is unacceptable to introduce pesticides into our environment that will have significant effects on our Progeny medically.

INTEGRATED PEST MANAGEMENT (1 PM)

The battle against pest is a never ending one. Pest management is rather complicated, because the advantages and dis-advantages of all pest control measures must be considered before attempting to control the pest. A well designed and carefully executed combination of chemical, biological, mechanical, physical, cultural and legislative techniques are being recommended to minimize adverse effects on the environment conserving natural control methods. This combined technique is termed Integrated control or Integrated Pest Management. This is the ecological approach to pest control and is the only way to curtail the pesticide pollution. In this method besides the combination of above methods resistant crop, microbial agents, genetic manipulation and messenger chemicals such as sex-attractants become mutually augmentative.

Entomologists, agronomists, geneticists and other research scientists are constantly working to develop new cultivars that are resistant to pest attack in possessing harder, tough tissue, excessive hair on stems and leaves and bitter or distaste to pests. There must be proper organization for the effective transmission of results of research to the farmer.

STATUS AND IMPACT OF I PM IN INDIA

I PM programmes are being led by the Directorate of plant protection, quarantine and storage. I PM has brought the changes like :

- *Policy Change :* Government has with drawn all kinds of subsidy and encouragement aimed for the enhanced use of pesticides. One third of total money allotted for pest management in agriculture is using for the establishment of bio-control laboratories and lot of money is being funded by the department of Biotechnology and ICAR for research activities particularly other than application of pesticides.
- *Awareness towards Health of Environment and Man:* Educating and giving training to farmers in taking utmost care while making Pest management decision especially pesticide use. So that there is the possibility of declining in Pesticide consumption.
- *Banning of Hazardous Pesticides:* Government banned already registered but most hazardous Pesticides. Consequently some pesticides have been refuged registration and some are under review and few are allowed for restricted use only.
- *Promotion of Bio Pesticides:* Microbial pesticides and pesticides of plant origin like Neem products and Bacillus have been granted registration.

New Challenge and Future Prospects: Emphasis should be placed on the development of Pesticides that are active at low doses, more specific for the target organisms, less toxic to the user, consumer, wild life, bio control agents and less Persistent in the environment. Continued improvements are needed in

Pesticide application technology and in methods to prevent Pesticide resistance.

Research must continue on genetic approach by encouraging Genetic engineering that will play a vital role in Production of transgenic bio-control agents and transgenic plants which have high bio control potential and ecological acceptability.

The challenge before us is to develop new science, new technology, new management skills and new concepts of integration in order to control plant pests, Protech our environment and provide a continuous supply of safe and nutritious food in abundance for a rapidly expanding 'world population'.

REFERENCES

De Bach, P. (1974), 'Biological Control of Natural Enemies'. Cambridge University Press, pp. 323.

Edwards, C.A. (1978), Environmental Problems caused by Pesticides presented at all India Symposium on 'Pesticide Residues in the Environment' conducted at University of Agriculture, Hebbal, Bangalore in November, 1978.

Jayaraj, S. (1985), Integrated Pest and Disease Management Proceedings of the National Seminar, Tamilnadu Agricultural University (Jayaraj, S. ed.) pp. 423.

Mary L.F. and Robert, V.D.B. (1977), A Source Book on 'Integrated Pest Management', Department of Health Education and Welfare, Office of Education, International center for Integrated and Biological Control of the University of California, pp 392.

Singh, S.P. (1995 a), 'Experience in Classical Biocontrol in India. In: Workshop on "Biological Control as a Corner Stone of Integrated Pest Management for Sustainable Agriculture in South East Asia" (September 11-15, 1995) Malaysia Agricultural Research and Development Institute and Palm Oil Research Institute of Malaysia, Kaula Lumpur, Malaysia, pp. 1-42.

Singh. S.P. (1995 b), Compatible Natural Enemies and Synthetic Pesticides for use in Integrated Pest Management in India. Pesticide Research Journal 7 (1): 8-28.

7

BIOTECHNOLOGY–A TOOL FOR ENVIRONMENT PROTECTION

M.Vijaya Koteswari

Biotechnology as the word indicates, is the product of interaction between the science of biology and technology. Already the products of biotechnology are used in diagnosis, prevention and cure of diseases.

Advances in the fields of molecular biology and microbiology have been exploited in a variety of ways some important fields are for production of industrially important biochemicals including enzymes and basic studies in molecular biology. Therefore, a new commercial environment has been created in which many famous scientists including some Nobel laureates opted to work for biotechnology companies. There are now at least 30 institutions in the country, where a strong infrastructure for training and research in biotechnology has been established with the help of DBT some programmes are now in operation.

The environmental problems of a country depend with its state of development, structure of its economy, productivity, technologies in use and its environmental policies.

Biotechnology is also helping in dealing with environmental problems. Biotechnological methods have been devised for some environmental problems like (I). Pollution

Control, (II). Depletion of natural resources for nonrenewable energy, (III). Restoration of degraded lands and (IV) biodiversity conservation.

POLLUTION CONTROL

Due to rapid industrialization, urbanization and other developments, there is a constant threat to the clean environment and to the depleting natural resources. Resource is a raw material as it enters economy. Environmental biotechnology is concerned, both with the implications and applications of biotechnology in the wider context of environment. In this connection reference should be made to– (a) The first conference on the human environment held in 1972 at Stockholm, where late Smt. Indira Gandhi, the then Prime Minister of India called poverty to be the biggest pollutant. (b) After 20 years in June, 1992 United Nations Conference on Environment and Development (UNCED) as held in Brazil where heads of the states from 166 countries participated to examine the issues involved and the possible solutions.

The time may be ripe for using 'Sci-tech' tools to solve the most pressing needs of the world's poorest countries in food, water, natural resources management, environment pollution, climate change and health fields. It is therefore necessary that the developing and developed countries jointly find a path of development, which "meets the needs of the present without compromising the abilities of future generations to meet their needs," (world commission on environment and development). Efforts are being made to achieve this objective through a variety of approaches, and biotechnology is certainly one of them. There have been rapid developments in the applications of biotechnology, which may help in controlling environmental pollution, thus giving a cleaner and sustainable environment in future. Major areas of applications of biotechnology in pollution control are:

– Cleaner technologies in fermentation technology, paper industry, plastic industry. Bioreactors have been designed where these have replaced environmentally problematic processes, which are environmental friendly. Arrangements have been made to treat the effluents from this system.

- Reducing environmental impact of industrial effluents of distilleries and paper industry by changing old technologies .
- Toxic site reclamation.
- Removal of spilled oil and grease deposits. In this use of Oleophilic fertilizers (oil loving) a mixture a bacterial strains, use of genetically engineered microbes are very important areas.
- Reducing environmental impact of chemical herbicides, pesticides and fertilizers. In this bio-rational or 'environmentally safe' weed and pest control herbicides, pest control and bio-pesticides and viral pesticides are important issues.
- Biosensors to detect environmental pollutants, and environmental monitoring and bio monitoring.

ENVIRONMENT AND ENERGY

The economic prosperity of any region in the world is closely linked with the level of its energy consumption. Industrial revolution led to the consumption of fossil fuels like coal, gas, petroleum etc. The energy demand is alarming and poses a great challenge to our technical and managerial abilities and also to our environment, which is under pressure.

The renewable energy sources offer less polluting alternatives and the following aspects can be considered in this thrust area. The renewable sources of energy are:

- Biomass production and its utilization for energy
- Waste materials for energy
- Bio-gas production
- Large Scale growing of energy crops like *Euphoria asclepiads* etc.
- Short rotation forestry
- Cellulose as a source of energy

– Using hydrogen as a fuel
– Conservation of energy

RESTORATION OF DEGRADED LANDS

Increased human activity has affected the different ecosystems, which led to degradation of habitats including cultivable lands. Degradation is mainly due to salinity, acidity, toxicity etc., Restoration of these degraded lands is a major concern for both developed and developing countries. With the advent of biotechnology, however unprecedented opportunities for recovery of degraded ecosystem have become available through the manipulation of biological systems. The following are some of the biotechnological methods available for the restoration of degraded lands. (1) Reforestation through micro propagation and use of micorrhae, (2) Improvement of soil fertility through the use of nitrogen fixing bacteria, Rhizobium in association with leguminous plants Frankie in association with non-leguminous species, (3) Development of plants tolerant to abiotic stress, so that they may be grown on degraded lands and, (4) use of select and engineered microbes for removal and recovery of strategic and precious metals from contaminated and degraded lands.

BIODIVERSITY AND ITS CONSERVATION

Biotechnology involves the use of life forms for human welfare. Therefore extinction of wild species and destruction of ecosystems has been a major concern of policy makers and biotechnologists. One of the efforts is surveying and conserving biodiversity. National parks and sanctuaries have been established in many countries to meet this objective. Several biodiversity conventions were held in 1992. In a formulated treaty an agreement was sought by the developed countries to allow, as a matter of right, access of every country on the gemplasm or biodiversity available any where in the world. Since tropical countries are far richer than temperate developed countries, such a treaty would have benefited only the developed nations. So the south particularly India had rejected this treaty. In this connection the issue of patents and intellectual property rights was much in debate. Similarly plant breeders rights was recognized in the North ignoring the farmers rights for compensation desired to be given to poor farmers in the developing countries.

Although most countries agree to the need of preserving biodiversity, there is disagreement on the issue of who will pay for it. While the developing countries feel that the conservation efforts will depend on flow of money from rich nations, the latter reject such a treaty to avoid payment of compensation for the losses, which the poor nations suffer due to inadequacy of their efforts towards biodiversity conservation.

Human being has already obtained enormous direct economic benefits from biodiversity in the form of food, clothes, medicines, industrial products etc. Most of our crops were originally wild plants and could be developed into productive crops through selection and breeding. About 7000 plant species have been used as food, but several times this number has been reported to have edible parts and therefore can be used in future. Similarly a large number of medicines have their origin in plants or microorganisms. With the advent of biotechnology, in future, genes from many species will be utilized for a variety of purposes. If biodiversity is lost future possibilities of conservation will disappear.

CONCLUSION

The choice between major energy sources, mining agricultural strategies, industrial development urbanization growing concerns about global climate etc., is the need of the hour related to environment and economy.

There is genuine potential for economic development in the field of biotechnology. The fruits of the efforts made are becoming visible now and it is desired that in the 21st century India should make significant contribution and may also become a leader in South Asia at least in some areas of biotechnology research.

REFERENCES

B.D. Singh (2001), Biotechnology, Kalyani Publishers, New Delhi.

R.C. Dubey (2001), A Text Book of Biotechnology, S. Chand & Company Ltd., Ramnagar, New Delhi.

S.S. Purohit (2001), Biotechnology, Fundamentals and Applications, Agrobios, Jodhpur.

P.K. Gupta (2003), Elements of Biotechnology, Rastogi Publications, Meerut.

8

NEED FOR DEVELOPING NON-CONVENTIONAL ENERGY RESOURCES – THE CASE OF SOLAR ENERGY IN INDIAN CONTEXT

T. Susilendra Sarma

Energy may be defined as any property which can be produced from or Converted into work. Consumption and production of energy indicate the level of progress of any country. Energy is a prerequisite, not only for the comforts of modern life, but also to fulfill the necessaries of life of all people. This energy becomes a 'life line' to any nation.

TRENDS IN PRODUCTION & CONSUMPTION OF ENERGY IN INDIA

Over the past two centuries, there has been significant change in the quantity, quality and complexity of energy resources. Wood and Coal were established as important fuels in nineteenth century. By 1950s oil has become an important fuel and in 1960s nuclear energy began to contribute for human development. The use of cola, mineral oils and gas and hydel power increased enormously as commercial energy in the twentieth century, accelerating the growth in industries, transport and services sectors. On the other hand, the biotic energy resources, which are animal, agricultural and forest based are in wide use in the rural sector, which forms the large proportion in Indian Economy. Animals have been used as important source for agricultural and transport purposes in rural areas. It is estimated that each bullock can produce 0.25 horsepower and generally work daily six hours. Animal dung, agricultural residues and forest produce have been significant sources of energy for the village people. In India over 40% of the total energy consumption is on account of these bio-mass products. This also forms 75 percent of all rural energy 1) Easy availability and non-monitized nature are the major factors for the highest share of bio-mass products in rural energy consumption. However, with the rapid course of deforestation and the mode of social forestry and afforestation programmes the rural people have been losing access to the forest and agricultural residence for their fuel requirements. The poor and landless millions have become poorer in terms of energy says the second citizens report on "The State of India's Environment". 2) Energy plays a dual role. It is used as input in the productive sectors like agriculture, industry and services. It is also a consumer good and is used by the households for lighting, cooking and space warming and for several other uses. It has direct impact on the quality of life of people. With the increase in population and increased development efforts, the demand for energy has also increased immensely during the last century, particularly in the second half. Various conventional energy sources like Wood, Coal, Oil, Gas and Power (Thermal, Hydro & Nucleus) are being harnessed to meet the fast growing energy requirements of growing economy as well as population. The trends in production of various commercial energy sources are given in Table-1. Though there is considerable progress in the production of various types of energy it is a glaring fact that the per capita consumption of energy is very low in India. It is about ¼ th of world average and 1/25th that of U.S.A. 3) Per Capita, consumption of energy in India, in comparison with some selected countries, both advanced and backward is shown in Table-2. Regarding consumption, the proportion of various sectors in total energy consumption are resented in Table-3, which shows, that industries and transport consume major proportion of the commercial energy. Their share in

Table 1
Production of Primary Commercial Energy

Energy from	*Unit*	*Production (year)* 1970-71	1980-81	1990-91	1999-2000
Coal	Million Tonnes	72.95	114.00	211.73	299.97
Lignite	"	3.40	4.80	15.80	22.12
Crude Oil	"	6.82	10.52	33.35	31.90
Natural gas	MCM	1445	2358	18280	--
Hydro Power	Billion KWH	25.25	46.55	71.70	82.80
Thermal Power	"	28.20	61.30	186.50	386.80
Nuclear Power	"	2.42	3.00	6.10	13.30
Power as total (5+6+7)	"	55.80	110.80	264.30	480.70

Source : Economic Survey, GOI, 2000-2001

Table 2
Percapita Income and Percapita Consumption of Energy
(for selected countries 1997)

Country	*Percapita Income GNP(In U.S. Dollars) yy.1999*	*Percapita Consumption of energy (kgs of oil equivalent 1997)*
India	2,149	479
Indonesia	2,439	693
Egypt	3,303	656
U.K.	20,883	3,863
Japan	24,041	4,084
U.S.A.	30,600	8,076

Source: World Development Report 2000-2001

Table 3
Selectoral Trends in Commercial Energy Consumption
(in percentage)

Sector	*1970-71*	*1990-91*	*1996-97*
Household sector	12	12	12
Agriculture	3	8	9
Industries	50	42	42
Transport	28	22	22
Others	7	13	15
Total	100	100	100

Source: Ninth Five Year Plan–Vol. II

consumption which was 78 percent in 1971 declined to 66 percent by the end of the century. Proportion of Agricultural sector has been increasing steadily. However, there is still dominance of traditional fuel usage such as fuel wood, crop residues and animal dung in rural sector.

Table 4
Proportions of Commercial Energy Consumption

(in percentage)

Type	*1953-54*	*1970-71*	*1990-91*	*1996-97*
Coal	80	56	36	29
Oil & Gas	17	35	49	54
Electricity	3	9	15	17
Total	100	100	100	100

Source: Ninth Five Year Plan Vol. II

Table–4 shows the changing pattern of energy consumption of various types. There has been rapid increase in the proportion of oil, gas and electricity from 20 percent to 71 per cent during the period 1953-54 to 1996-97, replacing coal. Proportion of coal consumption declined from 80 to 29 per cent during this period.

PROBLEMS OF CONVENTIONAL ENERGY SOURCES

Conventional sources of energy compromise of coal, oil, petroleum, thermal power, hydel power and nuclear power along with firewood, farm wastes and animal dung. Out of the conventional sources of energy fossil fuels like coal, oil, petroleum and natural gas are non-renewable resources in the sense that they cannot be replaced for a long time, once they are consumed. Hence their supply is limited. On the other hand, the non-conventional sources of energy like solar energy, wind energy, ocean energy, biogas etc. are renewable sources, since they non-exhaustible. Solar energy particularly is the primary source of the energy forms on the earth and it continues to be renewable or inexhaustible source of energy.

The problems implied in the conventional energy sources are broadly two fold. 1) Scarcity of these resource 2)

Externalities involved in their production as well as consumption.

SCARCITY OF COAL, OIL, GAS AND POWER

During the planning period (1950-51 to 2000-01) coal production had increased by nearly 10 times, crude oil production by 110 times and installed capacity of electricity by more than 50 times. (Economic Survey 2001-02) But with higher intensity of economic growth, and rapid population, the demand for these commercial energy sources has been rapidly rising, leaving the supply behind-vigorous steps have been taken by the Government to increase the indigenous crude oil but the consumption of petroleum and oil products has far exceeded the domestic production, and refining capacity. The known oil reserves in India form only 0.3 percent of world's known reserves and it is estimated these reserves will end up within 30-40 years. This situation has led to regular imports of petroleum. The value of imports of petroleum and its products increased from Rs.136 crores to Rs. 45,400 crores during 1970-71 to 1999-2000 (Economic Survey 2000-01). Shortage of electricity has become severe in Agriculture and Industries. The demand supply gap in coal has been increasing due to critical situation faced by coal industry. Thus there is mounting energy crisis due to the short fall of non-renewable conventional resources. There is yet deeper crisis due to fire wood shortage to millions of rural poor, due to indiscriminate deforestation and lopsided afforestation measures.

Secondly and equally serious problem has been the environment damage caused by the energy resources. Mining activity and Thermal power generation are highly polluting activities. Oil production, refining and consumption imply large scale atmosphere pollution, which has risen to irreversible proportions. Hydel Power projects have become a threat to the environmental balance pollution of air, water, soil, has increased enormously. Thus over dependence on traditional fuels led to several ecological and health problems.

In this context renewable energy technologies like wind, solar and biomass become significant.

SOLAR ENERGY AS AN ALTERNATIVE

The importance of solar energy cannot be over emphasized particularly in view of the fact that fossil fuels and other conventional sources are not free from environmental problems. Solar energy is universal and clean source of energy. It has none of the effects found in combustion of fossil fuels. It helps in maintaining ecological balance through the process of photosynthesis and green house effect.

India which lies in the sunny region receives 4 to 7 KWH of solar radiation on per square metre per day with 250 kw 300 clear sunny days in a year.

Solar energy can be used in various ways as follows:

1. Solar energy is converted into thermal or heat energy with the help of solar collectors. This can be used for Solar cookers, Solar water heating, Solar Air heating solar Desalination, Solar Refrigeration etc.
2. Solar energy can be used for Green house effect for growing vegetables, flowers and fruits and also for rearing poultry, or birds. These have been found very useful in hilly areas of Jammu & Kashmir, Himachal Pradesh, U.P. etc.,
3. Solar radiant energy is converted directly into electrical energy by using photovoltaic solar cells are used. But this technique has certain defects. These cells require lot of space and they are not capable of storing energy. This is more costly also. The solar cells are used in aeroplanes, space aircrafts and satellites also.
4. Solar energy can be used for PV Street lighting system, rural radio telephone system, water pumping systems and power plants. In India 10,000 domestic and 5000 Industrial solar water heating systems, 2.25 Lakhs solar cookers, 10,000 solar stills and 200 solar huts have been installed already.
5. Solar pond technology is utilised by suing sunshine, water and salt, which is very cheap device.

6. Solar ponds are installed in India in Bhavanagar, and Bhuj in Gujarat when salt is available. In Karnataka and Pondicherry also Solar ponds were setup. In U.S., Argentina & Israel, they are commercially in use. Scientists have a proposed to trap the abundant solar energy from space, by setting up a solar power station in space.

LIMITATIONS OF SOLAR ENERGY

1. The density of solar energy is low as compared to oil, gas or coal.
2. The intensity of solar energy is not constant. It varies from morning to evening.

However solar technology needs to be developed. India has been pioneering in the utilisation of solar power. In 1972, "Department of Non-Conventional Energy Sources" was setup by Government to promote research and development.

SUGGESTIONS FOR DEVELOPMENT OF SOLAR ENERGY

1. Since photo-voltaic technology is costly a cheaper technology is to be developed. There is possibility to replace PV technology by photo-electro chemical cells, this should be popularised. (This method involves coating with thin film of titanium dioxide).
2. One of the reasons for solar installation failure is the selection of unsuitable materials. This should be rectified.
3. Careful engineering techniques and proper equipment would help better functioning of solar systems.
4. Proper care should be taken in installing the solar plants and proper maintenance is required for efficient functioning.
5. Government should provide funds liberally for R & D operations in the solar technology.
6. Solar products will have to gain market image Measures are to be taken to promote marketing of solar products. Provision of subsidies, demonstrations and propaganda will help the solar technology to be attracted by the people.

The potential availability of solar energy is estimated as 5 x 1015 Whr/year, and potential exploitation is only 25 MW, which is very insignificant quantity. Let us hope that Government's financial assistance and initiative and Scientific Research would lead to fuller utilisation of the solar energy in India in coming future and the energy crisis will be tackled efficiently and adequately by this safest and abundant non-conventional source of energy.

REFERENCES

Ibrahim Hafeezur, Rehman, Kurukshetra (2002), "Energy Demand in Rural Areas Status Agenda for Future Policies and Programmes", Ministry of Rural Development, New Delhi, October, pp. 44-47

The State of India's Environment (1984-85), The Second Citizen's Report, Centre for Science and Environment, New Delhi, p. 49.

B.K. Sharma, H. Kaur (1997-98), Environmental Chemistry, Krishna Prakasam Media (p) Ltd., Meerut.

Ruddar Dutt and Sundara (2002), Indian Economy, S. Chand Publications, New Delhi, p. 118.

Dr. G.D. Sooltha (1993), Meeting Our Requirements through Solar Energy, Yojana, Jan 26, pp. 22-27.

Environment Chemistry, Ibid – p. 35, (Ch. Energy)

B.P. Chanrasia (1993), Environmental Degradation and Global Awakening (Ed.), Chugh Publication, Allahabad.

S.P. Asthna (1993), Environment Resource Planning, 2006, A.D., Chugh Publications, Allahabad.

R.R. Prasad, M.P. Jahagirdar (1992), Social Factors in Social Forestry, Chugh Publications, Allahabad.

Economic Survey, Govt. of India, Various Issues. Source : Ninth Five Year Plan Vol. II.

9

SOLAR ENERGY–ENVIRONMENTALLY SAFE

M. Syamala

INTRODUCTION

Energy in a simple way is defined as the capacity to do work. Many a times energy and power are used in a synonymous way. But power represents the time rate of energy production. Man has been using energy in one or the other form right from time immemorial. Energy is the basic element of human civilization and an indispensable input for economic development. In spite, of the great advances made in science the world has been facing acute economic and social crisis. There is growing population and the pressure on the world's resources namely energy, food, etc., continues to increase threatening the environment and the ecological balance. Energy is the backbone to all the economic activities of the society. Without energy all activities may come to a stand still. There is a very close relation between Energy, the Gross Domestic Product, Consumption, Development and Growth. It is to say that there is a linkage between energy and economy, energy and development and the income of the country. The link between the energy and economy seems to be little complicated and complex in nature.

There are four primary sources of energy namely - petroleum, natural gas and natural gas liquids, coal and wood. But the life span of these sources is not infinite. They are finite suppliers of energy with a life span of nearly 15 years (natural gas) to 300 years (coal). As they are non-renewable in nature and highly polluting, it is necessary to use an alternative energy source to reduce this pollution. So, there is a need for renewable sources, as one cannot depend on non-renewable sources for a longer duration. Such long term, permanent types of energy source are solar energy. Solar energy is a very promising and reliable source of energy, which does not require any high level techniques or specialization for its wide spread utilization. The positive thing in using solar energy is that it is not at all polluting in nature.

The energy scene in India is characterized by–

1. A low per capita consumption of energy.
2. Non-Commercial fuel is used in dome activities like animal dung, agricultural waste etc.
3. Predominance if direct thermal application.
4. A large and dispersed clientele with a limited purchasing power.
5. Poor capacity to manufacture and market technological products at local level

Basically energy can be of two types namely - conventional and non- conventional energy sources. Various economist and scientists have defined them in their own way, which is listed below. Dostrovsky (1988) says - " Any source of energy having the potential of lasting a million or so many years can be regarded as a perpetual source, whether that source is renewable or not." World Bank (1980) viewed - "Energy sources, which hitherto provided the bulk of requirements for modern industrial society that is coal, petroleum, fuel oil, gasoline, kerosene, diesel and electricity generated by burning one or other of these fuels or from hydro or nuclear power is called conventional energy or commercial energy ".

The energy of sun was used as a source from time immemorial. It is a main source of energy which is free of cost, abundant, clean and available everywhere. The energy is generated due to interior nuclear collusion of hydrogen and helium. Indians today have one more reason to worship the Sun, apart from its religious significance. Modern technology has helped to develop gadgets that are improvisations on the crude methods of either heating water or drying the agricultural produce. Solar energy is manifest in two forms namely heat and light. While the solar thermal route is used for heating, cooling, drying, water purification and power generation, the solar photovoltaic route converts sunlight into useful electricity. At present, solar generated electricity finds use in a variety of applications, such as lighting, water pumping and battery charging in rural India. India is fortunate to receive sunshine for about 250-300 days in a year. This solar energy is equivalent to over 50,000 trillion kWh/year, which exceeds the total energy consumption of the country. The total solar energy that is received by India is around 6000 billion MWh per year. If only 1% of this energy can be trapped at around 10% the total potential solar energy works out to be 6000 twh. This is equivalent to around 35 times the present electricity generation in India.

The total energy received by earth is around 5.6 million EJ/yr, which is nearly 12,000 times than the present world absorbed by the earth, which is 790,000Ej/yr and the energy that reaches the hot deserts are about 93,000 EJ (Bockris, 1980). A square foot of earth facing sun receives a flux of 1372 W. The mass of sun is 1.97 x 10^{30} kg. The gravitational pull of sun is 28 times more than earth. It is expected to last another 4.5 billion years. The sun's rays reaches earth in eight minutes. The atmosphere does not allow the ultra violet rays to reach the earth, thus saving all the living things on earth. The incoming of solar radiation is called Insulation, it is measured in BTUs/ft^2/hour. Its density is 1.41 - g cm-3. It is estimated that nearly 1.5 Quadrillion-megawatt hour of solar energy arrives at the outer layer of atmosphere each year.) The solar energy is so useful that even if just 0.01% of its radiation could be turned into high-grade energy, it would be sufficient to satisfy the present need of mankind.

Solar energy is everlasting and non-polluting. It is clean, abundant and inexhaustible. Solar energy is erratic. The sun's rays are vertical in equator. So, it is advantageous to collect solar energy there itself. But then if it is transported then the capital will be spent more on the transport. Since pre-historic time's man has been depending on sun as it provides warmth, energy for photosynthesis, rains, earth's rotation and heating of earth combine to form wind, waves etc. Nearly 0.2% of solar energy striking earth cannot be partially be collected and converted to useful energy. But solar energy cannot be used, as it has to be converted to heat or electricity. For example, if solar energy is collected through mirrors it will be in heat form but if it is collected through photovoltaic cells, it will be in electric form.

Solar energy technologies can convert solar rays into four principle modes namely-

- Low temperature,
- High temperature
- Electricity
- Chemical energy.

The basic problem of solar energy is that it is not available 24 hours. Another problem is with collecting, storage and transporting the converted energy. To convert sun's rays too useful energy costs a lot. But once converted and established, it is of great help and free from pollution. Solar energy is more useful in the rural and remote areas. Solar energy can be collected and used either in direct or indirect way. The former includes heating of water for domestic use, industrial and commercial use, evaporation of seawater, desalination, storage for short time, refrigeration, etc. Latter is used in biogas windmills, small-scale hydropower generation.

Solar energy can be converted to electricity in two ways:

1) Solar photovoltaic, 2) Solar Thermal Power

Solar Thermal Collectors- Solar Cookers, Solar Water Heater, Solar Dryers, Solar Stills, Solar Ponds, Solar Water Pumps, Solar Furnaces, flat plate etc.

Solar Photovoltaic Cells– Streetlights, domestic lights, industrial use, use in satellites, etc.

USES

- For cooking food through – solar cookers for domestic and community purpose.
- For heating water through – solar water heater for hotels, domestic and hospital use.
- For Space Satellites through – solar cells.
- Solar cells used in calculators and watches etc.
- Electricity
- Industrial use – Solar water heater for hot water and Solar furnace.
- Agricultural purpose – Solar water pumps.
- For drinking water solar energy can be used in the form of solar water pumps, solar stills.
- It can also be used the hospitals for sterilization.

A SWOT analysis has been made on solar energy. The details are listed below –

Strength

– Never ending source.
– Pollution free.
– Can be utilized for all purposes.
– Scope of decentralization.
– Easy to operate.
– Can be utilized in any form.
– Minimum working expenditure.
– Saves fossil fuels.
– Economically self-sufficient.
– Less hazardous.

Weakness

– Problem of storage.

- Not available on cloudy and eclipse days
- Quantum varies according to season.
- Initial investment is high.
- Needs subsidy.
- Spares not easily available.
- Not taken in priority list.
- Sometimes, it creates urban planning.

Opportunities

- It can reduce the cost
- It is non-polluting
- Saves conventional sources
- Helpful in the rural areas to face energy crisis
- Available most of the time
- Free and abundantly available

Threat

- Threats oil lobby.
- Threats coal lobby.
- Lake of knowledge of common consumers.
- Fluctuation due to seasons or weather may discourage consumers.
- Opposite from the different forces due to subsidy.

The following table shows the estimated unit cost of electricity generation of both conventional and non-conventional energy sources.

From the table it is understood that the cost of producing the electricity through solar energy is little costly compared to the conventional sources, but in the long run the cost can be brought down. By using the solar energy for such purposes the environmental pollution can be avoided to a very great extent. There are various solar collectors, which help in saving the conventional sources and also help in protecting the environment. That is to say many things of pollution like sound,

Estimated Unit Cost of Electricity Generation

Generation Source	*Unit cost US cents Per KWh*	*Long-term expectations US cents per KWh*
Coal	5.0	
Oil	6.0	May rise gradually with rise in Prices.
Gas	4.5	
Nuclear	5.5	May rise with growing environ mental concern.
Photovoltaic	30 - 40	7.0
Solar thermal	15.0	7.0
Biomass	9.0	4.0 - 6.0

Source: Tapan Bhattacharya, pp. 244, 1998.

water, air can be avoided to a very large extent by using solar collectors. For instance solar water heaters are useful for heating the water. The main uses are listed below -

- Individual residential and apartment buildings;
- Restaurants and canteens;
- Guest houses, lodges, hotels and hostels;
- Hospitals and nursing homes
- Boiler feed water for commercial and industrial applications;
- Process feed water for paint industry, electroplating, galvanizing industry etc. involving direct feed to the various process baths at 70 to 80 C;
- Bottling plants and distilleries for syrup making, bottle cleanings etc.;
- Pharmaceutical, chemical and fertilizer industries;
- Textile industry;
- Food processing industry

The use of solar water heaters in both commercial and non-commercial areas can reduce the use of non-renewable sources and even pollution. Like for example in the industries to heat the water for various processes they may use coal or oil and even electricity. By doing so many unwanted particles go into the air and create air pollution. These can emit sulphur, carbondioxide, dust particles, smoke etc, which are very harmful both for human beings and plants. Similarly in the residence especially in the rural areas to boil the water they may use wood or coal that emits similar waste into the air creating air pollution. To avoid these things it is advised to use solar heater and the cost ranges between Rs.18,000 to Rs.60,000. The cost factor in this respect is shown below -

The annual savings of a 100 LPD System by 60 Degrees C is-

Fuel (Kg)	*Calorific Value (kcal/kg)*	*Thermal Efficiency*	*Fuel Saved*
Firewood	4708	17.3	2213
Cow-dung	2033	11.0	7726
Charcoal	6930	28.0	893
Kerosene	9122	50.0	380
LPG	10882	60.0	265
Soft coke	6252	28.0	990
Electricity	–	90.0	1500KWh

Similarly for cooking purpose much of the conventional energy is used that pollutes air and water, so in order to avoid this the clean and non polluting source that is solar energy must be used . The saving of conventional sources by using solar cookers is quite similar to that of the use of solar water heaters. Solar cookers can save nearly 6 LPG cylinders in a year, 600 Kg of wood and nearly 12 liters of kerosene. So, by using solar energy the level of pollution through these conventional sources for cooking purposes can be reduced.

CONCLUSION

This article clearly explains as how solar energy is clean, abundant and non-polluting. It can be concluded that solar energy must be used as an alternative to the these polluting conventional energy sources.

REFERENCE

Bansal. N.K. and Otehrs (1988), "Energy Options for the 90s", Tata Mc Graw Hill Publishig Company Ltd, New Delhi.

Bhattacharya; Tapan (1998), "Terrestrial Solar Photoratlies", Narasa Publishing House, New Delhi.

Chauncay Starr (1979), "Current Issue in Energy", Pergamon Press, Oxford.

Desai, A.V. (1990), "Non-conventional Energy", Wiley Eastern Limited.

Deb, Kumr, Bose (1989), "Energy Economics", Indian Council of Social Science Research.

Dastrovsky, L. (1988), "Energy and Missing Resources: A View from the Laboratory", Cambridge University Press.

Rai, G.D. (1990), "Solar Energy", Himalayan Publications, New Delhi.

Symala, M. (1999), "Non-coventional Energy Sources as an Alternative for the New Millennium", Dissertation submitted to the Department of Economics, School of Social Science, University of Hyderabad, Hyderabad.

World Bank, Discussion paper No. 391, Amsterdam, Netherlands.

Bockris, M. (1980), "How to Obtain Abundant Clear Energy", Plenum Press, New York.

10

BIO-PESTICIDES AND BIO FERTILIZERS FOR SUSTAINABLE DEVELOPMENT

V. Jaya

Twenty First Century is the age of Biotechnology. The oldest of all Biotechnologies is plant Biotechnology heralded by the introduction of crop rotation. Plant Biotechnology has affected all avenues of human life. Agriculture has always been under pressure to cope with the needs of the ever expanding human population. World grain production has to increase at the rate of 50 billion tonnes per annum to match population growth. Green revolution has enhanced productivity in rice, wheat, cereals, vegetables and fruits. The increased use of fertilizers to boost the yield of crops and the use of pesticides to control pest has become necessary, which is cost effective.

Plants besides being used as food; serve as raw material for the production of fabrics, Medicines, chemicals, oils, dyes, paper and timber. With the rapid depletion of fossil fuels such as oil, coal and natural gas greater attention is now being paid to the possibilities of utilizing plants or plant derived products as substitutes for coal and oil for the generation and production of chemicals. Genetic Engineering, one of the newly emerging area of Biotechnology will pave the way for increased food production and also allow modification of plants for industrial needs.

Using genetic engineering herbicide resistance, virus resistance, male infertility, pest resistance towards fungal pathogens in plants can be brought to use. Conventional farming techniques including chemical application as fertilizers and pesticides are becoming out dated because of ecological constraints. Hence is the need for stress on the substitutes for these conventional methods of cultivation. We are lucky to have several modern technologies and that to principles from biology to serve the purpose. These have stood as the ultimate solution for the existing ecological and economical problems and to ensure. "Development without Deterioration"

BIOPESTICIDES

Biopesticides are pest management tools that are based on beneficial micro organisms, beneficial nematodes or other safe biologically released active ingredients. Benefits of bio pesticides, include effective control of insects, plant diseases and weeds, as well as human and environmental safety. Bio-pesticides are also known as biological pesticides. These are certain types of pesticides derived from such materials as animals, plants, bacteria and certain minerals. For example garlic, mint and baking soda all have pesticidal applications and are considered as biopesticides. The insects harm the crop plants both directly by damaging the leaves and other parts, and indirectly by acting as vectors of many plant pathogens, especially viral pathogens. Hence to control insect pests and insect borne diseases of the crop plants chemical pesticides are extensively used. The chemical pesticides themselves pose many problems, especially affecting non-target pests and environmental pollution. Further the chemical pesticides are highly expensive. Many pesticides are resistant to microbial degradation and persist in soil for long periods. Massive application of insecticides leave residue in food and fodder and pose serious health problems in man and animals.

In the 20th century alternative pest control methods, came to light. These biological methods of pest control are effectively used to eradicate the insect pests. In the year 1915 Berliner discovered *Bacillus thuringeins* which effectively inhibits the growth of the larvae-the possibility of using microbes as biopesticide brightened. At present a number of bacteria, especially species of Bacillus and viruses especially baculo viruses group are used as bio-insecticides.

Bacillus thuringeins is is the most important species for its use as bio-pesticide. Other species are B.popillae, B.lentimorbus and B. sphaericus. Bt a common soil borne bacterium produces toxic crystals described as parasporal bodies during the process of sporulation. These crystalline proteins are toxic to certain insect pests and are called endotoxins. The toxin production is controlled by plasmid genes. Different strains of Bt have different crystal morphologies and they also differ in their insecticidal properties. The parasporal bodies are of two types (1) Bipyramidal crystals and (2) cuboidal crystals. These crystals act against Lepidopteran insects, Dipterans and mosquitoes. The larvae are paralysed due to the destruction of gut and ultimately die. For mosquitoes which cause malaria, filaria and Encephalitis two major microbes are employed Bt var Israelensis and Bacillus sphaerius. With the advent of genetic engineering and advances in molecular techniques the scenario has changed. Biopesticide sales have attained 10% sales of world global pesticide market. The control of breeding of mosquito larvae is achieved through the use of Bacillus strains Bt var israelensis and Bt kurstaki. These bio pesticides are preferable biological alternatives to environmental toxic chemicals. There are many advantages in the use of these biopesticides. The important plant species of target pests are cabbage, cotton, potato and vegetables.

Bt strains are extensively used in genetic engineering to develop biopesticides. Research workers of Monsanto group of companies of USA have successfully engineered Bt toxin gene into crop plants to confer resistance to insects. Insect resistant transgenic plants have so far been developed in cotton, tobacco, tomato, potato, soyabean, rice and maize. There are certain advantages and limitations of transgenic plants. One of the limitations is high cost. The cost of producing pest resistance transgenic plants is very high. (2) performance limitation (3) Secondary pest problems, for example Bt toxin is inefficient against pests like leaf hoppers, mites, root feeders etc (4) Gene escape into the environment. Pseudomonas aeruginosa is effective in controlling adult grass hoppers, locusts caterpillars, and wax moths. A large number of Baculo viruses, and a few Retroviruses are used as biopesticides. These viruses are affective against nearly 200 different types of insects including butterflies and moths. Baculo viruses are used for the control of cotton boll worm, moths, alfalfa looper, saw fly. The first commercial viral pesticide was Baculo virus heliothis marketed under the trade name Elcar for the control of cotton boll worm. Heliothis zea under the Integrated pest management control IPM, bio pesticides, genetically modified crops are used to control pests. I PM is the call of modern day agriculture.

BIOFERTILIZERS

Biotechnology can contribute positively towards the sustainability of the environment the techniques are widely employed in the areas of agriculture, energy use and production, treatment of waste and Bio remediation.

Use of Biofertilsers in Agriculture

The population of the world has been alarmingly increasing during the last few decades and the global cry is for food. To meet the needs of growing population the agricultural production is also needed to be increased: Chemical fertilizers are consumed to increase the yield of crops. The cost of chemical fertilizers is not only expensive but the wide use of these fertilizers causes environments and ecological problems. Alternate methods to increase agricultural productivity is the use of biofertilizers which are less cost supplements to chemicals under IPM. Biofertilizers are preparations containing live/latent cells of efficient strains of nitrogen fixing, phosphorus solubilizing bacteria. Biofertilizers are applied to seed, soil or composting. The main objective is to increase the micro organisms population and there by increasing the agricultural productivity.

The various micro organisms having realized / potential applications as biofertilizers are bacteria - Rhizobium species Azospirillum, Azotobacter, among fungi Mycorhiza like Glomus, Blue green algae or cyanobacteria - Anabaena, Nostoc. Rhizobium as a legume innoculant was first developed and marketed in USA. Azo spirillum occurs in the roots and rhizosphere of many tropical grasses such as maize, sorghum, sugarcane etc. It is capable of atmospheric nitrogen fixation and also known to produce growth substance like IAA and gibberellins. Azotobacter-a non symbiotic bacteria fixes atmospheric nitrogen and produces growth substances like vitamins, coenzymes, oximes etc.

Phosphate Solubilizers : Next to nitrogen, phosphorus is the important element required for plant growth. Most of the phosphorus applied to the soil remains insoluble, unavailable to the plants. A number of micro organisms Bacillus species (Bacteria) Aspergillus, Penicillium (Fungi) are capable of solubilizing insoluble phosphorus.

Mycorrhizae : The symbiotic association between Fungi and root system of higher plants is termed mycorrhizae. It was reported by FRANK in the roots of cupuliferae. There are three types.

- Ecto mycorrhizae
- Endomycorrhizae
- Ectendomycorrhizae

Realising the importance of Biofertilizers in supplementing the use of chemical fertilizers the Government of India has launched the national project on development and use of biofertilizers, during the 6th five year plan. Under this project - 800 tonnes of Rhizobium and 600 tonnes of Blue green alga was produced annually.

The bio-fertilizers serve in bringing ecological balance as well as clearing the harmful residual chemical pesticides and fertilizers by acting as biological scavengers through their myriad of physiological functions. These living tools deserve their position because of their self perpetuating capacity.

Use of Chemical fertilizers has certain disadvantages. (1) cost of production is high (2) source of energy is fossil fuel (3) causes air pollution, (4) increase ground water pollution (5) decreases soil fertility. Advantages are Biofertilizers are Biodegradable, increase yield, eco-friendly and above all economical sustainable. Eco-friendly agriculture can be practiced by using bio-fertilizers. Finally judicious and efficient use of renewable source of energy has to be a special focus in the 21st century.

CONCLUSIONS

Plant Biotechnology has emerged an existing area of plant sciences by creating unprecedented opportunities for the manipulation of biological systems plant breeders are striving to meet the challenge or increased production by developing plants with higher yields, resistance to pests, diseases and needs and tolerance to various abiotic stresses. Advent of biotechnology has generated new opportunities for skilled employment in villages through biological software industries such as manufacture of biofertilizers and biopesticides and establishment of biomass refineries research work of major concern is to preserve genetic heterogeneity in cultivated trees and plants and animals in order to avoid genetic vulnerability to pests and diseases.

Major factors behind determination of environment in India is population growth and pattern of human settlement, destruction forest lands, shifting agricultural lands for construction purposes. Feeding the growing population can be attained by using new technology in agriculture along with inputs like chemical fertilizers and pesticides, etc. Excessive and indiscriminate use of these chemicals resulted in pollution of our natural resources like soil and water, and also a threat aquatic fauna.

Ecofriendly economical, sustainable agriculture can be practiced can using bioferlizers.

REFERENCES

H.S. Chowla (2003), "Introduction to Plant Biotechnology (2nd edn.)", Oxford and IBH Publishing Co. Pvt. Ltd., New Delhi.

Dr. S. Ignacimuthu (1996), "Applied Plant Biotechnology", Tata Mc. Graw Hill Published Co., New Delhi.

H.D. Kumar, "Text Book of Biotechnology 2nd edn.", EWP New Delhi.

Dr. Balaswaramiam and others, "Concepts in Biotechnology Costed", IBN University, CFA Bryce, Kunthala, Jayaraman.

11

PUBLIC HEALTH AND ENVIRONMENT SAFETY

Talluru Sreenivas

Where ever we go in India from North to South or East to West, we find accumulated garbage roads, uncleanly environment and hazardous disposal waste places. We come across the same situation, almost all metros, cities, towns and even the villages of our country. In fact, majority of the Indians do not bother about surroundings. Some in India try to keep their houses clean but through the waste on the road or in the house of next door fellow.

While disobeying the general situation, we find certain public places like hospitals, vegetable, fish and other market places, Railway Stations, Bus stand, parks and Cinema Halls where maintained unhygienic and infectious places. It is really wonder to not even the allied people like doctors and higher officials who stay in other public places that are mentioned above spend major part of their time in a day in these places and become immune to the environment. It is in this context an attempt is made in this paper to discuss about the problem of disposal of wastage in Indian hospitals and suggest some measures for the effective management of waste disposal.

HOSPITALS AND WASTE MANAGEMENT

Hospitals generate an enormous amount of waste. The amount of solved waste generated by hospitals has been increasing rapidly and may now range from 2 - 5 kg/bed/day in developed economics and 0.5 - 2.0 kg/bed/day in developing countries. Of course, the total amount waste produced in a hospital each day depends on the degree of specialization and the standard of the hospital. Hospital waste has increased to such proportions that it can no longer be ignore. Increasing concern for community health standards and pollution requirements demands that the mass of infectious waste be rendered as harmless as possible before it leaves the hospital.

It has been established beyond doubt that improper management of hospital waste has been responsible for spread of infections and diseases. Improper disposal of waste is a health hazard for Hospital employees. Patients and Society at large. Hospital employees come in close contact with infected tissues, biological fluids, and infected materials of patients. The risk of accidental infection is faced by : doctors, nurses, labour staff and technical staff working in laboratories. As far as patients are concerned the risk of cross infection and hospital acquired infection and hospital acquired infection increases, if adequate precautions are not observed.

It has been observed that many hospitals and nursing homes dump all the waste at the garbage collection site from where garbage is taken away by the vehicles for final disposal. Most of the sites are visited by rag pickers who may get infected while handling infected items. The items picked up are often cleaned and sold in the market by them. For eg. Used needles, syringes, gloves, discarded drugs etc. Those who use these items face the sick of infection.

TYPES OF HOSPITAL WASTE

Clinical Waste

It is generated during routine patient care, surgery and in high risk units. It is potentially dangerous and presents a high risk of infection to the general population and to the hospital staff. Eg. Solid dressing, body fluids, needles and syringes, drainage bags, blood products and amputated limbs.

Non-clinical Waste

This includes wrapping paper, office paper, plastic that has not been in contact with patient body fluids. It is bulky, and therefore, difficult to dispose of, although it is of no potential harm.

Kitchen Waste

This includes swill, left over food, and dirty water. It is a potential source of pests and vermin such as cockroaches, rats and is thus an indirect potential hazard to the staff and patients in the hospital.

Radio Active Waste

This includes low-level radioactive waste arising from medical diagnosis, medical research and disease treatment. The radiation hazard is small due to the low level of activity, but if infectious material is contaminated with radioactivity and if it is stored at the hospital, this could present a greater hazard.

WHO CLASSIFICATION

World Health Organization (WHO) has classified bio-medical wastes into following categories :

1. General waste : All non-hazardous domestic wastes like peels of vegetables, fruits, papers, packing material etc.
2. Pathological Wastes include tissues, organs, body pars, human fetus , products of conception - aborts, body fluids, blood etc.
3. Radio active waste includes solids, gases, liquids, body organs imaging, tumor localization etc.,
4. Chemical Waste: This may be hazardous or non hazardous
   - Hazardous includes toxic, flammable, reactive
   - Non-hazardous include antiseptics
5. Infectious waste includes culture from laboratories, waste from surgery, waste from patients in isolation wards.

6. Sharps include needles, blades, broken syringe and glass pieces.
7. Pharmaceutical waste include degraded raw material, outdated drug, spilled drug or chemical, contaminated drug.
8. Pressurized containers.

EFFECTS OF EXPOSURE TO HOSPITAL WASTE

- Porters and maintenance staff could at risk due to improper storage, handling and transport of clinical waste.
- Personnel involved in final disposal of waste may be at risk due to improper wrapping or loose pathological waste
- Personnel handling waste that contains blood soaked objects from patients in dialysis units need protection against Hepatitis B infection.
- Injury by infected sharp can cause HIV infection.

LEGISLATION RELATING TO DISPOSAL OF WASTE

Hospitals should act not only as 'healer' but also not become a source of spreading diseases. The responsibility to ensure that the hospital's premises not only attend to the health needs of patients but also maintain acceptable hygienic conditions squarely rest on hospital authorities. Scientist ever in search of new products for mankind has succeeded in maing products of convenience. The entrepreneurs and industrialists in turn engage in mass production of these products. This process creates pollution. Even though hospitals do not manufacture such products their services produce considerable amount of waste that are toxic as well as non-toxic and more importantly could multiply diseases due to infection. By and large, the hospital waste is currently disposed conveniently along with the municipal waste, thus creating a dangerous situation that could imbalance the health of the society. Consequent to a public interest litigation filled in the Supreme Court regarding proper method of disposal of waste produced in hospitals, the Supreme Court took the initiative and entrusted the Ministry of Environment and Forests to come out with suitable guidelines for proper disposal of medical waste. Consequently, the Central Pollution Control Board (CPCB) has framed rules to properly dispose the bio-medical wastes. Subsequently these rules have become Act. The biomedical waste (management and handling) Rules 1998, which have come into force from December 31, 1999, gives clear guidelines for segregating, handling, transporting and disposal of biomedical waste.

Highlights of Biomedical Waste (Management and Handling) Rules, 1998

Rule 2 says that the rules given apply to all persons who generate, collect, receive, store, transport, treat, dispose or handle biomedical waste in any form.

Rule 3 provides the meaning of biomedical waste, biomedical waste treatment and operator of a biomedical waste facility. Biomedical waste means any waste, which is generated during the diagnosis, treatment or immunization of human beings or animals or in research activities or in the production or testing of biological. Biomedical waste treatment facility means any facility where in treatment, disposal of biomedical waste or processes incidental to such treatment or disposal is carried out. Occupier in relation to any institution generating biomedical waste means a person who has control over that institution. Operator of a biomedical waste facility means a person who owns or controls or operates a facility for the collection, reception, storage, transport, treatment, disposal or any other form of handling of biomedical waste.

Rule 4 stresses on the responsibility of an occupier of an institution. It shall be the duty of every occupier of an institution generating biomedical waste which includes a hospital, nursing home, clinic, dispensary, veterinary institution, pathological laboratory, blood bank, by what ever name called, to take all steps to ensure that such waste is handled without any adverse effect to human health and the environment.

Rule 5 states that biomedical waste shall be treated and disposed of in compliance with the standards prescribed.

Every occupier shall setup requisite treatment facilities and ensure requisite treatment of waste at a common waste treatment facility.

Rule 6 says that biomedical waste shall not be mixed with other wastes. It shall be segregated into containers at the point of generation. Untreated biomedical waste shall be transported only in such vehicles as may be authorized. No untreated biomedical waste shall be kept stored beyond a period of 48 hours.

Rule 7 provides authority to the Government of every state for establishing a prescribed authority.

Rule 9 states that Government of every state has to constitute an advisory committee. It includes experts in the fields of medical and health, environmental management, municipal administration and other non governmental organizations. This advisory board shall advice the government of state.

Rule 10 stresses on the responsibility of every occupier regarding submission of annual report by every year January 31st. This report should include information about the categories and quantities of biomedical wastes handled during the preceding year.

Rule 11 specifies that every authorized person shall maintain records related to generation, collection, reception, storage, transportation, treatment, disposal or any form of handling of biomedical waste. These records should be ready subject to inspection and verification at any time.

Rule 12 states that any accident occurs at any institution or facility or any other site where biomedical waste is handled or during transportation of such waste, the authorized person should report.

HIGHLIGHTS OF THE ENVIRONMENT (PROTECTION) ACT, 1986

- Section 3 deals with the powers of the Central Government to take measures to protect and improve environment.
- Section 6 gives the rules to regulate environment pollution.
- Section 8 presents the persons handling hazardous substances to comply with procedural safeguards.

- Section 15 provides the information relating to the penalty for contravention of the provisions of the act and the rules, orders, directions.
- Section 16 fixes criminal liability on the directors and the principal officers of a company where an offence is committed by a company.
- Section 17 gives authority to fix criminal liability on the heads of the departments of Governments where an offence is committed by the concerned department.
- Section 25 delegates the powers to the concerned for carrying out the purposes of the proposed legislation.

INCREASING ENVIRONMENTAL AWARENESS

The Indian macro environment consisting of demographic, economic, technological, political, legal, physical and socio-cultural environments have been changing very rapidly resulting in changes in every walk of life of Indian people. The doctors or the patients did not bother that much about the physical environment prevailing in the hospitals. They used to show much interest about the curing aspects than the cleanliness and beauty of the surroundings. The origin of the Corporate Hospitals, there is tremendous change in the attitude of the doctors as well as patients. In Corporate Hospitals, separate departments are being maintained for in-house maintenance and interior decoration. These hospitals almost all built and arranged like Five star hotels an they are taking all care in the management of all types of wastes. In fact, they have professionals to destroy or manage not only biological wastes but also for providing cleanliness and interior decoration. Unfortunately, the managers of the public hospitals are unable to cope up to the changing environments and the demands of the patients. The doctors including the specialists, para-medical staff, IV class employees, patients and the visitors is even today responsible for the bad management of the increase of the waste and environmental pollution. Probably the first change, we have to bring in the functioning of majority of the hospitals in India is not on the matters relating to the curing process or the equipment but the maintenance and cleanliness of these hospitals.

SUGGESTIONS FOR BETTER MANAGEMENT OF WASTE IN HOSPITALS

Attitudinal Change: Management of hospital waste requires diligence and care from a chain of people starting with nurse, doctor, labour staff, persons transporting waste, persons handling mechanical and technical aspects. If need for safe disposal is stressed, cooperation for segregation, storage, disinfections will not be difficult.

Truly speaking, attitudinal change is required at the level of top management but not the lower level management. Chief Executive Officer or the Doctors are to be held responsible but not the IV class employees. They are continually failing in motivating the employees. Instead of throwing responsibility on to the IV class employees, we have to look into the practical work being undertaken by the top management. Instead of teaching morals, first there is a necessity on the part of the top people to participate in the waste management programmes. Because environment in which they are living should be kept clean and they should be kept clean they should be made accountable for bad environment.

Responsibility: It is desirable to specify job responsibility. If there are failures or problems, proper communication will sort out the same and decide on better alternatives.

Occupational Health: health hazard due to improper handling of hospital waste, i.e., without taking precautions must be known by the employees. The hazards are not faced by the society alone; they are faced more by the staff.

Financial Management: Steps required for safe disposal of hospital waste require some expenditure. If proper system is evolved and implemented the cost of safe disposal works out to be 0.1% to 0.2% of the total running cost of the hospital. Saving on this activity is of little significance in proportion to total expenditure.

Surveillance: The following steps are to be taken to help rag pickers

- Emphasis on dangers of handling infected waste and recycling
- Train rag pickers in acquiring recyclable waste
- Public awareness about segregation of waste and role of rag picker's activities, must be created
- Establishment of linkages between formal system and rag pickers
- Medical assistance and health education for rag pickers and their families
- General public must be convinced about reducing the quantity of garbage by utilizing reusable and recyclable items.

Training : Those who handle garbage are often not aware of the risk and hazard of the activity. They are also not aware of the importance of their contribution. Training of the staff is therefore necessary. The goals of training should be

- Clarify the components of the waste management system
- Explain the assigned roles and responsibilities to the personnel involved
- Educate and ensure proper use of the personal protective equipment
- Information regarding the procedure to be followed for a needle stick or other exposures
- Get an honest feedback from the workers
- Suggest remedies to their problems alter the processes, if required

Co-operation: The most important factor in successful implementation of medical waste management lies in the cooperation of the hospital staff and medical personnel. The proper management of hospital wastes calls for a well-coordinated approach and the role that the administration plays in this, is of vital importance. Ideally a hospital should form a waste management committee, which has the responsibility to design and implement a policy.

Committee Management : The committee should consist of representatives from the following :

- Administration
- Clinical services
- Hospital Infection Control Committee
- Nursing
- Housekeeping
- Maintenance
- Microbiology
- Accounts

12

HEALTH HAZARDS OF THERMAL POWR PLANT POLLUTANTS – A CASE STUDY OF KOTHEGUDEM THERMAL POWR STATION

M.V. Narasimha Sarma G. Pramila Kumari, G.B. Franklin

Energy and economic development move together, but demand for more energy leads to greater emission of pollutants into the atmosphere. Energy is treated as a fuel of economic progress and can also be called as fourth factor of production. Among the three principal sources of commercial fuels viz., coal, oil and electricity, consumption of electricity is the highest because of flexibility, amenability and versatility attracted economists to go for electricity rather than the other two. In addition, it is more convenient in its transmission.

Electricity is obtained mainly from three sources viz., thermal, hydel and nuclear. Generation of electricity has extensive disastrous effects on the eco-system. In particular, coal has the greatest potential for environmental damages. Particulate matter, harmful gasses emissions and trade metals come from thermal power stations, which is the main source of energy in India. As such, Indian government formulated a few guidelines for selecting thermal power stations.

(a) Plant should not be preferably set up with 25 kms, of metropolitan cities or tropical forests or national part of wild life sanctuary or of important lakes.

(b) They should be no commercial and residential area with in 1.6 kms, exclusive zone surrounding a thermal plant.

(c) They should be at least 10 kms, away from defense installations, archeological structures and important tourist spots.

(d) They should be at least 500 mts, away from national highways.

(e) For setting up a thermal plant or for ash disposal, no agricultural land should be used.

THERMAL POWER PLANTS – POLLUTION

During the production process, thermal power stations give out large amounts of particular matter, ash and sulfur and nitrous oxide, creates inseparable adverse effects on environment. Gases such as So_2 and No_2 mixes with atmosphere and come back to earth in the form of acid rains.

Fly ash, which comes out during energy production process, causes respiratory problems, which ultimately create heart problems. Waste heat that produces in energy plants and hot water causes thermal pollution. There is another pollutant known as noise pollution. All these pollutants creates various health hazards to those people living in the surrounding areas of the thermal power plant.

Economic development needs energy. But energy producing process creates pollution that pollutes the atmosphere. For cleaning the environment, a country needs more and more energy.

METHODOLOGY

Kothegudem Thermal Power Station is taken as sample to study the evil effects of pollutants that released during the process of energy generation. Totally, 233 respondents living in the surrounding area of the plant are selected to get the required information for the study. Primary data is collected through direct personal investigation by canvassing a questionnaire. Statistical tools such as percentage and cross tabulation are used to analyse the collected data.

Kothegudem Thermal Power Station is situated near Paloncha in Khammam district of Andhra Pradesh. This complex contains eight units. This plant is very closer to Singereni collieries, which are just six kilometers away.

SERIOUS HEALTH PROBLEMS OF POLLUTION

Health problems such as tuberculosis, indigestion, constipation, frequent attacks of jaundice, urinary problems, anemia, blood pressure, heart problems and cancer are some serious problems prevalent in the area of thermal power plants due to the result of pollutants released during the course of energy production.

HEALTH PROBLEMS IN KOTHEGUDEM THERMAL POWER STATION

Table No. 1 shows cross tabulation between health problems and distance, sex and age. There is negative correlation between distance of the plant and health problem.

FINDINGS

The study observed the following based on the analysis made in Table-1.

1. People living below 2 kms. Distance from the plant are most effected followed by 2-5 kms. And more than 5 kms.
2. It is found that male are effected more than that of the female.
3. Most of the respondents in various age groups are suffering from indigestion, constipation, anemia and tuberculosis.

SUGGESTIONS

Basing on the analysis of the study, the following are suggested for reducing the evil effects that are resultant of pollutants during the production of energy.

1. It may be suggested to made serious efforts to tap less polluting energy sources such as bio-energy, photo-energy, tidal energy and geo-energy.

Table 1
Cross Tabulation Between Health Hazards And Distance, Sex and Age in Kothegudem Thermal Power Station Area

Problem	*Less than Two kms.*	*Two to Five kms.*	*More than Five kms*	*Female*	*Male*	*Less than Thirty Years*	*Thirty to Fifty Years*	*More than Fifty Years*
Tuberculosis	72	16	2	8	82	43	43	5
% in the variable	42.86	34.04	11.11	33.33	39.23	42.57	37.84	23.81
Percentage in total sample	30.9	6.87	0.86	3.43	35.19	18.45	18.03	2.15
Indigestion	100	23	5	11	117	54	65	9
% in the variable	59.52	48.84	27.78	45.83	55.98	53.47	58.56	42.86
Percentage in total sample	42.92	9.87	2.15	4.72	50.21	23.18	27.9	3.86
Constipation	72	18	6	7	89	39	48	9
% in the variable	42.86	38.3	33.33	29.17	42.58	38.61	43.24	42.86
Percentage in total sample	30.9	7.73	2.59	3	38.2	16.74	20.6	3.86
Frequent attck of Jaundice	55	7	4	7	59	32	34	0
% in the variable	32.84	14.89	22.22	29.17	28.23	31.68	30.63	0
Percentage in total sample	23.61	3	1.72	3	25.32	13.73	14.59	0
Urenary Problems	53	9	1	6	57	30	29	4
% in the variable	31.55	19.15	5.56	25	27.27	29.7	26.13	19.05
Percentage in total sample	22.75	3.86	0.43	2.58	24.46	12.88	12.45	1.72

Contd.

Problem	*Less than Two kms.*	*Two to Five kms.*	*More than Five kms*	*Female*	*Male*	*Less than Thirty Years*	*Thirty to Fifty Years*	*More than Fifty Years*
Anaemia	71	14	5	7	83	36	50	4
% in the variable	42.26	29.79	27.78	29.17	39.71	35.64	45.05	19.05
Percentage in total sample	30.47	6.10	2.15	3	35.62	15.45	21.46	1.72
Blood Pressure	88	16	5	12	97	41	61	7
% in the variable	52.38	34.04	27.78	50	46.41	40.59	54.95	33.33
Percentage in total sample	37.77	6.87	2.15	5.15	41.63	17.6	26.18	3
Heart Problems	35	11	4	7	43	17	29	4
% in the variable	20.83	23.4	22.22	29.17	20.57	16.83	26.13	19.05
Percentage in total sample11	15.02	4.72	1.72	3	18.45	7.3	12.45	1.72
Cancer	12	7	0	3	16	8	11	0
% in the variable	7.14	14.89	0	12.5	7.66	7.92	9.91	0
Percentage in total sample	5.15	3	0	1.29	6.87	3.43	4.72	0

2. Residential area should be attest 5 kilometers from the plant because most of the effected cases are from below five kilometers.
3. As worn out, torn out or outdated machinery release more pollutants, it may be suggested to replace them with new and up to date machinery.

SECTION - II

Economic Development and Environment

13

ENVIRONMENT AND DEVELOPMENT ISSUES AND CONCERNS

G. Raghava Reddy

INTRODUCTION

Economic development continues to be a major challenge before the developing world. It is being pursed with grater vigor in order to make political democracy meaningful. In the course of economic development several social and environmental issues arise and generate adverse effects on human and social development. They impose a sense far den on the weaker sections of society by depleting natural resources polluting the environment. Environmental degradation is the net result. It has a negative effect on social welfare. Hence, protection of environment becomes necessary to safe guard the long run interests of society and ensure sustainability of the development process itself.

In this paper, a few concerns and issues of environmental degradation are touched upon and suitable techniques and measures of tackling environmental degradation are pointed out. The coverage of the theme is relative and peripheral due to its vast scope. Although the approach of the paper is global the focus is on India. It needs hardly to be mentioned that environmental degradation is a global problem with far reaching negative externalities which are to be tackled at the global level by forming and ratifying conventions and agreements on the elimination and control of environmental degradation of all types.

FACTS OF ENVIRONMENTAL DEGRADATION

It is well known that economic development involves rapid industrialization and urbanization. The exploitation of mineral resources goes on unabated and get exhausted sooner later. Air surrounding the industrial and urban units, automatically gets polluted. Water in the surrounding rivers, lakes, tanks and ponds gets polluted. Solid waste management poses several issues. Public authorities find it difficult to mobilize resources to meet the increasing cost of clean, safe, protected water supply to the urban habitations. The rural urban dichotomy is ever present and the needs of the rural society receive less priority. Agriculture becomes industrialized and commercialized wherever assured irrigation systems are operative and functional. Green revolution of the second generation with its emphasis on modern inputs results in environmental pollution. For example aquaculture in coastal Andhra poses a threat to biodiversity. Leather tanning units in Dindigal and Vellore area of Tamilnadu are damaging agricultural production in their neighbourhood.

The denundation of forests and overuse and misuse of common property resources (CPRs) have led to the degradation of the soil, climate changes and the green house effect with its deleterious consequences. Traditional fuel consumption in less developed countries is 65% of total energy use. But in high income countries it is only 34%. On the other side per capita electricity consumption is 69 and 8481 kilowatt hours in 1999 in less developed and high income countries respectively (UNDP, HDR 2002). It is only 1.1 metric tons per capita in India in 1999.

Forest Cover

It is well known that forests have a many-faceted ecological role to play which affects human life directly in a variety of ways. They the vast dangers of cloud drifting, soil erosion, floods, wind erosion and ground water evaporation. They also protect a wide variety of flora and fauna, provide recreation, and also generate several positive benefits to the communities that live in and nearly by forest areas such as tribals (IDR 1997). But India has only 2% of World's geographical area, 1% of forest area and 0.5% of pastureland. India's forest cover is hardly 20% of geographical area as against 33% prescribed by the national forest policy of 1988. Moreover a large part of these forests is degraded and destroyed by vested interests and prodúctivity is very low. As a consequence of this several negative externalities are generated disturbing the livelihood system of people linked up with forest areas. The construction of big dams in forest areas have also displaced the people.

Policy Frame Work

In the context of uneven development across the globe, the persistence of extreme poverty and un-employment in the less developed countries, there is a need to safeguard the environment and natural resources from over exploitation and denudation. The destruction of the environment tends to aggravate the incidence of mass poverty and unemployment in less developed countries. The developed countries have a responsibility to initiate measures for environmental protection because they are the major players in the area of environmental pollution and degradation. The future of mankind is at stake if the government, NGO's and other stake holders do not play their role responsibly and on time environmental threat is more severe than that of terrorism, either, domestic or cross-border.

The public authority in protecting the environment is fundamental. There are several legal and administrative mechanisms to initiate action and ensure results that are favorable to the society at large. But in less developed countries public governance systems are weak and are prone to corruption. Gunnar Myrdal's soft state is generally found to be operative at least on the environment front. Hence, there is a need for the encouragement and active participation of the agencies of civil society and the stake holders themselves.

Fortunately self-help groups (SHG's) are springing up either spontaneously or by the facilities of government of non-government agencies to shoulder the responsibility for safeguarding the natural and physical environment.

Self-Help Groups and their Role

Self help groups are emerging to promote social mobilization for community action to safeguard their environment for development. DWACRA Groups are well known through out India now. They take their origin from the success of Grameena Bank of Bangladesh. Not only in the promotion of thrift and savings but also in family welfare, nutrition and health, education and sanitation they are playing an important role. Water users and water shed associations and communities are already there with several success stories. Vana Samrakshna Samithis (VSS) are there to protect forest cover. Mothers committees, education committees, hospital advertising committees and several other agencies are involved in promoting human development and environmental safety.

Concluding Remarks

Dispite the rapid strides made on the economic front, problems of income, human, environmental, poverty persist on a large scale. Development and depreciation are found side by side. But the theory of poverty and deprivation is still evolving. The numbers affected are assetless, voiceless, powerless, and jobless. They are highly disadvantaged on the political, social, economic and cultural front. The governance systems are generally elitist and pro-ruling. Fortunately there is a change in the scenarios. SHG's are emerging and playing an important role to safe guard the environment and there by protect their own interests. The poor nations and people have to protect their interests by social mobilization and community action.

REFERENCES

UNDP, "Human Development Reports", 2000, 2001, 2002 Oxford, New Delhi.

IGIDR, "India Development Reports", 1997, 1998, 1999, 2000, Oxford, New Delhi.

Network, "India Infrastructure Report", 2001, Oxford, New Delhi.

The World Bank, "India: Reducing Poverty, Accelerating Development", 2000, Oxford, New Delhi.

14

ENVIRONMENTAL PROBLEMS AND AGRICULTURE: A MICRO-LEVEL STUDY

K. Nageswara Rao

It is estimated that one sixth of the population in India, with forty per cent of the cultivated area, live in drought prone areas. These areas miss the priorities of planned development and experience the problems of environmental balance. Recurring droughts left devasting impact in these areas in the form of degradation and destruction of soil, water and forest resources and displacement and deprivation of the dependent people on agriculture. In view of this, prevention of environmental degradation and sustainability of agriculture and irrigation under minor sources like percolation tanks and check dams constitute the major concerns of the policy-makers in the drought prone regions.

PURPOSE OF THE STUDY

The present study is an attempt to highlight the environmental impact of irrigation development as it is practiced in drought prone areas with specific reference to a village in Anantapur district of Andhra Pradesh State. This study is based on the preliminary information obtained on a visit to Atmakur village as a prelude to a larger study on droughts and sustainable agriculture. This paper is divided into three sections–first section dealing with a brief description of a village and the crisis faced by it, the second section explores the underlying causes and the last section is an attempt to raise larger questions regarding drought and sustainability of agriculture.

SECTION – I

Anantapur, geographically the largest district in Andhra Pradesh state is a chronically drought prone district which attracted the attention of both the Central and State Governments. A series of beneficiary oriented and area specific programmes were implemented in the district to mitigate the adverse effects of droughts in the last three decades. Minor irrigation schemes and soil conservation works are the important programmes implemented for the sustainability of agriculture in the district.

Atmakur, along with its hamlets Kurpalapalli and Kothapalli, is an unusually large village with a population of 7,667 and a geographical area of 233 sq.miles. With no irrigation tank, the village is entirely dependent on rainfall and well irrigation for cultivation. Over the years the village has been undergoing severe ecological stress which may be seen from the changes in population growth, work force composition, drinking water for human beings and the livestock, land use, cropping pattern and the use of common lands.

The data relating to changes in population and work force over three decades 1971-2001. The rate of growth of population has been lower than the National average. This is not unusual for a drought-prone area. But, compared to 1.4 per cent in 1970s, the growth rate declined to 1.1 per cent in 1990s, further decreased by 2001. The changing definition of workers from Census to Census make comparison of the work force data, without proper adjustment, rather tenuous. A cursory look at the data does reveal that there has been slowing down of the growth of work force indicating the possibility of migration.

It is of interest to note that in 1961 there was a Weavers' Cooperative Society and Neera and Jaggery Cooperative Society in the village but there was none when we visited in

January 1999. With the decline of the household industry, the proportion of work force in agriculture (cultivators and agricultural labourers). This remained at 70.0 per cent in 1971 declined to 68.0 per cent in 1991, similarly by 2001. It would be interesting to look into the wage rates, the intensity of employment etc., but as yet we have no data.

Until late 1970s the villagers were drawing water for their domestic and drinking requirements from open dug well which had oil engine for irrigation. This was the source of drinking water for livestock also. Besides, there were about 5 wells in houses supplying water for domestic use. But by the end of 1970s most of the dug wells and the household wells dried-up. Since 1980 the only source of water supply has been a dug well with an in-well bore. Piped water is supplied to the village from an overhead tank through tap outlets at important corners. There was enormous pressure on this single source for water supply resulting in acute scarcity.

Atmakur and the neighbouring villages were known for sheep rearing. But, in recent years lack of adequate grazing land and drinking water resulted in many sheep cooperatives financed under DPAP became defunct. Scarcity of fodder and water forced the farmers to resort to distress selling of cattle. The residential area of Atmakur is surrounded by tamarind trees which constituted the common property of the village. But in recent years many of these trees have been drying up because of depletion of the water table to the depths beyond the reach of these trees. This is èxperienced ever since there has been competitive drilling of in-well bores.

SECTION – II

In understanding the present ominous crisis in Atmakur we have to take a close look at the changes in the moisture regime as an important explanatory factor. These changes may best be analysed by considering them in their components of rainfall, surface water use, ground water exploitation and cropping pattern.

RAINFALL

Rainfall in Atmakur has not only been low but extremely variable ranging from 225 mm in 1992-93 to 1000 mm in 2000-01, with mean of about 700 mm. However, there is no secular trend, though one may notice an increase in the fluctuation for the later period of 1990-2000. it would be too much of a speculation at this stage to consider these increasing variations in the later period as a consequence of deteriorating vegetative cover affecting the convective rainfall, though not that of monsoon. In other words the changes in Atmakur economy and ecology cannot be blamed for declining rainfall. This leaves us with the human interventions with the moisture regime in the form of storage of run-off, use of ground water and the nature of crops grown.

SURFACE WATER

Atmakur village has no irrigation tanks but two large percolation tanks which have been converted into private lands for cultivation. One of the major causes for the present water crisis in the village appears to be the conversion of the two public percolation tanks into private property. One of these two percolation tanks is located close to the village at an elevated area supposed to hold the run off from the up-lands and the other is located at a distance of two kilometers at a lower end of the village with a catchments of some hillocks and uplands. Though the exact years are yet be found out, the information from the villages suggests that up until the 1950s these two percolation tanks were effective in collecting the run-off from the South-West monsoon and the storage served not only as effective percolation to maintain the water-table in the dug wells but also as a source of drinking water for livestock.

Though it is not exactly known how these percolation tanks, the common prosperity of the village, became private land, one may conjuncture that during the Grow More Food Campaign when tank-bed lands were assigned to cultivators for raising food crops, lands in these two tank beds might have passed into the private hands. These hands must have caused the breaches, which have never been repaired. For over three decades now these percolation tanks have only huge bunds, which are the public property and tank beds which are 'patta' private land. The major claimants to these tank bed lands happen to be the two dominant land owners, one in each of the two tanks. And besides the privilege of owning the tank beds, they share among themselves and their in-laws the position of democratically elected offices of Panchayat Presidentship, Cooperative Bank Directorship, positions for their children in civil services etc. The gravity of this process of privatization of public property now threatens the very survival of the village economy. And this is related to the ground water exploitation for irrigation.

GROUND WATER EXPLOITATION

Since there are no irrigation tanks, the only source of irrigation is wells which are dependent on private investment. With the given rainfall, and deliberate encroachment upon the percolation tanks in favour of private gain of a few individuals, the crux of the scarcity of water in the village depends entirely on the behaviour of the exploitation of groundwater by wells. Information from the village suggests that there were as many as 170 dug wells with at least one-third of them fixed with diesel engines before 1971. But by 2000-01, the number of wells declined to 141 and the diesel engines to about 35. The number of well as well as area irrigated both in kharif and rabi seasons show a clear declining trend, reaching the lowest level by 1979-80. It was during this period that there was increasing realization of the depleting impact of the breached and privatized percolation tank on the water table. The abandoning of the surface storage in the percolation tank combined with the lifting of water from the wells with diesel engines precipitated a crisis which resulted in drying up of dug wells and the decline in their number to 120 and dismantling of as many as 35 diesel engines. This phase also witnessed serious drinking water problem both for human and livestock population.

1980-81 marks the beginning of the revival phase. The revival in the number of irrigation wells and the area irrigated during the kharif and rabi seasons was ushered by the extension of electric power for water lifting and the introduction of in-well-bore technology. By 2000-01 the number of wells increased to 130. All but one well, were equipped with an in-well bore and electric pumps. There were liberal institutional credit and in certain cases subsidies to the well owners for executing in-well-bores. This competitive spirit was further aided by the state policy of fixing the power tariff for agriculture in terms of flat rate per horse power regardless of the energy consumed. The gross area irrigated has been increasing gradually and so are the disastrous consequences. The water table is depleting so fast that a few in-well bores have dried up. At least three wells have already been fixed with two motors each to lift water in two stages. Some of the tamarind trees in village commons have started drying up in the recent years.

A close analysis of aspects of the irrigation achieved at a heavy investment to the private well owners and a grave ecological threat to the very sustenance of human, animal and plant life of the village. It is observed that during 1990-2000 period, the area irrigated was higher during the kharif compared to the rabi. The latter never exceeded one-third of the gross irrigated areas. A word of explanation is necessary here. Atmakur lies in the rain-shadow area and receives even the meager rainfall only during the South-West monsoon which falls in the kharif. The entire season is therefore a singe season i.e., kharif crop area and the irrigated area under kharif have been more.

In spite of this fact the area irrigated to the area cultivated during the 2000-01 has been in the range of only 4 to 5 per cent (Table 3). In other words the grave dangers to which the village economy and ecology are subjected to are in return for the benefit a small fraction of the total area cultivated. During the survey period, the village has about 1300 households and only 138 wells with bores drilled and energized are the sources of the problem. Given the fact that there are a few households with two or three wells, about 10 per cent of the households irrigating about five per cent of the net sown area and among themselves only a few occupying the percolation tanks, have been responsible for pushing the entire village to the brink of the sustainability. Further, the area irrigated per well fluctuated during the period. One of the contributing factors to this small increase may be the power tariff policy, which has all the incentives for overuse of the installed power capacity. This phenomenon also may have induced the well owners to prefer water-intensive crops. However, average irrigated area under a well still remains at a low level of four acres even in the best of the seasons like kharif of 2000-01. The limits to the exploitation may be seen from the rabi irrigation which never exceeds an average of 2.04 acres per well.

CROPPING PATTERN

Cropping pattern is an other important aspect of the moisture regime which has often been looked upon as a possible source of effecting some conservation. Data also shows that there was a marginal increase in the area irrigated under wells and the area cultivated. This is rather surprising in the light of the fact that irrigation accounts only for a small fraction of the net sown area and rainfall, though fluctuated, did not show any declining trend during the period. The cropping pattern also experienced rapid changes, jowar declining from its place of primacy accounting for over 70 per cent of the kharif crop in 1990-91 to about 28 per cent in 2000-01 and groundnut expanding from about 11 to 58 per cent during the same period.

SECTION – III

Atmakur is thus a clear and conspicuous case of gross neglect of surface water and over exploitation of groundwater, causing severe and potent irreversible ecological degradation of resources and deprivation of livelihood activities to the people. It is a clear evidence of man-made hazard in the absence of protecting institutional system. One wishes that Atmakur is an exception and the experience of other drought prone areas are different. But the evidence is to the contrary. The question therefore is how to make development sustainable in the sense of not only providing for the basic needs of the present and future generations of people in these areas but also for improvement of their quality of life. With increasing proportion of population depending on agriculture which is characterized by low and very widely fluctuating rainfall of 225 mm to 100 mm, with per capita cultivated dry land varying from half to one and a half acres between the good and the bad monsoons, with no prospect of the area irrigated exceeding not more than ten per cent of the cultivated area, with the ground and drinking water at the brink of exhaustion i.e., water itself acquiring the characteristics of an exhaustible resource, with pastures and forests disappearing into the records merely as data, how to sustain life in the areas like Atmakur, what kind of an approach would help in understanding and arriving at the right strategy? Could it be looked upon merely as an "economic problem, which must be understood in economic terms." Or, would one approach it in game-theoretic terms which suggest that the outcome "is caused by the operation of 'the isolation paradox' whereby a socially irrational outcome is caused by the sum of uncoordinated individual actions none of which may be irrational within the narrowness of the individual frame of reference"? Can the 'tragedy of commons'– here the surface and groundwater be solved by the Olsonian solution of 'collective action'? Or can one think in terms of a technological solution of diverting water from other basins? Given the existing institutional set up, would it result in sustainable development? Or, is 'in-situ' water conservation a reality? Or, would it not be possible to see more productive use of the very existing resources if there is change in the relationship between the producers and resources?

NOTES

Prabab Bardhan (1984), "The Political Economy of Development", Delhi, OUP, p.6.

The World Commission on Environment and Development (1987), "Our Common Future", Delhi, OUP, pp. 43-66.

Jeffrey James: Growth, Technology and the Environment in Less Developed Countries : A Survey" in P. Streeten (ed.), Recent Issues in World Development.

G. Hardin (1973), "The Tragedy of Commons" in H.E. Daly (ed.) Towards a Steady-State Economy, W.H.Freeman.

M.Olson (1977), "Logic of Collection Action", Harvard.

B. Venkatarami Reddy, Reddy, Op.cit.

Jayanto Bandhyopadhyaya, "Ecology and Drought", Op.cit.

The Global Analysis of 'delinking' is set out in Samir Amin (1983), The Future of Maoism MRP.

D. Senghaas (1988), "The European Experience: A Historical Critique of Development Theory", Dover, NH, 1985 and D.Senghaas "European Development and the Third World", Review, Winter.

15

MINING AND ENVIRONMENTAL EXTERNALITIES IN IB VALLEY COAL FIELD OF ORISSA

Prajna Paramita Mishra

INTRODUCTION

During the closing decades of the 20th century environmental issues have emerged as a major concern for the survival and welfare of mankind through out the world. Modern civilization armed with rapidly advancing technology and fast growing economic system is under increasing threat from its own activities causing pollution of air, water and soil. The fast eroding life support system of our biosphere not only endangers the future of human race as such but also is a major threat to life itself.

The UN Conference on Environment at Stockholm in June 1972 heralded the first serious effort to take note of the environmental issues at the global level. Ever since then concepts like environmental sustainability and carrying capacity of earth have become central themes for policy making around the world. Environmental problems remain acute in most countries and continue to escalate in many parts of the world. There has been a quantum increase in awareness of the magnitude of the problem and of the need for action during the last few years. The UNCED in 1992, in Rio, known as the Earth Summit provided further momentum for change.

Although the desirability of development is universally recognized, recent years have witnessed rising concern about whether environmental constraints will limit development and whether development will cause serious environmental damage in turn impairing the quality of life of this and future generations. A number of environmental problems require urgent attention. The protection of the environment is an essential part of development. With out adequate environmental protection, development is undermined; without development, resources will be inadequate for needed investment, and environmental protection will fail (World Development Report: 1992).

The quality of environment and ecosystem in India is declining at an alarming rate as India is trying to bridge the gap between the status of 'developing' and 'developed' in the field of industries and economy. After independence in 1947, India has implemented Nine Five-year plans and three Annual plans, as a result, it has achieved the unique distinction of a developing country and now it is on the threshold of achieving the status of developed countries. With improvement in science and technology India has earned international prestige amongst the community of nations. However, in the process, with less effort to conserve the natural resources, India is rapidly becoming a vast wasteland.

Environmental pollution is multidimensional. It is affecting land, water, forests, people, wildlife, and the entire habitat and the atmosphere. Mining is among the worst polluting activities. At the same time mining is the main economic activities. In fact, happens to be the single most contributing the economy in some countries. Being poorly managed it is causing considerable environmental damage risk human health, ecosystem and economic infrastructure.

Coal is the most important and abundant amongst minerals. At present fossil fuels, coal; oil and natural gas supply more than 90% of world's energy demand. This situation is not likely to last as oil's share of the energy market diminishes and it has to be replaced by an energy source, which is abundant, flexible in use and easily extracted. Coal can satisfy all these requirements. Coal has been and will continue to be the prime source of energy in India due to abundance of coal reserves, fast diminishing petroleum reserves in the world and therefore rising prices of kerosene, disel and petrol, foreign exchange difficulties and inadequate exploitation of the hydropower potential. Taking into consideration the alarming environmental problems in general and that of mining in particular this paper concentrates on the affects of coalmines on environment.

Coal mining commenced in India in 1845 in Raniganj coalfields in Bihar. The growth of coal industry was not only slow but also unsystematic and inefficient based on pure consideration of short-term profit maximized by private mine owners till 1971-72, when the coal industry was nationalized. After nationalization exploration for coal and coal mining was taken up in a more systematic way to take care of long term requirements of the country.

OBJECTIVES OF THE STUDY

The study has the following main objectives.

1. To find out the environmental externalities of mining in general and that of IB valley coal field in particular.
2. To find out what measures have been taken by the company to improve and protect the environment.
3. To suggest some actions to be taken to counteract and neutralize the adverse impacts on the environment.

ENVIRONMENTAL IMPACTS OF MINING: A REVIEW

Mineral deposits are to be mined where they are. While the developed countries are in what might be called "recycling phase" waging war with dirty air, polluted water, noise, congestion, energy shortage, etc., the developing countries which are primarily of agriculture or mineral based are accelerating their pace of industrialization and exploitation of resources in the footsteps of the former. Having awaken from the experience of environmental damage to air, water and soil, undergone by the developed nations due to large scale industrialization in the level of primary goods production, the latest fad (conspiracy) is to push this activity to the natural resources based developing countries and concentrate on the relatively cleaner high tech industries. Thus, richer countries tends to be cleaner and the poorer continues to be dirties in the same parady of the technological exploitation in the present system (Mihajlo Mesarovic et al, 1976).

One of the visible expressions of mining activities on earth is its affects on health. Occupational diseases like silicosis, fluorosis, asbestosis, manganism, plumbirm, Itai-Itai etc., have been well-known to be associated with mining societies the world over (Sahu, 1990). Open cast mining activity has played havoc with the environment and is killing workers slowly. 25% of the workers suffer from silicosis, bronchitis, asthma and tuberculosis and 50% from malaria, which has spread as a result of mosquitoes breeding in the open pits. Noise levels touch 96-125 decibels, way above the permissible limit of 75 decibels causing stress and affecting the mental health of workers (Khurana, 1997).

Miners in asbestos mines are suffering from asbestosis, a disease of the lungs caused by inhaling asbestos particles that ultimately lead to death due to suffocation (Yadav, 2002). The Orissa Voluntary Health Association (OVHA), an NGO, conducted a survey in the chromites mining areas of Sukinda Valley in 1995 under the Orissa Environment Programme, funded by the Norwegian government. It reported the health hazards related to hexavalent chromium are acute, causing irreparable loss to human health. It has the potential to cause ulcers in the pulmonary system and gastrointestinal tract and may also lead to cancer (Barik, 2002).

Prolonged exposure to coal dust causes coal miners pneumos-coniosis (CMP). It is a very unpleasant disease. The lungs lose their natural flexibility and it becomes increasingly difficult to breath. Simple tasks like walking up stairs become impossible. It is a slow and painful death from suffocation (Smith, 2001). There has been 800 deaths in the country over the past two decades in mine accidents, but in the rush to meet ever higher production targets, mine safety measures receive inadequate attention (Choudhuri, 2001). Among major hazards are roof falls in underground mines, and accidents of workers being run over by machinery in open cast mines. Inundations have caused some of the most serious disasters in Indian mines (Smith, 2001).

Sand mining is posing a serious threat to mining districts of Tamil Nadu. People in the region are exposed to lungs related diseases because of the dust emanating from the sand laden lorries. Informal gold mining in Brazil warns a danger. Mercury vapor is the most hazardous of the inorganic forms because it can diffuse through the lung in to the blood and then the brain, where serious damage can occur. Early effects of the central nervous system, including loss of appetite and weight, insomnia were detected on workers exposed to higher concentrations (Biller, 1994).

The exploitation of mineral resources through surface and underground mining has caused wide ranging environmental problem such as air, water and noise pollution. All methods of surface and underground mining results in the generation of wastes that can affect surface water quality. The erosion of dumps and its flow can give rise to silting and choking of existing natural watercourses. It affected ground water table in many areas with the result that the yield of water from the wells of adjoining villages drastically reduced (Areeparampil, 1996).

The magnitude of air pollution in mining areas varies with methods of mining type of minerals and level of mechanization. The problem of dust, fumes and moistures gases, which are the sources of air pollution, are more common in the large mechanized mines. Due to unscientific coal mining in Meghalaya there is an increase in air pollution level, and the weather has become unusually warm in the coal belt of the state (Ghosal, 1998). Open cast and underground mining often exposes large amounts of pyrite and other sulphide minerals to the air, which accelerates their oxidation. Once oxidized to sulphates, they form an acid in water that can severely damage plant and animal life if it leaks from the mine (Harries, 1999). Open cast quarries, coal washeries, thermal power plants, coke oven plants, cement factories, fertilizer plant etc. contribute to serious air pollution (Areepampil, 1996). Continued sand mining in Tamil Nadu has led to obstruction in the free flow of water during the monsoon. It has also hindered the flow of water into the heavily silted Red Hills and Cholavaram lakes, thereby posing a serious threat to Chennai's water supply system (Viswanathan, 2002).

Mining and allied operations also cause serious noise pollution. Mining operation such as drilling, blasting, loading and dumping generates significant noise especially in the work environment. The sound levels in both audible and ultrasound range produced due to the above activities are known to have adverse affect on the human being and livestock.

Pollution of the streams that originate in the mining area affected agriculture and the farmer class. Paddy yield declined because of the accumulation of silt and waste tailings in the fields. During monsoon water brings with it silt and tailings. This solidity hardens in summer. Nothing grows on the field. The tailings rendered the sand unfit even for construction purposes (Sharma, 2001). Extensive illegal mining of silicon sand has resulted in depletion of ground water and consequently affected agriculture. With drain canals blocked, agricultural lands were getting flooded in several places.

Mining and associated activities resulted in the loss of habitat and the fragmentation of the contiguous block of tropical moist forest and grasslands. In the mining area biodiversity is at a low level. Although several species of grass and herbs have sprung up in areas abandoned after mining, they are insufficient to stabilize the broken soil (Sharma, 2002). Mining especially opencast mining would disturb the land mass. Slope stability problems give rise to landslides and rapid soil erosion. Blanketing of topsoil in the nearly agricultural grazing land results in poor yield. Due to open cast mining forest land and consequently flora and fauna would get disturbed. Extensive damage to the national wealth without any compensatory aforestation disturb the ecosystem greatly.

Extensive mining of coastal sand for uranium and construction purposes is damaging the coastal ecology and livelihoods of Tamil Nadu. Mining operations have the potential to cause severe sea erosion, which will have an adverse impact on the fishing communities on the coast. The disappearance of sand dunes owing to indiscriminate mining has made interior land vulnerable to storms and cyclones. (Viswanathan, 2002). Shrinking habitat due to deforestation and mining activities disturbs the tranquility of elephant habitation. As a result they entere human territory and cause widespread destruction (Barik, 2001).

There have been many instances when people in the vicinity of mining industry have complained of vibration problems. Unsound blasting operation results in vibration. It damages houses and other surface structures due to blast vibration. It results in acceleration of landslides in hilly areas, destruction or weakening of structures, rattling and breaking of window pans, annoyance to human beings and livestock. Underground mining operations; especially of coal have created unsafe surface conditions in many areas warranting diversion of roads, railway lines, etc., and the shifting of a number of townships. Most of the localities are unsafe for human habitation (Areeparamphil, 1996).

Growth of mining activities has acted as the most powerful stimulant in the emergence of new industries and in the growth of new urban centers. There in turn have caused further alienation of indigenous people land and their displacement. Private contractors illegally mine a lot of land. Land is also converted into roads, townships of miners, infrastructure for administrative purposes. Further disposal of mining debris creates pollution and makes agricultural fields infertile forcing the people to abandon or alienate their lands and move out of the areas.

IB VALLEY COAL FIELD

According to the Geological Survey of India (GSI) a total of 234.11 billion tones of coal reserves are estimated as on 1-1-2002. Jharkhand has the highest 70.52 BT, placing Orissa in second place with 58.01 BT. Out of 57 Gondwana and 14 tertiary coalfields for the national inventory of coal, Orissa state has only two coalfields. Talcher coalfield and Ib valley coalfield.

IB valley coalfield located in Jharsuguda and Sundargarh districts of Orissa. The main Howrah-Bombay railway line passes through this coalfield. The Madras-Calcutta railway line also connects the coalfields at Jharsuguda. This coalfield is also connected to state highway, which in turn, joins the National Highway No.6 at Sambalpur. B.N. Railway first discovered IB valley coalfield while constructing a bridge over IB river in the year 1990. M/S Himgir Rampur Coal Company opened colliery in the year 1909. Many more mines were opened in the year 1940, 1954 and after the nationalization of coalmines, the mines came under WEL. Later on it came under SECL and than under MCL (Mahanadi Coalfield Limited) in the year 1992 after it's formation. Production of this field was 0.55 MT in 1972-73, which has increased up to 14.70 MT in the year 2001-02. IB valley coalfield has four areas. IB valley area, Orient area, Lakhanpur area, and Basundhara area.

ENVIRONMENTAL PROBLEMS IN IB VALLEY AREA :

Mining activities in IB valley area is now more than half a century old. MCL is trying to be the largest producer of coal in the world, while the state government is worried about the royalties and taxes from this sector. In such a situation no one seems to care for the environment and the indigenous people. The following are some of the major environmental hazards, which people of that area are facing.

Water Pollution: With the starting of coal mines water pollution has become a major problem. Availability of a ground water in wells of the adjoining villages is reduced drastically. People are facing of acute scarcity of water for their fields and daily needs. Depletion of ground water and pollution of surface water is the basic cause for that.

Noise Pollution: Blasting for coal, drilling and other related activities are causing noise pollution. It is causing stress and affecting the mental health of the workers. Blast vibrations are damaging the houses and other surface structures.

Air Pollution : Due to operation of mining and other allied activities air pollution in this area is increasing. With operation of CHP, along with transportation of coal the amount of dust in air is increasing.

Impacts on health : Human beings and animals are inhaling small sized coal dust particle equal to 5 micron (1000 micron= 1 mm) as a result asthma and bronchitis has became a major health problem of this area. Cases of malaria, tuberculosis and skin diseases areon the increase as a result human and animal death rate has increased.

Deforestation: Before mining started this area was a dense forest. The state government has given nearly 10,231 hector of land to MCL for coal mining of IB valley. For aforestation programme MCL has given Rs.1,95,88,188 to Sambalpur District Forest Officer (DFO) between 1991 to 1993. But not a single plant has been planted (Bitarka, 2000). Although aforestation programme in the OB dump is going on by MCL, that is not sufficient to keep the ecological balance of that area. Temperature of this area has raisen to 48 degree Celsius, posing a serious threat to the life of that area. A significant change has also been seen in the amount of rainfall.

Loss in Productivity : Polluted water from mines is entering the nearby agricultural field, resulting in the deterioration of soil quality. As a result agricultural productivity is also declining. It is also affecting the grazing land of the nearby area.

Displacement: Exploitation of mineral resources has resulted in large-scale displacement and the displaced persons are not properly resettled or rehabilitated. Though resettlement colonies have been established there is no sufficient infrastructural facilities.

Socio-economic Impact: With additional employment opportunities being created population of that area has suddenly increased. Jobs available in mines generally require skilled people. So there is large-scale immigration of people to this area. Due to their higher demand and requirements the cost of essential items materials automatically up higher in the coal markets-creating problems for the local people. Children are encouraged to earn their livelihood at the cost of their studies.

Geological Problem: As thousand tonnes of coal are being extracted daily, it is expected to have an adverse impact in the nearby Hirakud dam. People are also complaining of mild earthquake.

Coal India Limited (CIL), as a matter of policy is committed to ameliorate the ill effects of mining in a systematic way. This has necessitated the evolving of a corporate environmental policy.

CORPORATE ENVIRONMENTAL POLICY OF COAL INDIA LIMITED

The objective of this policy is to lay down guidelines for its subsidiary companies, enabling them to develop methodologies and work plans to match guiding principles of sustainable development. The policy entails a compliance of environmental statues, guidelines, instructions of legal agencies and implementation of the provisions of the Environmental Management Plan (EMP).

The Environmental Policy aims at building up an organizational capacity at all levels to meet the challenge. Besides this it also integrates Environmental Impact Assessment (EIA) and EMP with mine planning, designing, operation, mitigation of adverse environmental impact to the best possibel extent, training environmental personnel and arousing awareness at all levels.

CIL has laid down strategies in order to achieve the desired results. The strategy envisages that all mine planning and design must have the EMP as its integral part to be environmentally acceptable. CIL through its policy plans to continuously strive to help its technical capability for environmental protection and development of organizational capability to address the impact of mining. It also proposes to give annual awards for achieving excellence in environmental programmes to its subsidiary companies.

CIL intends to place in position environment cells at all levels. It plans to have environmental cells at Unit, Colliery, Area, Company Headquarters, CIL corporate level and

CMPDIL. The first phase of the plan is to obtain environmental clearance by the Ministry of Environment and Forest (MOEF). The second would comprise of mines having EMP cleared by CIL or Company Boards.

MEASURES TAKEN BY MCL TO PROTECT AND IMPROVE ENVIRONMENT

According to the Annual Report 2001-02 of MCL the following measures have been taken to protect and improve environment.

Aforestation and Land Reclamation: Afforestation drive in the mines of MCL continued vigorously and 2,60,000 saplings of mixed species have been planted during 2001-02. Special attention is being given to vegetating the slopes. OB Dump Reclamation Plan, approved by the expert of IIT, Kanpur appointed under World Bank assistance to CIL for 23 Old External dumps was implemented. Spice, dry fruit and fruit bearing trees were planted on dumps along with other multipurpose trees.

Air Pollution Control Measures: Provision of fixed point, auto start, fine nozzle mounted water sprinklers on roads, railway siding and CHPs. Installation of Dust Control System and Dust Extraction System. In CHPs and at transfer points elsewhere. Green belts have been created between residential area and mine infrastructure for dust control. Tender was opened for procurement of 6 Nos of Multipurpose Hydroseeder-cum-Fire-Water Tender which will be used for throwing of seeds on the OB dumps with the help of water, for watering the plants on the slope of OB dumps and also to be used as water sprinkler.

Water Pollution Control Measures: Effluents from mines, Workshop, settling ponds and spoil dumps are made to conform to standards of MOEF before being discharged into the natural drains and steams/ nalas. Mine seepage water is made to settle in big sedimentation lagoons created in the quarry bed. Mine Discharge Treatment Plants (MDTPs) have been provided in each mine before the water discharge point to surface or nalas. Garland drains have been provided near the toe of OB dumps as well as quarry boundaries. Water is monitored at all discharge points and all the parameters remain within prescribed limit.

Noise and Ground Vibration Control Measures : Green belts have been created between the residential colonies and the mines and their infrastructural facilities like CHPs, Railway Siding, Workshop etc. To attenuate the noise level and to arrest the movement of dust. Workers exposed to noise beyond permissible limits have been provided with earmuffs and earplugs. No electric detonators are used for blasting. Controlled blasting practice is adopted whenever it is necessary.

Environmental Monitoring and Environmental Audit: Regular monitoring of Air, Water, Noise and Soil are carried out including micro meteorological studies through Government agencies whose laboratories are duly recognized by MOEF in this regard. The results or monitoring are scrutinized by a senior officer at headquarter and any upward trend is immediately brought to the notice of the project authorities for taking corrective measures. Results of monitoring are submitted to State Pollution Control Board (SPCB) on monthly basis and to MOEF on half-yearly basis. Environmental audit was conducted in each project by a multi disciplinary audit team and environmental statement was submitted to SPCB and MOEF.

Environmental Awareness: Environment week was celebrated in June 2001 starting with World Environment Day on 5th June in all the mines of MCL. Month long Van Mahotsav was also celebrated which was inaugurated on 5th July. Environmental awareness training programme are conducted at regular intervals for the employees of MCL on the subject of Environmental Management in Mining Areas. Basically the programmes undertaken during the Environment week/ Van-Mahostav include fruit tree plantation, painting, essay competition among the school children, wide circulation of environmental booklets. Training manuals, screening of videocassettes on Environment theme, organizing cycle rally, street plays etc.

Environmental Award and Recognition: Indo-German Environment Excellence Awarded for 2000-01, organized by Greentech Foundation, New Delhi and Centre for the

International Transfer of Environmental Technologies, Germany was bagged by MCL for outstanding achievement in the field of Environmental Management. TERI has extended special invitation for MCL to join as a member of Corporate Roundtable Development of Strategies for the Environment (CORE), an exclusive group of companies, which included NTPC, TISCO, TELCO, and ONGC etc. MCL was short listed by the award committee for "TERI Corporate Environment Award" 2001-02.

Though the coal companies are sincere to implement the various measures as envisaged in the environmental management plans, they are also facing some problems. Generally the coalfield has other industries in the vicinity, which equally contribute to the pollution of land, air, water and the immediate surroundings. The State Pollution Control Board and state government should act as an overall coordinator to maintain a healthy environment pin pointing the responsibility to various industries (Patnaik, 1990).

M/s. Envirocare, Rourkela, Orissa has published a report on environmental monitoring in this area. The Suspended Particulate Matter (SPM) concentration at 8 hourly intervals for 24 hours for continuously 8 days in a season gives a clear status of pollution caused by SPM in the atmosphere. SPM concentration in some area varies from 102 microgram/m^3 to 425 microgram/m^3. Surface water was compared with drinking water quality, IS: 10500, and mine discharge was compared with IS : 2490. It is observed that the drinking water quality sometimes does not meet the prescribed standard for suspended solids.

CONCLUSION

Though the company has been telling that a lot of work is going on for the protection of the environment, but only a visit to the site reveals the true story of the area and it's people. For this the state pollution control board has to play an important role. Another significant role has to be played by media to bring environmental awareness among people. Social work organizations and trade unions have also a significant role.

The concept of carrying capacity will have to taken into consideration in decision making for mining projects. Carrying capacity of any ecosystem is an important parameter in selecting the modes to sustainable development.

Carrying capacity is defined as the physical limit for economic development or maximum rate of resource utilization and waste discharge, which can be supported or assimilated by regional environment indefinitely without affecting the ecological integrity (Khanna, 1991). The prediction of impacts of mining using mathematical models or expert opinion can be done. Better management of mining activity is expected to enhance the economic and ecological value addition. However, costs and benefits of such management practices need to be assessed in order to arrive at feasible policy intervention.

A proper balance needs to be struck between two needs namely urgent economic development and protection and preservation of the environment. It is thus necessary to start a comprehensive programme of data compilation and analysis in the mining industry for this purpose. Suitable guidelines are to be evolved as regards the methodologies of environmental impact analysis and assessment in the mining industry and steps to be taken right from the planning and implementation stage, for the protection of the environment (Mahapatro, 1990).

The mining industry professional must find ways of mining with the minimum possible impact on the environment, and where such damage is inevitable steps should be taken to reclaim the land and afforestate the area as long as possible after mining is over. Industrial activity creates environmental hazards but this can be controlled very efficiently if the society cooperates the industry. If the society and the industry plan together and work the improvement of the country as well as of the area will be much better. We should try for developments with protection of the environment instead of development at the cost of environment.

REFERENCES

Agrawal Anil and Narain Sunita (edt. 1997), "Dying Wisdom", Centre for Science and Environment, New Delhi.

Areeparampil Mathew (1996), "Displacement due to Mining in Jharkhand", Economic and Political Weekly, No.24, pp. 1524-1528.

Ayres Wendy, S, Andersion Katheleen, Hanrahan David (1998), "Setting Priorities for Environmental Management: An Application to the Mining Sector in Bolivia, World Bank Technical Paper No. 398, The World Bank, Washington, D.C.

Barik Satyasundar (2002), "Polluter's Heaven", Down to Earth, April 30 pp.10.

Barik Satyasundar (2001), "Driven up the Trees", Down to Earth, May 15, pp. 18,19.

Barik Satyasundar (2002), "Valley of Despair", Down to Earth, July 31, pp. 38,39.

Bennagen Ma. Eugenia C. (1997), "Estimation of Environmental Damages from Mining Pollution: The Marindague Island Mining Accident, IDRC, Ottawa, Canada.

Bertelmus Peter (1994), "Environment, Growth and Development: The Concepts and Strategy of Sustainability", Routledge, London.

Hangara Ratnakar (1996), "Coal Mining Displacement", Economic and Political Weekly, No.11, pp. 647-651.

Bhatachrya Rabindra N. (edt 2001), "Environmental Economics An Indian Perspective", Oxford University Press, New Delhi.

Biller Dan (1994), "Informal Gold Mining and Mercury Pollution in Brazil", Policy Research Working Paper No.1304, The World Bank.

Bojo Jan, Maler Karl Goran, Unemo Lena (1992), "Environment and Development: An Economic Approach", Kluwer Academic Publishers (1992), London.

Bosson Rex, Varion Bension (1977), "The Mining Industry and the Developing Countries", Oxford Economic Papers.

Brown Barbara E, Dunne Richard P. (1988), "The Environmental Impact of Coral Reefs in the Maldives,Environmental Conservation, Vol.15, No.2, pp. 159-166.

Brown Lester R, Flavin Christopher, Postal Sandra (1994), "Saving the Planet", Orient Longman Limited, Bombay.

Carson Richard T, Wilks Leanne, David Imber (1994), "vAluing the Preservation of Australia's Kakadu Conservation Zone", Oxford Economic Papers, Vol.46 Supplement, pp. 727-749.

Common Micheal (1998), "Environmental and Resource Economics", Longman, London.

Das Vidya (1995), Development or Destruction? New Mining Projects in Orissa", Economic and Political Weekly, No.22. pp.1281-1282.

Das Vidya (2001), "Mining Bauxite, Maiming People", Economic and Political Weekly No.28, pp.2612-2614.

Folmer Henk, Gabel H. Landis, Gerking Shelby, Rose Adam (edt. 2001), "Frontiers of Environmental Economics", Edward Elgar Publishing Limited, Cheltenham, UK.

Goodstein Eban S. (1995), "Economics and the Environment", Prentice-Hal, Inc. Englewood Cliffs, New Jersey.

Khanna, P. (1990), "Role of EIA in Sustainable Development", Workshop on EIA of Multipurpose River Valley Projects, Kosi, India.

Kothari Ashish (1995), "Environment and New Economic Policies", Economic and Political Weekly, No.17, pp.924-928.

Mahapatra, R.K. (1990), "Project Report on Study of Environmental Pollution in IB Valley Coal Fields.

Mittal.D.K. (1994), "Coal Industry", Anmol Publications Pvt. Ltd., New Delhi.

Mohapatra Richard (1999), "Confrontation Mine", Down to Earth, April 15, pp.20-23.

Mukul (1995), "Destruction of Mining and Miners", Economic and Political Weekly, No.38, pp.2365-2366.

Patnaik Lalit N (edt.1990), "Environmental Impacts of Industrial and Mining Activities, Ashish Publishing House, New Delhi.

Panayotou Theodore (1993), "Green Markets: The Economics of Sustainable Development", Institute for Contemporary Studies Press, San Francisco.

Pearce, D.W. (1976), "Environmental Economics", Longman Inc, New York.

Sharma Ravi (2001), "Kudremukh Concerns", Frontline, September 14, pp.64-71.

Tanzen Micheal (1980), "The Race for Resources, Continuing Struggles Over Minerals and Fuels", Monthly Review Press, New York.

Tietenberg, T. (1988), "Environment and Natural Resource Economics", Foresman and Company, London.

World Bank (1992), "World Development Report: Development and Environment.

Yadav Kushal P.S. (2002), "Sitting Ducks", Down to Earth, April 15, pp. 34-37.

16

DEFORESTATION AND ENVIRONMENT

Babu, B.S. Rao

Forest are the very basis of our survival as they maintain the proper balance of organisms, chemicals, in the environment by producing or absorbing them and preventing soil erosion, floods and draughts, etc. In olden days we had plenty of forests and vegetation. But now the area of forests was decreased to a greater extent. The forests of a country make a natural asset of immense value. Forests are the only source of timber, wood, fuel, bamboos and rich source of a variety of a valuable products including fodder, which are indispensable requirements of the people living in close proximity of forest.

DEFORESTATION

Forests in developing countries are going to be reduced at an alarming rate. Deforestation breaks the delicate environmental balance, which is maintained by nature itself, floods or broughts are the terrible consequences. The process of deforestation is a serious threat to economy, quality of life and future of the Environment in our country. The total forest area of the world was estimated to be 7000 million hectares in 1900. By 1975 it was reduced to 2890 million hectares and if the trend of reduction continues it is expected that only 2370 million hectares by 2000 A.D.

Maximum reduction has been estimated in India, Burma, and Srilanka. The rate of destruction of forests is thus alarming in developing countries like India. Table-1 shows the comparative situation of forest cover 1993 and 1991 assessment in square kilometers. In total Himachal Pradesh is increasing forest area, while Andhra Pradesh is decreasing its area to an extent of 34 sq. km. In this paper an attempt is made to study:

Table 1
Comprative Situation of Forest Cover-1993 and 1991 Assessment

(sq.km.)

State/Uts	*1991 Assessment*	*1993 Assessment*	*Change in 1993*
Andhra Pradesh	47290	47256	-34
Arunachal Pradesh	68757	68661	-96
Assam	24751	24508	-43
Bihar	26668	26587	-81
Goa (including DIU)	1255	1250	-5
Gujarat	11907	12044	+137
Haryana	513	513	-
Himachal Pradesh	11780	12502	+722
Jammu & Kashmir	20064	20443	+379
Karnataka	32199	32343	+144
Kerala	10292	10336	+44
Madhya Pradesh	135785	135396	-389
Maharashtra	40044	43859	-185
Manipur	17685	17621	-64
Meghalaya	15875	15769	-106
Mizoram	18853	18697	-156
Nagland	14321	14348	+27
Orissa	47205	47145	-60
Punjab	1343	1343	-
Rajasthan	12835	13099	+264
Sikkim	3033	3119	+86
Tamilnadu	174713	17726	+13
Tripura	5535	5538	+3
Uttar Pradesh	33609	33961	+252
West Bengal	8015	8186	+171
Andaman & Nikobar	7622	7624	+2
Chandigarh	5	5	-
Dodra & Nagar Haveli	206	206	-
Delhi	22	22	-
Lakshdweep	-	-	-
Pandicherry	-	-	-
Total	639182	640107	+925

Source: Environmental Chemistry : P:F-10

- the reasons for deforestation and
- effects of deforestation on Environment.

The process of forest destruction is a world wide tragedy. It is estimated that a forest of the size of Cuba is being destroyed every year. Global 2000 described as a gloom and doom report, is a warning and a call to action. If the deforestation rate continues at the same rate, the present multiple strains on the earth resource base and Environment could become much worse. The important cares of deforestation in India are

(a) Rapid explosion of human and livestock population
(b) Increased requirement of timber and fuel wood because of increase in population,
(c) Expansion of agricultural crop lands for farming and enhanced grazing by cattle,
(d) Construction of dams, power stations, roads, highways, stone mines and other similar projects,
(e) Development of industries, quarrying, irrigation and agriculture,
(f) Increased demand for fuel wood, wooden crates, paper, new prints, medicines etc.,

Table 2
The Area and Reason of Deforestation between 1951-1972 in India

Reason	*Area (Hect.)*
River valley project	401000
Agriculture	2433000
Road Construction and Transport	55000
Industries	125000
Others	388000
Total	3402000

Source: Conservation of Forests : F.19

Table–2 depicts about he are and reasons of deforestation between 1951-1972 in India. The table shows about 3,80,000 hectares of forest area was destroyed for other purposes. This tells that for the non-agricultural reasons also deforestation is going on. During this period (1951-72) about 34, lakh hectares of forest was destroyed.

It should be noted that deforestation is also responsible for soil erosion. Deforestation is the main cause of floods, droughts, loss of precious, wild life, change in land scape, wind direction, temperature and humidity of the surrounding area. It also changes the composition of air in atmosphere on which all life depends. As a result of deforestation, the economy of the country, quality of life of human beings and future of environment have been much deteriorated. In himalayan regions shortage of fire wood and water causes great hardship to people living in that region. They have to spend almost whole of the day in the collection of fire wood for cooking meals of the day. If the trend continues, the time will come when the lost of food would be much lesser than the cost of fuel to cook it.

FOREST–THE VANISHING WEALTH

Today the World's ecological mess is growing at an alarming rate and the acute forest depletion problems are causing concern all over the globe. In fact, a new unforeseen crisis in threatening the man kind. The murder of the environment which involves, senseless poisoning of the earth, air and water as well as destruction of forest wealth may be called as 'Ecocide'. The maximum deforestation was in Punjab, followed by Rajasthan, Gujarat and Harayana.

Deforestation is a Heavy loss to green wealth and some aspects of the brightening scenario would be

- Erosion of million of tones of productive soil and of gene deposits which are essential for crops.
- A ten fold increases in flood damage which is already very heavy.
- Degradation of more than 70 percent of Agricultural land.
- Regional decrease in rain fall, exacerbating desertification.

- Global increase in temperature becuase of the rise in atmospheric carbon leading to a rise in sea levels.
- Loss of precious wild life.

To sum up, environmental education is essential for the proper management. Critics look at the sustainable logging and foresting as mere sugar coated pills for the continued exploitation of the rain forests and of the poor tribal lives. What we need today, is an ecologically sound and socially just forest convention that totally bans deforestation for any reason what so ever, and that would safe guard the last, chances for the survival of the forest tribals. Aforestation is necessary because there is general shortage of forests. Unless the people control the deforestation, the day will come that people in this country may not die of hunger in near future, but may die due to their inability to cook the food because of scarcity of fire wood.

"We have to live on earth
we cannot go live on the planets.
Let us keep the earth clean
Let us keep the earth peaceful"

REFERENCES

B.D. Naga Choudari and S. Bhalt (1987), The Global Environment Movement, Sterling Publications Pvt. Ltd.

K.A. Longman and J. Jenik (1974), Tropical Forest and Its Environment, Longman, London.

Danbenmire, R.F. (1974), Plants and Environment, 3rd ed. John Wiley, New York.

Kumar, V.K. (1982), A Study in Environment Pollution, Tara Book Agency, Varanasi.

17

TRADE RELATED GLOBAL ENVIRONMENTAL ISSUES AND WORLD TRADE ORGANISATION

M. Sundara Rao, A. Sailaja Devi

INTRODUCTION

International trade is in "engine of growth" has been the belief of many countries and also international organizations. This belief originated in Adam Smith and has continued to influence the policies of a large number of countries in the mid-twentieth century. In recent years many new issues have come to the forefront to influence the trade patterns. The concern of environment is one, which has been exerting dominant influences in the world trade.

Global economy has adopted the path of overall development. Development implies increase in GNP, per capita, income, improvement the levels of standard of living, political stability, and environmental balance. Modern economic development is based on maximization of consumption and exploitation of resources, which have resulted in environmental imbalance in developing economics. Environment is the composite effect of all elements involved in the process of development.

The concern about environmental pollution and its degradation has been growing over the recent years. Matters relating to improvement in the environmental situation are areas of major anxiety by the policy makers, industrial establishments as well as the academics. The increasing interest on the subject of environment has been caused due to various kinds of problems arising out of the development and growth process which are threatening the healthy living of the people of the world as a whole. But the environmental problems are often thought of as being unique characteristics of highly developed industrialized society and it is not certainly true. But, within the next few decades, the environment in developing countries will become at least as large as issue as it is in the developed world today.

Some Global Issues

The broader global issues such as global warming, biodiversity and ozone layer depletion have dominated global protocols. It has emphasized that an increase in average global temperature would induce a number of natural changes with significant effects on population. Depletion of the ozone layer has also been a source of anxiety as it results in ultra violet light penetrating the atmosphere. This could have devastating effects on human beings, animals and the natural environment. There is a need to examine the ways in which developed and developing economies perceive environmental pollution.

The present day policies dealing with environment are inadequate and they are inherently incapable of tackling the escalating degradation of the human environment. A time has come when serious debate must start to emphasize that the taxation should be levied in proportion human endeavour. This requires a major shift in our thinking, a careful policy formulation and designing of an appropriate institutional framework to safeguard the common prosperity resources for promoting sustainable development. Therefore, environmental issues should not be viewed from a sectoral perspective or regarded as an add on consideration, because they form an integral part of all human activities. There is an urgent need to include the concept of "Environmental Burden" in international trade and commerce.

Specific Problems of Third World Countries

Transforming developing countries from an agricultural to an industrial economy has been the focus of the planners, underpinned by goals of stimulating growth and reducing poverty. But environmental degradation has emerged as a major global concern for human survival. As part of political agenda, environmental issues are raised in a particular way, often notoriously based towards the interest of industrial nations. Thus, the stringent measures applicable to these developed countries may not be necessary to be the same for developing countries.

It is futile to attempt to deal environmental problems without a broader perspective that encompasses the factors underlying world poverty and international inequality. It makes sense to ask those countries, which have the largest responsibility for the damage to the world environment, and these happen to be the rich countries. Developing countries obviously cannot be expected to accept that their growth should be held in check if the result is damage to environment. Developing countries may view global policies as an imposition on their goal of development. A key aspect of this is the contribution of developed and developing countries to the main forms of environmental pollution and in turn the relative responsibility of both groups in minimizing production and consumption activities which intensify environmental problems. Against this background an attempt is made to examine the trade related global environmental issues under the regimes of World Trade Organization. In this direction it is planned to discuss about the issues relating to environment and International Trade (Section 1.1), GATT and WTO on environment and trade (Section 1.2), specific environmental issues of the Indian economy (Section 1.3), and a package of policy suggestions are presented at the end (Section 1.4).

Environment and International Trade

International trade and environment have the issues at debate ever since the developed countries became industrialized. In the process of rapid industrialization, the developed countries had prospered at the cost of exploitation of natural resources. Cities and towns have become polluted, forests denudation have led to climatic changes, ozone layer is being depleted, fertility of earth is getting reduced, oceans are polluted and are getting shorn of their natural wealth and so on. In the Uruguay Round, a relationship between trade and sustainable development was emphasized.

Through International trade environmental externalities can transcend national boundaries, trade flows can be affected by the environmental policies; and environmental policies can affect the trade flows. Thus, trade and environment can be complemental policies can affect the trade flows. Thus, trade and environment can be complementary or competitive. The World Development Report, 1992 reports that the world can hope for a better and cleaner environment through the reduction of polluting industries and adoption of cleaner technologies, and international trade could foster this. According to the signatories of the Uruguay Round of GATT, there should be no such; conflicts between international trade and environment.

GATT and WTO on Environment and Trade

Although the issue of trade and environmental was not directly included in the Uruguay Round of negotiations, yet certain environmental conclusions were addressed. Towards the end of the Uruguay Round, a Ministerial Decision on trade and Environment was adopted (April 1994) calling for the establishment of a Committee on Trade and Environment (CTE). A broad based mandate was agreed upon for the CTE consisting of identifying the relationship between trade measures and environmental measures in order to promote sustainable development and of making appropriate recommendations on whether any modifications of the provisions of the multilateral trading system are required.

In the Uruguay Round two agreements were formulated, agreements on Technical Barries to Trade, agreement on Sanitary and Phyto-Sanitary measures (SPS). These agreements deal with the measures to be taken by governments to protect human, animal and plant life along with domestic environment and health. Besides, agreements on the following had undergone some alternations having some bearing on environment and trade.

Agreement on Agriculture

Under this agreement, WTO members are exempted from direct payment under environmental programmes (to reduce domestic support for agricultural production), subject to certain conditions.

Agreement on Subsides & Countervailing Measures

Thus, we find that whilst developed countries were subjected to increased pressure from vocal environmental interest groups to reconcile what they perceived as 'incompatibilities' between trade and environmental policies, developing countries feared that environmental concerns would be addressed at the expense of international trade. In particular, fears that a new 'green' conditionality would be attached to marked access opportunities, emerged. Within this context, certain parameters that have guided trade and environment discussions in the WTO. That the WTO is not an environmental protection agency and that is competence for policy coordination in this area is limited to trade policies, and those trade-related aspects of environmental policies which may result in a significant effect on trade. That GATT/WTO Agreement already provide significant scope for national environmental protection policies, provided that they are non-discriminatory. That secure market access opportunities are essential to help developing countries work towards sustainable development. That increased national coordination as well as multilateral cooperation is necessary to adequately address trade-related environmental concerns.

To address the complementarily between trade and environment, the WTO's role is to continue to liberalize trade as well as to ensure that environmental policies do not act as obstacles to trade and that trade rules do not stand in the way of adequate domestic environmental protection. WTO members believe that WTO rules already provide significant scope for members to adopt national environmental protection policies. Non-discrimination is one of the main principles on which multilateral trading system has been founded. It is a principle, which guarantees secure and access to markets, protects the economically weak from the more powerful, and guarantees consumer choice.

From the point of view of the developing countries, where poverty is the number one policy preoccupation and the most important obstacle to environmental protection, the opening up of world markets to their exports is extremely essential. WTO members recognize that trade liberalization for developing countries generate the resources they need to protect the environment and work towards their sustainable development. As many developing countries are heavily dependent on the export of natural resources for foreign exchange earnings; trade liberalization is expected to contribute towards their improved allocation and more efficient use of resources, as also to enhanced export opportunities for their manufactured.

WTO Committee on Trade and Environment (CTE)

To decisions were adopted during the Uruguay Round, which address environmental issues. The Ministerial Decision on Trade and Environment, created the CTE with the aim to making international trade and environmental policies mutually supportive. The Decision contains the work programme of the CTE. Ministers also adopted a Decision on Trade in Service and Environment. The decision has instructed the CTE to examine the relationship between trade and the environment including the issue of sustainable development.

Specific Environment Related Areas Under WTO

- Dispute Settlement and WTO transparency Provisions. When a dispute arises between WTO members who are parties of MEA over the use of trade measures pursuant to MEA. Then this has to be resolved through dispute settlement mechanism available forum for dispute settlement. This provides proper functioning of multilateral trading system to prevent unnecessary trade restriction and distortions in providing information about market opportunities and to avoid trade disputes from arising. The WTO provisions also ensure that trade and environmental policies are developed and implemented in a mutually supportive way. Transparency should not be more onerous in trade-related environmental measures in that the CTE states that no modifications to WTO rules are required for other measures that also affect trade.

- Issues of export of Domestically Prohibited goods and trade liberalization. Developing countries raised the concern that hazardous or toxic products were being exported in their country, which are domestically prohibited, and without informing them fully about environment or public health hazards of the products. GATT stipulates that the importing country should be fully aware of the product it was receiving and has the right to reject them subject to the importing country's health hazard problems. WTO members are moving forward to full implementation of trade liberalization after the Round. UNCED recognized an open non-discriminatory trading system as a pre-requisite for effective action to protect environment and to generate sustainable development. Developing countries depend on trade as the main source of continued growth and prosperity.
- Trade in Services, TRIPS and Eco-labeling. CTE was to require to examine WTO's role in relation to the links between environmental measures and the new trade agreements on services and intellectual property reached in the Uruguay Round. CTE's report states that the discussions in CTE have not led identifications of any measure that members fee may be applied for environmental purposes to trade in services. The TRIPS is a provision of GATT, which seeks to impose certain minimum standards of property of intellectual property rights (IPRs) among WTO members. IPRs are crucial in the context of environmental standards: e.g., patents, plant

rights and trade secrets. TRIPS dealing with multilateral trade agreements are crucial.

Programmes for environmental protection promoting environment - friendly products and processes are the main content of Eco-labeling. It is essentially a type of certification (either by a private organization or by a mixed public-private organization) of goods which are environmentally eco-friendly. These programmes are voluntary in nature, except in a few cases where labeling is mandatory. Programmes should be opened to both domestic and foreign manufactures. Trade experts, however, think eco-discrimination between home produced and imports or between imports from and imports to the trading partners. Environmental policies, that incorporate trade provisions or affect trade significantly should be based on the principle of non-discrimination.

Implications of WTO's Environmental Standards on India

The Implications of WTO's environmental standards for the Indian economy could be discussed from two angles: effect of trade reforms on environment, and effect of domestic environmental policies on international trade. On the first account, it is argued that recent trade policies like liberalization in the form of drastic reduction in tariff rates and subsidies are likely to have adverse consequences on environmental degradation in industries like leather and leather products, pharmaceutical and drugs, etc. But such an environmental degradation can possibly be avoided through the use of appropriate economic instruments. In this regard, certain factors are worth nothing. First of all, stricter environmental regulations might lead to higher costs to producers, thus affecting their comparative advantage in international markets. Similarly, India has expressed concern about the German packaging order, which are not readily available in India. The other industries, which are likely to be adversely affected, are motor vehicles and pharmaceuticals. Industries which are identified as creating above average environmental pollution include primary metallurgical producing industries including zinc, lead, copper, aluminum and steel, paper, pulp and newsprint/pesticides/insecticides/refineries/fertilizers: paints/dyes: leather tanning/ rayon: sodium/potassium cyanide/basic drugs/ foundry/ storage batteries/ acids/ industry/ and electroplating industry.

These are likely to affect India's exports of these articles. In general, the production conditions of Indian agriculture may be dubbed as unhygienic and pollutive by international standards, and adherence to such norms would nullify much of our comparative advantages in these products, so that liberalization of agricultural trade, as per the WTO directions, could be counter productive to the Indian economy.

In the case of marine products, the Indian exporters of shrimps to USA had to face a major crisis when USA stipulated that it would not impart shrimp if during the process of catching fish endangered species of sea-turtle are being harmed. It is unlikely that in the near future the WTO would change its stance on environmental standards, such that the Indian exports in a number of products are threatened with discriminatory deals.

However, the awareness to produce eco-friendly goods among Indian should be raised through campaigning of eco-labeling programmes. Indian industry has to go for higher level of environmental standards in future to meet the domestic environmental needs and the importing partner's demand. Moreover, CTE's stand for free - trade will support Indian economy dependence on foreign trade for its continued growth and prosperity.

Conclusion and Policy Suggestions

Though there is a dilemma regarding development and environmental balance, some policy measures can be suggested for developing countries in this regard, such as, population control, minimization of human needs, stress on small/ cottage industries, national urban environmental policy, environmental conservation and planning, stress on rural and regional development etc. If developing economics want to have environmental balance attaining sustainable development, there should be rational combination of theory and practice for economic, social and ecological considerations.

The developing countries experience immediate environmental problems related to scarcity and safety of drinking water, inadequate sanitation facilities, air pollution in urban areas, soil depletion and degradation, indoor smoke from burning of wood, coal and dung and from burning of coal for industrial production. In contrast, the industrialized countries encounter different set of problems, such as carbon dioxide emissions, petro chemical smog and depletion of atmospheric ozone, acid rain and hazardous wastes. Thus, the third world countries must rely on their own resources and technology for protecting the environment, instead of joining hands with the outcry of developed countries on environmental issues. Developing countries like India will be better off, if we focus our attention to these immediate problems.

Thus, a pragmatic environmental policy should emphasize preventive measures instead of relying on curative approaches. A "paradigm shift" is called for to ensure a healthy environment for the well-being of present and future generations. We must have the wisdom and sense of responsibility so that a cleaner and "Safer Earth Planet" is handed over to the future generation and the pollution free environment is shared by all nations.

The challenges faced by the Indian economy in the globalization process are intricate and numerous. Of these, the domestic factors could be marshaled by the design of appropriate socio-economic policies for the country's development. But the external factors, like the environmental standards of WTO, impose restrictions, which are outside the domain of domestic policy experiments and the scope for international cooperation and coordination seems extremely difficult and time consuming in the present day context of global political economy. The positive aspects of trade liberalization under the WTO regime have to be counterbalanced against the stupendous task of enhancing the market access problem for Indian exports which are facing numerous non-tariff barriers in the garb of environmental protection.

REFERENCES

Anderson, Kym and Balckhurst, Richard eds. (1992), "The Greening of World Trade Issues", Harvester Wheatshef, Britain.

Bhagwati J.N. and T.N. Srivasan (1995), "Trade and the Environment", Mimeo.

Bhattacharya B and L.D. Mogo (1998), "Trade and Environment Issue in the WTO-Indian Experience", Foreign Trade Review, IIFT, New Delhi.

Chatterjee Biswajit (2000), "Environment, Trade and Globalisation-Emerging Issues and Policy Options", N.K. Prasad Memorial Lecture, delivered at the 4th Annual Conference of Economic Association of Bihar, Patna, May 28, 2000.

Chatterjee Biswajit and Asim Karmakar (1993), "Environment and Development in an Open Economic IEA Conference Volume", Gwalior, December, 1995.

Chimni B.S. (2000), "WTO and Environment-Shrimp-Trutle and Ec Hormones Cases", Economic and Political Weekly, Vo.35, May 13-19.

Http//www.wto.com (1999), Internet Website of WTO relating to Trade and Environment.

Markusen J.R. (1975), "International Externalities and Optimal Tax Structures", Journal of International Economics, Vol.5, 15-29.

Markusen J.R. Edward R. Morey and Nancy Olewiler (1993), "Environmental Policy when Market Structure and Plant Locations are Endogenous", Journal of Environmental Economics and Management.

Murthy M.N. et.al. (1998), "Environment and Trade: Developing Countries Perspective and Indian Experience", Working Paper IEG, February.

Ulliveppa H.H. (1999), "New Development in the Theory of International Economy-Trade and Environmental Issues", Foreign Trade Review, IIFT, New Delhi, July-September.

World Bank (1992), "World Development Report", Washington D.C.

18

ENVIRONMENTAL IMPACT ASSESSMENT (EIA) : A CASE STUDY

P. Vasudeva Rao, P. Murali Krishna

INTRODUCTION

Environment consists of two major elements: the biological environment and the physical environment. The biological environment refers to plants and animals and provides for man and fulfils his other needs. The physical environment includes the sum total of the non-living or inorganic mater such as the land, water and air. The physical environment provides favourable conditions for the existence and growth of different forms of life including man. Biosphere is a unique feature of the earth. Ecological balance is a natural phenomenon. But it is disturbed by the market forces in the process of economic development. Knowledge of the precise connection between each component of nature and human life is still rudimentary. Perhaps it is the reason why development projects in various parts of the world aimed at improving human well-being have had unintended detrimental effects on the people and natural resources (Vinish Kathuria, 2003). In this paper it is inferred to describe the value of natural resources and make out a case for environmental impact assessment (EIA) in the context of developing countries. It needs hardly to be stressed that the approach is explorative and not exhaustive. A few examples are cited to illustrate the point under consideration.

ENVIRONMENTAL SERVICES AND VALUES

Natural resources perform a number of environmental services and ecological functions that a society enjoys (Pandit, 1997). Examples are air, ecological balance, nutritional recycling, security, aesthetic beauty. These are in addition to the known economic functions such as energy supply from fossil oil and solids, timber and non-timber products from forests and so on. Many of these are instances of non-marketed and non-use functions performed by natural resources (G.K. Kade Kodi, 2001). Natural resources provide several use values and non-use values. The sum of use values and non-use values is total value i.e., UV + NUV = TV. Use values (UV) can be further classified into three groups: direct, indirect and optional values. Table gives a bird's eye view of the total value and its components.

Table 1
Total Value of Natural Resources

Use Values	*Non-use Values*
Direct Value	Intrinsic, Existence Values
Examples : (a) Sustainable Timber (b) Non-timber forest products (NTFP) (c) Recreation and Tourism (d) Medicine, Plant genetics (e) Education, Human habitat	Cultural, religious and heritage values Bio-diversity
Indirect Value	
Examples : (a) Water shed protection (b) Nutrient recycling (c) Air pollution reduction (d) Micro climatic functions (e) Carbon store, Bio diversity	
Option Value	
Future use as per (1) and (2)	

Source: Pearce and Moran, 1994.

NEGATIVE EFFECTS OF ENVIRONMENTAL DESTRUCTION

The degradation and destruction of the environment in the course of modern economic development releases several negative effects on human welfare. They are termed as negative externalities. They undermine the positive benefits of economic development. It is now increasingly realised that economic development is only a means and not an end in itself. Human development and welfare are the ends. The disruption of social harmony, loss of human livelihood and life as in the case of those displaced by the construction of dams but not properly rehabilitated, onslaught of new diseases, the destruction of renewable resources are some of the consequences that negated the positive benefits of economic development (Sohari et al 1997).

THE PURPOSE OF EIA

The main purpose of EIA is to provide information to decision makers and the public about the environmental implications of the purposed action/project before decisions are made. Besides providing information EIA also suggests measures for preventing or reducing those impacts. It also proposes mitigation plans so that negative impacts are minimised. The scope of EIA is rather wide. It can contribute effectively to environmentally sound and sustainable development. It is well-known that a number of developing countries including India are plagues by problems like wide spread deforestation land and soil resource degradation, industrial pollution, urban congestion and pollution and water resource problems. The incorporation of EIA can facilitate sustainable development (Vinish Kathuria).

PHASES OF EIA AND ISSUES IN ITS IMPLEMENTATION

EIA analysis has three phases which are sequential - identification, prediction and assessment. Identification involves characterising the existing physical, social, economic and ecological environment and identifying the components of the development project which are likely to impact the environment. Prediction involved quantification of project impacts based on accepted standards. The predictive functions demands a forecast of the positive and negative environmental impacts. Assessment includes a detailed design of mitigation measures. Though EIA is incorporated into the development project of developed countries, its implementation is facing several constraints. They include

- insufficient procedural guidance
- inadequate base line data
- high cost of EIA preparation
- delays in implementation
- lack of expertise
- inefficient communication
- Insufficient commitment to follow up (Sohani et al, 1991)

SUMMING UP

Nature has provided resources which are variously classified–renewable and non-renewable–is only one of the classifications. There is a difference between the concept of 'price' and 'value' in the case of natural resources. Though they do not command market price, many components of natural resources have value. Their total value (TV) consists of use values (UV) and non-use values (NUV). Environmental degradation and destruction reduces the value of these resources. Hence, the environment is to be safeguarded in the process of economic development. The conflict between issues of development and environment is to be harmonised by methods such as EIA.

REFERENCES

Vinish Kathuria (2003), "An Assessment of EIA", EPW, Feb.15, p.623

Pandit M.K., "Ecological Economics Towards a Synthesis of Two distinct Disciplines", Current Science Vol.72 No.2 pp.119-123.

Gopal K. Kade Kodi (2001), "Valuation of Natural Resources: What have learnt from Indian Experience?", IJAE Vol.56 No.3, p.287,45.

Peaarce and Moran (1997), "The Economic Value of Biodiversity", International Union for Conservation of Biological Diversity, Earthscan Publications Ltd., London.

Sohani B N J. W Evans, R.R. Everitt, H. Ludwig, RA (1997), "Carpenter and SLTU Environment Impact Assessment for Developing Countries in Asia", Vol.1 and 2 ADB, Manila.

Vinish Kathuria, Ibid.

19

RELOCATION OF PULLUTING INDUSTRIES : SOME ISSUES

NVR Jyothi Kumar

The supreme court has issued a series of orders since 1996 directing the Delhi Government to deal with the horrible levels of air and water pollution. Following such orders, hundreds of Small Scale Industries (SSI) have closed down in Delhi over the last seven years. This has generated a lot of heat because closure or relation would imply a loss of jobs to a significant proportion of the 1.5 million workers estimated to be employed by these units. In developing nations, therefore, a conflict exists between competing priorities–clean environment versus jobs for workers. The state government in India have promoted the SSIs with a view to create more jobs. But the polluting SSIs which operate in residential areas are making the urban life in India one of the more dirty in the world.

With over 2000 generators running every day, Moradabad, has the highest density of generators in Uttar Pradesh. These cause heavy noise and air pollution. Air pollution killed over 10,000 people and affected the health of 5.5 million people in Kolkata from 1995 to 1997. Most deaths were due to chronic exposure to polluted matter that cause respiratory disorders like bronchitis emphysema and asthma. The major contributors are industrial units and vehicular traffic. Howrah, the oldest industrial town in Asia, tops the official list of "Critically Polluted Areas" in India with over 570 large units of metal and steel-based industries. The estimated number of SSIs in Howrah is 32000. Many of these area polluting units. There are more than 200 units function in residential areas.

BENEFITS OF RELOCATION

The main benefit would be the control of environment pollution. In case the units producing similar products can be relocated together. It will felicitate to combined treatment of effluents and disposal of hazardous waste in a sound manner. Zoning can also lead to realisation of significant agglomeration of economics leading to increased competitiveness. Workers would be better off as industrial laws can be enforced.

At present Mumbai has more than 50% of the population as alum-dwellers, Kolkata 43% and Delhi 30%. Chennai has two million people living in slums followed by Ahemedabad (1.13 million), Hyderabad (1.1 million), Bangalore (1.03 million), Kanpur (0.8 million) and Pune (0.5 million). Relocation efforts would discourage migration into these cities resulting in decongestion. The supreme court observed: "By enacting a law and framing a Master Plan and then knowingly allowing where illegal industrial activities have grown with the active connivance of the authorities. This resulted in the breakdown of infrastructural services and environmental degradation. Any relocation would be a boon to the citizens of such cities. Similarly, water problem and low voltage due to power thefts by the nonconforming units also be dealt with to a greater extent.

ARGUMENTS AGAINST RELOCATION

There are certain storing arguments against relocation of industrial units:

The courts and governments have not taken into consideration those most affected by relocation - the workers. For example in London through a policy of relocation, lakhs of manufacturing jobs were lost in the 1950s and 1960s, and further from 1.4 million in 1961 to 5,83,000 in 1993. In New

York, they declined from one million in 1950 to about $1/4^{th}$ of that 2,86,000, in 1993. All these cities have been taken over by offices, commercial establishments, service industries and shopping complexes. If one were to view the closures in Delhi since 1996 as a part of relocation process, a similar pattern emerges. The conservative estimates suggest that one lakh or more manufacturing jobs have disappeared from the city in less than 5 years. The loss of jobs means the loss of self dignity, increased social tensions, loss of health and borrowing and department. In fact an inordinate burden at times like this falls on women and children.

Economists and sociologists opine that limiting of manufacturing in cities may appear to be a natural outcome of urban economics shifting to service and commerce. This process will lead to social dislocation, and a further contractualisation of the workforce. In Mumbai, such a 'de-manufacturing' process began in the 1980s – intensifying with the closure of its textile mills 00 with manufacturing jobs declining even as is economy was growing.

CONCLUSION

Industries go to remote areas where they get clean water at a lower rate. But, in less than 10 years, the place is left with irreversible environmental effects. Dispute the impoverishment, pollution and environmental hazards created, the government and public seems to believe Industrialisation at any cost is the way forward. As rightly pointed out by M.C. Mehta, a Magsaysay award winner, "the 74th amendment in the constitution has provided more powers to the urban local bodies and a more active public role and participation in planning and development of their respective areas. However due to political and administrative apathy, absence of environmental awareness and lack of technical, managerial, organisational and fiscal capabilities, the municipalities have not been able to take advantage of the 74th amendment and create a 'sustainable city' model in India. It is desirable, however, that regional and district plans should be urgently formulated with due consideration for environmental concerns, so that people can enjoy a healthy and decent quality of living"

REFERENCES

Nagaraj Adve (2001), "Politics of Closure: An Agenda of 'De-Manufacturing", The Hindu Survey of the Environment, pp. 39-45.

Vinish Kathuria (2001), "Location : Bane or Boon". The Hindu Survey of the Environment, pp. 31-38.

R. Ramachandran (2000), "The Lethal Zones", Frontline, Dec. 9-22.

H. Dembowski (1999), "Courts, Civil Society and Public Sphere: Environmental Litigation in Calcutta", Economic and Political Weekly, January 2-9.

M.C. Mehta (2001), "Capital Pollution: Wages of Violation", The Hindu Survey of the Environment, 47-51.

20

RENEWABLE ENERGY : SOME ENVIRONMENTAL ISSUES

C. Sailaja

India is in need of huge generating capacity of electric power for faster industrial growth, enhanced agricultural productivity and overall development and thus achieve the targets set in the planning process. Most of the energy we use in our country comes from non-renewable "fossil" fuels such as coal, oil and natural gas. High energy consumption and the ever increasing population will force residents to confront the critical problem of windling domestic fossil energy supplies. Supplies of these fuels will diminish over time and become more expensive to use. Undoubtedly new technologies will be developed that will make it possible to extract more oil and coal. However, this extra extraction can only be achieved at great energy and economic costs. When the energy input needed to power these methods, approaches the amount of energy mined, extraction will no longer be energy cost-effective. The mining processing, transportation and conversion of fossil fuels to energy have many environmental impacts. Many scientists believe that fossil fuel combustion, especially that based on oil and coal, is the major contributor to increasing carbon dioxide concentration in the atmosphere, thereby contributing to probable global warming. This climate change is considered one of the most serious environmental threats throughout the world because of its potential impact on food production and processes vital to a productive environment. Therefore, concerns about carbon dioxide emissions may discourage widespread dependence on coal use and encourage the development and use of renewable energy technologies.

RENEWABLE ENERGY TECHNOLOGIES

Renewable energy resources as sunlight, wind, water and plant material are self-replenishing or inexhaustible. The use of solar energy is, however, expected to grow. Renewable energy technologies that have the potential to provide future energy supplies include: bio-mass systems, hydroelectric systems, hydrogen fuel, wind power, photovoltaics, solar thermal systems, passive and active heating and cooling systems. The environmental impacts of renewable energy are less in comparison to those of non-renewable energy. Proper planning can usually reduce or eliminate most adverse impacts of renewable energy technologies. The following paper discusses some of the environmental benefits and impacts associated with renewable energy technologies.

BIO-MASS ENERGY AND BIO-FUELS

Worldwide, and especially in developing countries, biomass energy is more widely used. Forest is the most abundant biomass resource and the most concentrated form of biomass. The term biomass energy refers to the direct conversion of solid organic materials, such as wood, crops, manure, sewage and Municipal Solid Wastes(MSW) to heat and electricity. Bio-fuels are liquid or gaseous fuels made from biomass. Burning wood and agricultural residues produces almost no sulfur dioxide, but more particulates than most fossil fuels based on energy content to weight. Efficient combustion and treatment of the combustion gases will control particulates in air emissions. Sustainable production and harvesting of biomass for energy will result in no net increase in carbon dioxide production, since plants consume carbondioxide in photosynthesis.

Incinerating MSW is of more concern environmentally, mainly because of the non-biomass materials in MSW, like plastics, heavy metals and chemicals. Burning MSW releases numerous hazardous elements and compounds into the combustions gases. The ash may also be heavily contaminated. MSW incinerators must meet much stricter air emission and ash disposal regulations than facilities that burn pure biomass material.

The use of liquid bio-fuels for transportation, such as ethanol from corn and bio diesel from soyabeans and rapeseed, is increasing every year. The conversion of biomass to liquid biofuels poses few environmental hazards. The combustion of these fuels creates less overall air pollution than gasoline and petroleum, diesel, although the exact amount of specific pollutants is under question.

If natural forests are managed for maxiamal biomass energy production, loss of biodiversity can be expected. Studies conducted (1984) shows that biomass in the form of harvested crop residues is used for fuel, the soil is exposed to intense erosion by wind and water. In addition to the serious degradation of valuable agricultural land, the practice of burning crop residues as a fuel removes essential nutrients from the land and requires the application of costly fossil-based fertilizers if yields are to be maintained. However, the soil organic matter, soil biota, and water holding capacity of the soil cannot be replaced by applying fertilizers. Another study conducted (1992) states that crop residues should not be removed from the land for a fuel source. In response, biomass energy proponents argue that it is possible to grow and harvest bio-energy crops on an economically and ecologically sustainable basis on lands that have marginal agricultural value.

LIQUID FUELS

Petroleum is essential for the transportation sector as well as the chemical industry. The analysis in this section is focused on the potential of three liquid fuels: Ethanol, Methanol and Hydrogen.

ETHANOL

A wide variety of starch and sugar crops, food processing wastes and woody materials have been evaluate as raw materials for ethanol production. Corn appears to be the most feasible biomass feed stock for producing ethanol. Intensive corn production causes serious soil erosion and also requires the further draw-down of ground water resources. Another environmental problem is caused by the large quantity of stillage of effluent produced. During the fermentation process approximately 13 litres of sewage affluent is produced for each liter of ethanol produced. The production and use of Ethanol fuel contribute to the increase in atmospheric carbon dioxide and to global warming, because twice as much fossil energy is burned in ethanol production that is produced as ethanol.

Ethanol produced from corn clearly is not a renewable energy source. Its production adds to the depletion of agricultural resources and raises ethical questions at a time when food supplies must increase to meet the basic needs of the growing population.

METHANOL

Methanol is another potential fuel for internal combustion engines. Various raw materials used for methanol production including natural gas, coal, wood and Municipal solid wastes.

Compared to gasoline and diesel fuel, both methanol and ethanol reduce the amount of carbon monoxide and sulfur oxide pollutants produced, however both contribute other major air pollutants such as aldehydes and alcohol. A study conducted (1990) states that air pollutants from these fuels worsen the tropospheric ozone problem because of the emissions of Nitrogen oxides from the richer mixtures used in the combustion engines.

HYDROGEN

Gaseous hydrogen, produced by the electrolysis of water, is another alternative to petroleum fuels. Using Solar electric technologies for its production, hydrogen has the potential to serve as a renewable gaseous and liquid fuel for transportation vehicles.

To consider hydrogen as a substitute for gasoline, at present, commercial hydrogen is more expensive than gasoline. Some of the Oxygen gas produced during the electrolysis of water can be used to offset the cost of hydrogen. Also the oxygen can be combined with hydrogen in a fuel cell, like those used in the manned space flights.

Compared with ethanol, less land is required for hydrogen production that uses photovoltaics to produce the needed electricity. The environmental impact of hydrogen are minimal.

Water for the production of hydrogen may be problem in the arid regions, but the amount required is relatively small compared with the demand for irrigation water in agriculture. Based on this comparative analysis, hydrogen fuel may be a cost-effective alternative to gasoline, especially if the environmental and subsidy costs of gasoline are taken into account.

HYDROELECTRIC SYSTEMS

For centuries, water has been used to provide power for various systems. Hydroelectric plants require land for their water-storage reservoirs.

Reservoirs constructed for hydroelectric plants have the potential to cause major environmental problems. First, the impounded water frequently covers agriculturally productive, alluvial bottom land. This water cover represents a major loss of productive agricultural land. Dams may fail, resulting in loss of life and destruction of property. Further, dams alter the existing plant and animal species in the ecosystem. For example, cold water fishes may be replaced by warm water fishes, frequently blocking fish migration. Within the reservoirs, fluctuations of water levels alter shorelines and cause down-stream erosion and changes in physiochemical factors, as well as, the changes in aquatic communities. Beyond the reservoirs, discharge patterns may adversely reduce downstream water quality and biota, displace people and increase water evaporation losses. Because of widespread public environmental concerns, there appears to be little potential for greatly expanding either large or small hydroelectric power plants in the future.

WIND POWER

For many centuries, wind power like water power has provided energy to pump water and run mills and other machines. The availability of sites with sufficient wind limits the widespread development of wind farms. Another limitation of this energy resource is the number of wind machines that a site can accommodate.

An investigation of the environmental impact of wind energy production reveals a few hazards. For example, locating the wind turbines in or near the flyways of migrating birds and wild-life refuges may result in birds flying into the supporting structures and rotating blades. A study conducted in 1991 suggests that wind farms be located at least 300 meters from natural reserves to reduce this risk to birds. Insects striking turbine blades will probably have only a minor impact on the insect populations, except for some endangered species. However, significant insect accumulation on the blades may reduce turbine efficiency. Wind turbines create interference with electromagnetic transmission, and blade noise may be heard upto 1 km away.

Under certain circumstances shadow flicker has caused irritation disorientation, and seizures in humans. However, as with other environmental impacts, mitigation is usually possible through careful site selection away from homes and offices. This problem slightly limits the land area suitable for wind farms.

PHOTOVOLTAICS

Photovoltaic cells are likely to provide the nation with a significant portion of its future electrical energy. Photovoltaic cells produce electricity, when sunlight excites electrons in the cells, because the size of the units is flexible and adaptable. Photovoltaic cells are ideal for use in homes, industries and utilities. According to a study conducted (1992), locating the photovoltaic cells on the roofs of home, industries and other buildings would reduce the need for additional land by approximately 5%, as well as reduce the costs of energy transmission.

Photovoltaic technology offers several environmental advantages in producing electricity compared with fossil fuel technologies. For example, using present photovoltaic technology, carbon dioxide emissions and other pollutants are negligible. The major environmental problem associated with photovoltaic systems is the use of toxic chemicals such as Cadmium sulfide and gallium arsenide, in their manufacture. Because these chemicals are highly toxic and persist in the environment for centuries, disposal of inoperative cells could become a major environmental problem. However, the most promising cells in terms of low cost, mass production, and relatively high efficiency are those being manufactured using Silicon. This material makes the cells less expensive and environmentally safer than the heavy metal cells.

SOLAR THERMAL CONVERSION SYSTEMS

Solar thermal energy system collect the Sun's radiant energy and convert it into heat. This heat can be used for household and industrial purposes and also to drive a turbine and produce electricity.

SOLAR PONDS

Solar Ponds are used to capture solar radiation and store it at temperatures of nearly 1000c. Natural or man-made ponds can be made into solar ponds by creating a salt-concentration gradient made up of layers of increasing concentrations of salt. These layers prevent natural convection from occurring in the pond and enable heat collected from solar radiation to be trapped in the bottom brine (Brine solution-sodium chloride).

Some hazards are associated with solar ponds, but most can be prevented with careful management. For instance, it is essential to use plastic liners to make the ponds leak proof and thereby prevent contamination of the adjacent soil and groundwater with salt. Burrowing animals must be kept away from the ponds by buried screening. In addition, the ponds should be fenced to prevent people and other animals from coming in contact with them. Because some toxic chemicals are used to prevent algae growth on water surface.

SOLAR RECEIVER SYSTEM

Other solár thermal technologies that concentrate solar radiation for large scale energy production include distributed and central receivers. Distributed receiver technologies use rows of parabolic troughs to focus sunlight on a central pipe receiver that runs above the troughs. Pressurizes water and other fluids are heated in the pipe and are used to generate steam to drive a turbo generator for electricity production or provide industry with heat energy.

The potential environmental impact of solar thermal receivers are : the accidental or emergency release of toxic chemicals used in the heat transfer system, bird collisions with a heliostat and incineration of both birds and insects if they fly into the high temperature portion of the beams. One study conducted states that if one of the heliostate did not track properly but focused its high temperature beams on humans, other animals, or flammable materials-burns, retinal damages and fires. Flashes of light coming from the heliostats may pose hazards to air and ground traffic.

Other potential environmental impacts include micro-climate alteration, for example, reduced temperature and changes in wind speed and evapotranspiration beneath the heliostats or collecting troughs. This alteration may cause shifts in various plant and animal populations. The environmental benefits of receiver systems are significant when compared to fossil fuel electrical generation. Receiver systems cause no problems of acid rain, air pollution or global warming.

COMPARING SOLAR POWER TO COAL AND NUCLEAR POWER

Many environmental problems are associated with both coal and nuclear power generation. For coal, the problems include the substantial damage to land by mining, air pollution, acid rain, global warming as well as the safe disposal of large quantities of ash. For nuclear power, the environmental hazards consist mainly of radioactive waste that may last for thousands of years, accidents and the decommissioning of old nuclear plants.

The occupational and public health risks of both coal and nuclear plants are fairly high, due mainly to the hazards of mining, ore transportation and subsequent air pollution during the production of electricity, And, as important, coal produces more diffuse pollutants than nuclear fuels during normal operation of the generating plant. Coal fired plants produce air pollutants including sulfur oxides, nitrogen oxides, carbon dioxide and particulates-that adversely affect air quality and contribute to acid rain. Technologies do exist for removing most of the air pollutants, but their use increases the cost of a new plant by 20-25%. By comparison, nuclear power produces many fewer pollutants than do coal plants.

CONCLUSIONS

Solar energy alternatives to fossil fuels have the potential to meet a large portion of future energy needs, provided that the Governments are committed to the development and implementation of Solar energy technologies and that energy conservation is practiced. The implementation of Solar technologies will also reduce many of the current environmental problems associated with fossil fuel production and use.

An immediate priority is to shift from reliance on non-renewable energy sources to renewable, especially Solar based. Various combinations of solar technologies should be developed consistent with the characteristics of different geographic regions, taking into account the land and water availability and regional energy needs.

No energy technology is free of environmental impacts. Most renewable energy technologies produce very little air and water pollution relative to fossil fuels and nuclear power. It is paramount that all residents of the country must work together to conserve energy, land, water and biological resources. To ensure a reasonable standard of living in the future, there must be a fair balance between human population density and energy land, water and biological resources.

21

INDUSTRIAL DEVELOPMENT-ENVIRONMENT SAFETY

K. Kanaka Durga

There is direct link between Industrial Development and Environmental Safety. Industrialisation began with industrial revolution. It refers to the completion of the industrial revolution and the transfer of the economy to industrial methods of production. It is a system of economic development in which the major part of the national resources are used to develop a technology up to date diversified national industry capable of assuring a high rate of growth for the economy as a whole and of overcoming economic and social backwardness. This concept brings out clearly the importance and rationality of Industrialisation in the context of the developing countries. But as a result of rapid urbanization due to Industrialisation, huge qualities of liquid and solid wastes have been generated. As a general practice, these wastes are deposited off either on the ground surface for percolation/evaporation or into water streams without bothering about its after effects on environmental safety.

Environment is the complex of climate, edifice and biotic factors that act upon an organisms or an ecological community and ultimately determine its from and survival. It sustains all life; the plants and animals that provide us food, clothing, medicines, raw materials and all other human needs including a livable atmosphere; providing the basic life support system to us.

The objective of the environmental safety is to reduce pollution. The substances responsible for pollution are called pollutants. Main causes of pollution are use of fossil fuels in factories and industrial effluents. Pollution is an undesirable changes in the physical, chemical and biological constituents of air, water and soil to the extent of harming the living organisms, damaging the monuments of our cultural heritage, affecting our natural resources and interfering with comfortable existence.

PURPOSE OF OBJECTIVES OF THE STUDY

Analysing the degree of environmental safety and the extent of problem of pollution. Pollution hinders the social safety of the population and creates many problems. In view of this, it is proposed in this study to evaluate the impact of pollution on environmental safety. The main objectives of this study are

1. To analyse the severity of the problem of pollution.
2. To examine the impact of pollution on environmental safety.
3. To reveal the problems of pollution.
4. To suggest measures to reduce pollution problems and protect the environment.

The environmental issues have occupied the centre stage during the past few years. Environment consists of chemical components and Physical components such as the climatic conditions, salinity pressure, light, temperature, rainfall, solar radiation, geomagnetism and soil. Chemical components such as acids, alkalies, inorganic nutrients required by plants and animals. The population of a community interact not only among themselves but also with their environment. Industrialisation, Urbanisation and objective management of resources creating the problem of pollution which is disturbing the environmental safety. The expansion of cities under Industrialisation reduces forest area, agricultural land and water resources.

According to a recent survey Calcutta, Delhi and Mumbai find a place in the top ten of the most polluted cities of the world. The ash content is very high in Indian Coal. It ranges from 15 to 45% when used in the super thermal power plants, the coal produces large quantities of fly ash which is very difficult to get rid off. The cement factories release cement dust into the air causing air, water and land pollution problems. The textile industry is one of the largest energy consuming industries in India with an annual consumption of 4.5 million tonnes of Coal. About 90% is thermal energy that is in the form of steam and the rest is electricity. It is used in the boilers, rope washing, bleaching, cloth mercerising etc., tobacco curing, coffee drying and rice processing units. The cement factories also release cement dust into the air causing air, water and land pollution problems.

Andhra Pradesh has One lakh industries and out of these 1,500 are large and medium scale. Six hundred units are causing pollution and 231 units are releasing harmful wastage's. 69% of these are established in and around Hyderabad where there is no favourable naturel to absorb the wastage like sea. Medak district has 100 units releasing most dangerous wastes. The following pie diagram gives clear picture of pollution creating units of Andhra Pradesh.

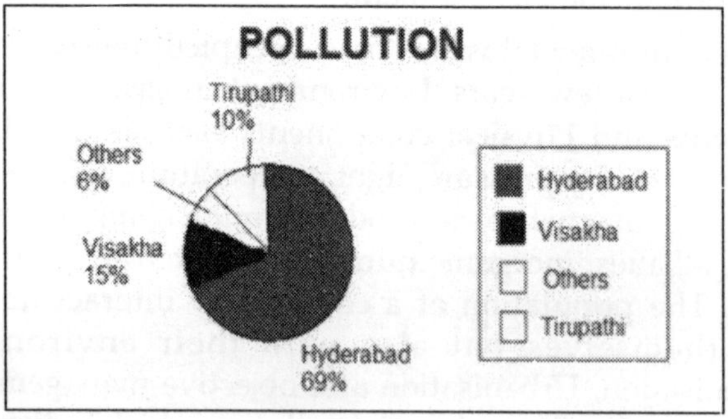

At the National Level, the National Conservation Strategy and Policy statement on abatement of pollution have been announced providing the basis for integration of environmental consideration in the policies and programmes of different ministries and departments under the Environmental Impact Assessment (EIA) notification. It has became mandatory for 29 categories of industries and projects to seek environmental clearance before expansion, modernisation or undertaking new projects.

A drive has been launched by the ministry during the last two years setting deadlines for 17 categories of grossly polluting industries in the large and medium sectors. Out of the 1551 such identified units, only 48 have yet to take steps to install the requisite pollution control facilities. Action is being initiated against the delinquent units. An industrial pollution on control project has been launched with World Bank Aid and its Phase-II has been approved at a cost of 330 Million Dollars. Under this project financial assistance is provided to install Pollution Control Equipment for Large Scale Industries. Government subsidy and soft loan is also made available for setting up common effluent treatment plants in clusters of Small Scale Units.

Besides environmental guidelines have been evolved for location and operation of industries. A net-work of ambient air and water supply monitoring stations has been setup. Standards for air and water quality have also been notified in 22 critically polluted areas all over the country have been identified and environmental management plans are being implemented for control of pollution and improvement of environment in these areas. Now it has become compulsory for any one carrying an industrial operation to statements to the State Pollution Control Board. The industries are also required to specify the impact of pollution control measures on conservation of natural resources.

Consumer benefit was sizeable in terms of higher fuel efficiency and less pollution. The more recent court verdict relates to the shifting of polluting industrial units in Delhi from residential areas to specifically designated industrial areas. The Delhi Government was forced to take measures to close down a large number of polluting units. Central Pollution Control Board would focus on a few key issues which govern environmental protection. Under Zoning Atlas Programme 150 more districts would be taken up and industrial estate planning activity be extended to about 20 cities to ensure that the location of industries and industrial estates are environmentally sound.

In Andhra Pradesh also APIIC (Andhra Pradesh Industrial Infrastructure Corporation) is shifting industries from residential localities to distant places to reduce pollution on the advice of pollution council. Recently i.e., in February 2003, APIIC decided to establish four more industrial estates in Guntur District at Mangalagiri, Bapatla, Ponnur and Repalle to shift industries from town area. Still there are so many obstacles and problems to provide safe environment. The problems are listed below:

- Natural Resources, which are vital for food, livelihood and environmental security are under intense presure today.
- Industrialisation is creating problems of environmental degradation through anthropogenic tropical deforestation, species extinction and pollution of water, soil and air.
- Pollution is disturbing the ozone layer.
- Bird migration to Kolleru lake is affected due to water pollution.
- Aquatic Water animals are affected due to water pollution.
- The direct release of wastes into water systems causes a rised a organic and inorganic contents to a significant level.
- Urbanisation and Industrialisation is causing reduction in water resources, agricultural land and forest area for example during 1973-91, nearly 100.43 SKM agricultural land, 5.97 SKM water resources have disappeared.
- Industrial Estates are not providing basic amenities such as facilities like Water, Transport, Electricity and Communication.

– In addition to these, agricultural land becoming unfit for cultivation. Fly ash also causing health hazards like cardiac problems and respiratory diseases.

SUGGESTIONS

By taking up the following preventive steps, the problem of pollution, a man created problem can be solved to a great extent.

1. Industries should decrease energy consumption with improve efficiency For example all Nokia Production sites have certified Environmental Management System (EMS). Nokia also expects suppliers to have a documented EMS in place. All these helped Nokia to decrease energy consumption and improve efficiency in waste management which results in cost savings.
2. One of the priority requirements for advising sustainable development is to create sustainable human societies. Environmental research and education are essential.
3. Need to develop environmentally friendly alternative sources of energy for industries with least pollution.
4. Only un-leaded petrol has to be marketed to prevent lead pollution.
5. Factories should use tall chimneys and release the smoke in the upper layers of air, so that it dissipates over a wide area and prevents air pollution.
6. Industries should use Electro Static Precipitators to reduce pollution.
7. Thermal power stations should develop ash ponds at low level areas to release the ash with water through pipes instead of releasing into air and rivers. Ex. VTPS is adopting this method.
8. Coal with low sulphur and ash content should be developed.
9. Dust particles present in the smoke released by the factories should be removed using filters and scrubbers.

10. The waste water generated in factories and industries should not be allowed to be released into water sources unless the harmful chemical substances present in it are separated through treatment plants. This water can be used for raising crops and trees. To prevent thermal pollution, the hot water generated in the factories has to be cooled as per the regulation with the help of cooling towers.
11. Oxidation, stabilization tanks purify the domestic water for re-usage. It is suggested by National Environment Engineering Research Organisation, Nagpur.
12. New techniques should be developed to recycle to polluted water.
13. Government should strictly enforce Environmental safety Act by imposing Environmental Tax, and compulsory of preparation of Green Balance Sheet.
14. There must be co-operation between industrialists and environmental scientists to protect environment.
15. There is need for shifting industrial units that had historically been located in the central business districts.

CONCLUSION

Thus environmental safety is essential for human existence, which influences social life, health, behaviour etc., Environmental quality is essential for quality of life. But there are threats to the environment from the use of un-sustainable resources.

Tenth plan aims to impart environmental education and training through seminars, symposia/workshops awareness campaign, eco clubs etc., with the sincere efforts and support from all sections of the society. India is all set to embark on a path of sustainable development and improved quality of life for our people without deranging the environment.

REFERENCES

Y. Anjaneyulu (2002), "Susthirabhiurubhiki Paryavarana Parrirakshne Margam", Yojana, June.

Eenadu Telugu Daily News Paper (2003), February.

Kamal Nath (1994), "Environment & Development", Kuruksehetra, December.

Srikanta K. Panigrah (2003), "Environment Protection and the 10th Plan", Yojana, January.

22

ENERGY–A BOON OR BANE

G. Sudhakar

The atmosphere is the life blanket of the earth. Energy is the chief pollutant of atmosphere. But energy is the ultimate resource for economic development. The use of it is inevitably significant and the bad effects of it are also inevitably on the welfare of human through environment. So energy is the ultimate resource and at the same times the ultimate pollutant. There are no means of harnessing energy, which is completely free of adverse environmental impacts. Consequently we thought to live in the dichotomy of energy roles as an ultimate resource and ultimate pollutant. Therefore the deepest of the dilemmas that make up the energy problem is generated. The present paper is a moderate attempt to study the impact of energy consumption, production and the other related activities on the atmosphere with special reference to burning of fossil fuels in automobiles and to find alternate strategies. The need of the study arises as the world community is striving to arrive at advanced methods for environmental safety form the bad effects of energy use for a sustained economic growth.

ENERGY- A BOON OR BANE

The expansion of civilization legitimately increased the use of energy for the production of goods and services in the economy to the well-being. The remarkable growth of human population and the development of civilizations can be attributed largely to the invention of fire(energy). Further accentuated by learning to harness natural flows and accumulations of energy and turn them to the human ends. Economic growth of the world communities is assessed basing on the consumption levels of energy.

Considering the commercial energy use percapita as the indicator of development, Table-1 shows the oil equivalent commercial energy use percapita for the year 1998 for a few developed countries and for a few developing countries. Here the commercial energy consumed in non-energy uses, i.e., excluding the energy consumed in the production of energy. Commercial form of primary energy (Eg. Petroleum, natural gas, sokidfuels etc.,) and primary electricity (Eg. Nuclear, thermal, hydel etc.,) all converted into oil equivalents. U.S.A. Canada, Australia, are in the top brass of developed countries using 16 times higher energy percapita of an average energy percapita of developing countries. It narrates the development pedagogy was built on the barrals of energy consumption. On the other hand the damages done by the increased consumption of energy on the well being of the economy through environment are also equivalently higher in developed countries.

There are huge emissions and affluents by the commercial energy use. These will pollute the environment particularly the air and water. The emissions and affluents are treated as indicators for the environment. Taking into account the Co2 emissions from the energy use as one of the main indicator for air pollution, the relation between energy use and pollution can be assessed. As per the Table-2 all the six developed countries are witnessing highly polluted atmosphere than the developing countries. The developed countries people are living in high pollution emissions like CO_2 Percapita ranging 20 toners per head. While the developing countries are loaded with CO_2 emission at an average of 1.2 toners per head only. These pollution figures are in collaboration with the levels of consumption of commercial energy of different countries.

Hence the negative impact of energy use observed is also most significant.

AIR POLLUTION- MORE DISASTROUS

The atmosphere is a gaseous substance enveloping the earth protecting it from abrupt changes in temperature and protecting all living beings from harmful solar and cosmic radiation. Problem of air or atmospheric pollution was chiefly connected with emissions of CO_2, H.C, and Non Sulphurous gas etc from energy use. Increasing industrialization, urbanization and automobiles are the primary sources of atmospheric pollution. The accumulation of waste gases and particles form combustion, production and other economic activities of energy use exceed the natural dispersion capacity of the atmosphere. The serious effects of it are holes to Ozone layer and chemical rains. On troposphere an increase in the absorption and radiation of infra-red rays which increase warmth, i.e., What is called as 'green house effect'. The emission form energy production and combustion have fatal effects on the different areas of environment like air, water, land and sound. But as a matter of fact the effects are more on air. The comparative effects of various energy sources presented in Table-3 shows that about 80 percent are solidified only on air. That is why the air pollution has become more disastrous than water and other pollution. Another bare fact from the table is that both conventional and non-conventional energy sources are effluent to a certain minimal degree of bad results.

AIR POLLUTION IN INDIA

The nature of environmental problem is quite different from that of the developing to developed countries. As per the environment indicators all the developed countries are facing major threats in the area of air pollution. So, also among the developing countries India and China are facing with high air pollution. The air pollutant emissions of carbondioxide in India stand at 1.1 metric tonne per head per year. The major sources of air pollution are industries, transport (automobile), irrigation, domestic waste and thermal power. Industrial activities, motor transport and bunking of fossil fuels have been emitting large quantities of pollutants into the atmosphere. This can be supported by the fact that the two sectors industry and transport are using major chunk of the total energy consumption in the economy. The Table–4 reveals the same thing that 82.33 percent of coal and lignite 91.79 percent of natural gas and 56.49 percent of electricity has been used by the industry.

Whereas 47.96 percent of petroleum products are being used by the transport sector. There by the chief pollutants agents of air are industry and transport sectors. Oil and natural gas consumption in India is 54 percent in the total energy consumption in India is 54 percent in the total energy consumption where in India stands as world's 8th largest consumer in oil and natural gas. The total oil and natural gas consumption for the year 2000–01 is more than 100m.ton. Almost 90 percent of this has been engulfed by industry and transport sectors. It was more than apparent that the major contributor to the haze and poisons in the air was not factories but automobiles. Fuels used by these two sectors will cause emission of two types i.e. Regulated and unregulated pollutants. Emission of regulated pollutants depend upon maintains, control and design. Whereas emissions of unregulated pollutants depend upon the quality of fuel. While the regulated pollutants are just pollutants, unregulated pollutants are toxic in nature. So far as the degree of emissions are concerned regulated pollutants are very high. These are spoiling the atmosphere drastically. The effect these emissions on atmosphere is known as 'green house effect'. And the chief agent causing this effect is CO, CO_2.

The Table–6 shows typical composition of oil exhaust per part load in percentage shows a high degree of CO-$_2$ emission from the combustion of fuels. Normal composition of atmosphere allows CO_2 at 0.03% only. An abnormal increase of CO_2 combination in the atmosphere at the cost of reducing Oxygen levels from 20.945% to 15% and Nitrogen levels from 78.09% to 75.21%. Another significant observation is the presence of unregulated pollutants and suspended particulates at 0.09% level. These two worried developments causes concern over the air pollution through fuel emissions.

AUTOMOBILE EMISSIONS AND AIR POLLUTION

Barring the CO_2 emissions from coal and lignite mostly used by the industry and Hydrogen sulfide emissions caused by Natural gas also mostly used by the industry. Major threat to the air pollution is caused by the emissions from automobile (transport) sector. Therefore the problem shifts towards vehicular traffic and pollution caused by it. There is enough evidence that the emissions from the vehicular traffic become greater concern for the urban areas of the economy. Results of a survey made in Hyderabad City tell that only 7% of the vehicles are emitting 50% of hydrogen carbons (SPM). This is because of badly managed and old vehicles. The severity of the problem arises out of the sporadic increase of vehicle traffic on the Indian roads. During the period from 1993–94 to 1999–2000 vehicle sales in India increased to around 112% over a period of 7 years, thus showing an average increase 16% per annum. Taking an average 23 lakh vehicles totaling to 3.45 corers are on the roads. Among which 10% means 34.5 lakh vehicles are aggravating the p0ollution problem.

MEASURES TAKEN TO RESTRAIN VEHICULAR POLLUTION

For over a decade there has been no comprehensive planning on how to check threat to the health of millions and decay of environment for future generations. But the following filthy measures are ensured by –

1. The introduction of unleaded petrol controlled lead emissions to a greater extent but did not find solutions to keep the levels of benzene in control.
2. Steps initiated to supply diesel with less sulfur content as it will brought down emissions of most poisonous sulphurous gasses.
3. Euro–III emission norms are followed for four wheeler vehicles. It prescribed maximum permutable emissions in grams/per/km.

4. Urban transport systems are planned as a part of sustainable development to evert the extreme congestion of vehicular traffic due to the spatial distribution of population and economic activities which rise the vehicular population.
5. Shift in the production of automobile engines from more pollutants two stroke to less pollutant four stroke.
6. Introducing better technology and fuel efficiency in four wheelers.
7. Use of non-polluting energy sources like compressed natural gas (CNG) and liquefied petroleum gas (LPG).
8. Particulate traps and particulate filter systems used in diesel system vehicles are giving good results.
9. Petrol tank and inlet manifold is connected to a canister to absorb the volatile fuel vapour that would other wise go out to pollute the atmosphere as an evaporative emission.
10. Sulfur in Indian gasoline is permitted upto 1% according to BIS specifications for the year 2000.

ALTERNATIVE STRATEGIES

Sustainable development involves not just ecological practices that enable meeting the needs of the future generations, but a change in production and consumption pattern of energy. The thrust area then is effective implementation of energy conservation policies aimed to more efficient energy use. These policies should aim at preservation of atmosphere and environment. The preservation of environment mostly depends upon the success of air pollution abasement programs. The following general and specific measures maybe considered to control air pollution air pollution as an alternate strategies.

1. Through mechanical devices like cyclones, scrubbers, bag uses and Electro-static precipitators suspend particle matter can be captured.

2. In the transport sector use of more fuel-efficient engines and multi axiable vehicle will contribute to energy conservation.
3. Certain standards should be developed for acceptable levels of Benzene. Additional care must be taken for the supply of diesel with less sulphurous content and form adulteration with naphtha.
4. A careful study of the right mix of solutions and standards has to be workout with regard to the fuel technologies and vehicle combustion technologies.
5. Looking into the possibility of using energy efficient mode of transport such as electric trolley buses and battery-operated vehicle would present a radically different direction in future.
6. Policies should also be directed towards segregation of mixed traffic modes through horizontal separation such as the provision of cycle trucks or for slow moving vehicles.
7. Modernisation of urban transport by means of balanced in generation of walking, non-motorized transport.
8. Indian fuel specifications should be changed to reduce sulphur in gasoline to less than 0.5%.
9. Above all the better way out is to provide effective public transport facilities, ensure movement of more passengers and fewer vehicles.

23

INDUSTRIAL DEVELOPMENT AND ENVIRONMENTAL SAFETY

P. Sridevi

INTRODUCTION

Nature and environment have always been man's benefactors. It is in and through his environment that man finds succor, and upon nature's bounties he has sustained himself. Man's progress and development towards higher forms of civilization is mainly owing to the utilization of his environment, nature and its abundant resources. But it is bitter fact that more civilized man has become, the more he has defiled the environment and nature. Man has indulged in indiscriminate plunder of his environment which has reached a stage when he is becoming growingly concerned with his own survival in the midst of all pervading 'pollution'.

INDUSTRIALIZATION - OVER VIEW

Industrialization is central to economic development and improved prospects for human well being. The benefits of industrial production can be seen in all aspects of life from the range of consumer goods available, to the efficiency of transportation systems, to the astounding advances made in computers and communications technology. Since the 18th

Century, wealth in the developed countries has paralleled industrial growth, and developed countries continue to produce the lion's share of manufacture. Today, many developing countries like India & China are experiencing an industrial revolution of their own, capturing an ever-increasing share of industrial growth. The positive economic and social results of industrial growth have been accompanied by serious environmental degradation, however, as well as growing threats to health from occupational hazards.

Industrialization has brought Significant Environmental Damage

Industrialization and its consequent processes of urbanisation, modernisation, rapid advancement in the sphere of science and technology, have not merely had an socio-economic, political and psychological impact on mankind. As a matter of fact, man had until very recently kept his eyes closed to the enormous damage he had done to his environment and the manner in which he had upset the 'ecological balance' through indiscriminate use of technology. Man has virtually 'poisoned' his environment and lives a highly unhygienic life by his own scientific standards. Scientists and ecologists along with other experts have established that nature's gifts of air, water and earth to man, have become terribly filthy and contaminated—courtesy man's inhumanity towards his environment. The advanced countries were perplexed and vexed to know that 'pollution' was detrimental to all forms and species of life on the earth.

A substantial share of industrial growth in developing countries revolves around the transformation of raw materials into industrial products such as steel, paper, and chemicals. The production of industrial chemicals, for instance, has been shifting to the developing world. From 1990 onwards this industry's annual rate of growth was 5.6 percent in developing countries, compared with a mere 1 percent in the developed world. Not only are these processes resource-intensive, but also industries such as electricity generation, chemicals and petroleum refining, mining, paper production, and leather tanning tend to produce a disproportionately large amount of hazardous and toxic wastes.

A wide range of pollutants is associated with these industries. In contrast, much of economic growth in developed countries is now in the service sector (e.g., education, entertainment, defense, and finance) and communication sector (e.g., computers, cellular phones, and electronics), which are inherently less polluting. This rapid industrial growth has made water pollution, air pollution, and hazardous wastes pressing environmental problems in many areas of the developing world. Industrial emissions along with vehicle exhausts cause air pollution, while concentrations of heavy metals and ammonia loads often cause major fish kills down th river in industrial areas. The lack of hazardous waste treatment facilities compounds the problem, with industrial wastes often discarded on fallow or public lands, in rivers, or in sewers designed to carry only municipal wastes.

POLLUTION CAUSED BY INDUSTRIALIZATION - OVER VIEW

Pollution may be defined as an undesirable and harmful change in the aboitic and biotic components of an ecosystem by the addition of an agent. The agent which causes pollution is called a pollutant There are a large number of pollutants which may be produced due to natural causes or due to human activities and they may pollute air, water and soil.

Air Pollution

Various gaseous pollutants are added to the air by industries and other human activities. For example chloroflourocarbons are released into air from refrigerators, spray bottles. Particulate pollutants are either solids or liquids and may be of various sizes and have boiling points above 200 degrees centigrade. Larger particles of solids and liquids settle down slowly. Very fine particles do not settle down at all. Ash produced by burning coal and wood; dust produced by quarries, cement and mining industries; metal vapours produced by various industries are typical examples of particulate pollutants. Tetraethyl lead and trimethyl lead are the particulate pollutants added by automobiles using petrol. Pollen grains, bacteria, fungi etc. are also particulate pollutants.

Gaseous and particulate pollutants cause health problems in animals and man, damage crops (thereby reduce the agricultural productivity), buildings, and monuments and changes climatic conditions locally. For example oxide of nitrogen and sulphur reduce the crop yield. Acid rain causes widespread damage to plants and animals. Hydrocarbons in air cause premature falling of leaves, flowers, fruits and also discolouration of various plant parts. Acid rain also causes wide spread damage to buildings. Gases like sulphur dioxide causes watering in eyes, throat irritation and drying of mouth. These gases enter the tissues and form acids inside the tissues. This injures and damages soft tissues. Carbon monoxide combines with hemoglobin present in red blood cells and reduces oxygen supply to tissues. This causes death of tissues and even man. Pollengrains, bacterial and fungal spores cause various types of allergic conditions in man. Lead compounds emitted by automobiles accumulate in the tissues and damages the nervous system. Dust particles in the mining, cement and asbestos industries enter the lungs and harden them. They cause several respiratory problems. The hydrocarbons liberated from industries are known cause for cancer. Pollutants also cause immense damage to the domestic live stock such as cattle and poultry. They reduce the production of meat, milk and eggs. The best example for the damage caused by air pollution is " Bhopal gas tragedy". Thousands of people died, many more are suffering even today because of this tragedy.

Remedial Measures

Realising the problems, efforts are being made to reduce air pollution. Unleaded petrol (petrol without lead) is now being used in automobiles to reduce lead pollution. Exhaust smoke from automobiles is made to pass over catalystic converters which burn hydrocarbons completely. Electrostatic precipitaters are used to reduce the particulate matter in the factory smoke.

Water Pollution

Water in the ponds, lakes, rivers and even in sea is polluted. Water is used, for cooking washing and in industries. Used water discharged from the industries is called industrial effluent. It contains a variety of chemicals depending on the type of the industry. These chemicals may be inorganic chemicals or organic substances. Industries which are established near water bodies such as lakes, rivers and sea , discharge the effluents directly into the water body. As a result, these chemicals causes immense damage to ecosystem. Most of the chemicals in industrial effluents are toxic and kill the aquatic organisms. They react with oxygen present in the water and reduce the oxygen level in the water. This affects the life of aquatic organisms. Industries located far away from water bodies, release the effluents into surrounding land or into pits. The effluents percolate and contaminates ground water. Making it unfit for drinking, washing and for cultivation. Contaminated ground water kills the plants either immediately or slowly. As a result, the entire land becomes unfit for cultivation. It is very difficult to remove the pollutants from ground water. Another type of pollution caused by industries is called thermal pollution. Water used for cooling absorbs heat and this hot water is discharged directly into water bodies such as lakes and rivers and even into the sea. This increases the temperature of water and adversely affects the stability of the ecosystem. Solubility of oxygen decreases with increase in temperature. This reduces the amount oxygen available in the aquatic ecosystem. Higher temperature also increases the metabolic activity of several aquatic animals and thereby increases their oxygen requirement. As a result, several animals die due to the lack of oxygen in aquatic ecosystem. Thermal pollution occurs near thermal and nuclear power plants. Thermal pollution can be reduced by cooling the water in cooling towers before it is released into water bodies.

Pollution of water resources is a major problem as it changes the quality of water. This kills aquatic micro organisms, plants and animals destroying the entire aquatic ecosystems. As both wild and domesticated terrestrial animals drink water from these water bodies, the health of these animals is also affected. Polluted water is unfit for human use. When man uses polluted water for drinking, bathing and washing, these pollutants enter into his body and cause health problems.

Remedial Measures

The only method to reduce water pollution is to treat and clean the sewage water and effluents from industries before releasing them into water bodies. For this purpose, waste water is to be filtered first to remove particulate material and stored in shallow tanks where bacterial degradation of organic compounds takes place. This water is then treated with chlorine gas to kill the bacteria. Nitrates and phosphates are finally removed by chemical treatments and this water is then released into the rivers. Similar procedure is to be adopted by industries. The effluent water is to be neutralised and chemical pollutants are to be removed before the effluent water is released from the industry. These processes are costly, time consuming and are non-productive. Hence, they are not adopted. Instead, effluents are untreated or treated partially and are released into rivers.

Soil Pollution

Soil pollution may occur directly or indirectly. Soil pollution may alter the physical, chemical and biological nature of soil and make it unfit for plant growth, animal and human use. Soil pollution in agricultural areas affects crop productivity and may even make land unfit for agriculture. Soil is formed by erosion of rocks by wind and water. This process is very slow and takes several years. Another way of soil formation is the cooling of lava coming out during volcanic eruptions. Large amounts of soil are formed by this in a short time where as soil pollution and degradation occur more rapidly. Taking all these into consideration, soil may be considered as a non-renewable natural resource, preventing soil pollution and promotion of soil conservation is an important task.

Soil is also polluted by the deposition of unwanted inorganic and organic substances. Several industries dispose off their waste products on near by land sites. These waste products include concrete, rubber, tin, iron, chromium, aluminum and other metals. In addition, several organic wastes such as paper, plastics, pesticides, discarded food and dead bodies of animals are also dumped by both industries and from domestic use. Land pollution by plastic materials has increased to an alarming proportion in recent years due to increased use of plastics for packing domestic products.

Remedial Measures

Soil pollution can be minimised by collecting the wastes properly. Several materials discarded from homes and industries such as metals, paper, certain types of plastics, glass can be recycled. Biological wastes such as discarded food, vegetables and fruits can be used for production of manure. Wastes containing pathogenic organisms and those which can not be easily recycled are burnt in a careful manner in places far away from residential areas.

Noise Pollution

In addition to these, pollution due to loud noise is also becoming a major problem in industrial areas, on busy streets, railway stations and in places near aerodromes.

Depletion of Ozone Layer

As chloroflourocarbons (CFC's) were used extensively in refrigeration air-conditioning, aerosol propellants, solvents, and fire suppressants. These chemicals are primarily responsible for the progressive depletion of the stratospheric ozone layer. The most dramatic manifestation of ozone depletion is the springtime ozone hole over Antarctica, first discovered in 1985. The major significance of stratospheric ozone depletion on health is reduced shielding of the earth's surface against incoming solar ultraviolet radiation, in particular ultraviolet-B. Ultra violet light can cause cataracts, skin cancer etc.

On the one hand, the advanced countries are advocating preventive measures against pollution, for bringing about ecological balance and on the other, they are reveling in nuclear, atomic, hydrogen and neutron energy experiments and explosions for destructive purposes which are the greatest and most corrupting elements of pollution and ecological imbalance. Pollution caused by nuclear reactors and radioactive elements last for many decades in the environment. The examples of Nagasaki and Hiroshima which were destroyed by Atom Bombs during World War II will forever cry of man's depravity, not only towards humanity, but also towards nature and his own environment. While many of the industrial products of industrial are known toxins, it is difficult to determine how these chemicals affect public health at the levels found in the environment. To what extent does environmental pollution from industrial wastes contribute to the observed increases in, for instance, birth defects and some cancers? This is an important question. Industrial chemicals can persist in the environment for many decades and accumulate in marine and terrestrial food chains, thus posing health hazards years after their use.

CONCLUSION

Environmental pollution is a problem which is going to increase with the increase of population and industrialization in the coming years but vegetation can reduce it upto some extent. Plants are not only the integral part of the biosphere, but are also essential for the existence of human civilisation. The impact of plants on nature and natural beings need no further vitiation. They are the primary producers of the food chain. Plants play the most important role in keeping the atmospheric balance of carbon-dioxide and oxygen.

Many countries are now trying to adopt anti-pollution measures although they are proving to be very costly. We in India must heed these warnings in time. Pollution has been increasing at an alarming rate in our cities due to industrialization. We must carefully examine our needs and the risks of industrial expansion. Abuse of science must be firmly controlled. The very science and technology that eases man's work and helps him control his environment must be directed towards finding ways and means to convert industrial waste into harmless products. All is not lost yet much can be saved and earth can be rescued from pollution. The result of man's unthinking, selfish "progress" towards material wellbeing. Pollution is the heavy price of rapid and thoughtless industrialization, but it need not be paid if we give a little attention to the environment.

24

FORESTS AND TRIBALS

P. Kodandarami Reddy, T.V. Ravindra Reddy

INTRODUCTION

Forests provide valuable products such as timber, wood pulp, gums, rubber etc. They play an important role in preventing soil erosion. They permit more water to seep though the soil and reduce the quantity of run-off on the surface. They provide suitable environment and necessary seclusion for the survival of wild animals and birds (N.A 1984). They provide energy (half of the world's population depends on fuel wood), food, fodder, pharmaceutical products and other non-wood products such as fibers, rubber and resins. Forests are priceless ecological resources. They constitute rich stock of valuable genetic resources, a common heritage of mankind. But forests cover hardly 30 percent of the land surface of the world. They were many more extensive in the past. Deforestation is a continuous process. During 1990-95, it was of the order of 0-7 and 0.3 percent in the case of low income and middle income countries (World bank, 2000). Deforestation refers to the permanent conversion of forest area to other uses including shifting cultivation, permanent agriculture, ranching, settlements and infrastructure development. Tribals or indigenous people who have been living near forest fringes have also suffered in the process of deforestation. In recent times several schemes have been launched to take of forests as also of tribals. We propose to deal with a few aspects of these schemes in the context of our country.

THE NEED TO PRESERVE ECOLOGICAL BALANCE

All organisms in the biosphere are interdependent. The lower organisms provide food for higher organisms. There is a balance in the relative numbers of different organisms in the environment. Man has interfered with the ecological balance in several ways in the course of economic development. He has cleared the forests and grassland for cultivation and other needs. Indiscriminate hunting for furs, feathers or skins and fishing have resulted in the extinction of some species. This has led to the realisation that conservation of wild life is important to preserve it for future. Wild life sanctuaries have been established in many parts of the world. The natural habitat is preserved in national parks and sanctuaries and hunting of wild life is prohibited.

NATIONALLY PROTECTED AREAS

These areas refers to totally or partially protected areas of atleast 1000 hectares that are designated as national parks, national monuments, nature resources, wild life sanctuaries, protected landscapes, and sea scapes with limited public areas. The indicator is calculated as a percentage of area. Table 1 gives the position of nationally protected areas for a set of countries.

Table 1
Nationally Protected Areas : 1996

Country	*Thousand Square KM*	*% of Total Land Area*
India	142.9	4.8
China	598.1	6.4
Indonesia	192.3	10.6
Pakistan	37.2	4.8
Srilanka	8.6	13.3
United Kingdom	50.6	20.9
United States	1226.7	13.4
World	8543.5	6.6

Source : World Development Report, 2000 P.291

It is clear that our populated developing countries like India, Pakistan and China have a lower proportion of nationally protected area compared with developed countries like U.K. and the U.S.A.

FOREST POLICY : PAST AND PRESENT

Traditionally forests have been the property of the state and the government was made responsible for its protection. Forest laws have been enacted to punish those who encroach into them for exploitation of its wealth. Those laws were enforced by the forest department. The tribals and other rural inhabitants who entered the forests were treated with suspicion and were punished. With all the checks and balances operated by the forest department, forest cover has been destroyed and commercially exploited. During the last two decades India witnessed annual depletion of forest cover at a pace of 235 square kilo metres (GOI, 1999).The causes of deforestation and environmental degradation are many. They boil down to the policy inadequacies and failures. It is now widely recognised that community participation is important in safeguarding forest resources.

COMMUNITY PARTICIPATION IN FOREST MANAGEMENT

Experiences of people's involvement and exclusion in forest management have established that people's participation in forest management can result in better forests and also in development of local communities. India (having 633,397 square kilometers of area under forest has lost 46,803 sq. kms. since Independence in 1947) is among the few leading countries which after realising the economic, social and environmental costs of excluding community partnership between the local community and the forest department was forced to introduce community participation in forest management. The government of India through its third forest policy (1988) and later through a resolution in 1990 identified local communities as the first claimant over forests and its various produce and provided specific guidelines for their involvement in forest management.

19 states of the country having more than 80 percent of the country's forest area and more than 92 per cent of country's population are implementing participatory forest management. More than 35 thousand local institutions are successfully involved in the management of allotted areas. The organisations that are involved in the forest management are called Joint Forest Management (JFM) Committees. They are called 'Vanasamrakshana Samithis'(VSS) in AP. Studies show that people living in forest fringe villages are more responsible to issues related to forest protection from biotic interference including human beings and disasters like forest fires etc. Several positive outcomes such as improvement in the quality of forests, water table, employment and earnings of the members of JFMs are reported.

SOCIAL FORESTRY

In addition to the protection of natural forests, social forestry has been launched on a large scale. The purpose is to improve the green cover and put to use the barren and waste lands to proper use. Avenue plantation is also a part of this programme. It is financially supported by the multilateral funding agencies and the government of India. It has certainly resulted in several positive externalities for the preservation of environment especially in drought prone areas. Social forestry is an important component of watershed programme which is very much emphasised.

SUMMING UP

Issues of environmental protection are becoming important in the context of development resulting in environmental pollution, degradation and destruction. Forests render several services which are valued economically and culturally. The preservation of forest wealth is an element of ecological balance. The policing of forests and their commercial exploitation have led to their depletion. Deforestation has to be stopped. Community participation in forest management and social forestry are the means of forest protection and enlarging the green cover. The local communities as stakeholders are the direct beneficiaries. The community at large also benefits. The participating approach to forest development is to be further expanded to safeguard our natural and physical environment.

REFERENCES

N. Anantha Padmanabhan (1984), "Man and Environment", NCERT, New Delhi, p.38.

The World Bank (2000-2001), "World Development Report", pp.290-291.

GOI (1999), "State of Forest Report Fourth Survey India", Ministry of Environment and Forests, Dehradun.

25

AGRICULTURE AND ENVIRONMENTAL SAFETY

Y. Sarada

Indian Agriculture had reached the stage of development and maturity before the now advanced countries of the world embarked on the path of progress. As the Planning Commission observes, agriculture has all alone been the most crucial sector of the Indian Economy. Agriculture contributes over 1/4th of India's GDP. It provides livelihood for about two thirds of the population, supplies raw materials for a number of important industries and contributes about one-fifth of the export earnings. Development of agriculture is necessary to help solve the twin problems of unemployment and poverty. In fact rural India represents one of the largest potential markets in the world for many manufactured products. The development of the industrial and other non-agriculture sectors depends to a very large extent on the prosperity of the agrarian sector. It is well recognized that fluctuation in agricultural income affects the fortunes of other sectors.

PHASES OF DEVELOPMENT

Sixth five year plan document points out, starting from the beginning of this century, three major phases in our agriculture evolution.

(a) The first phase from 1900 to 1947 was marked by a near stagnation in farming, as is clear from a growth rate of about 0.3% per annum achieve in agricultural production during this period.

(b) Phase two extending from 1950 to 1980, has been marked by considerable advance in the process of modernization of agriculture, thanks to the steps taken in the development and spread of –

- Technology based on scientific research
- Wide range services and
- Public policies.

(c) Third phase, which has begun in the eighties, is marked by the need for greater attention to marketing and trade, and to institutional framework that can help to minimize the handicaps of small and marginal farmers and maximize the benefits of intensive agriculture offered by small holdings.

DEVELOPMENT STRATEGY

Our five-year plans have emphasized the role of agriculture in national development and the Central and State Governments have taken a number of steps to develop the agrarian sector. Some of these important measures are reviewed in the following way.

Irrigation is one of the important inputs that significantly increase agricultural productivity and employment opportunities. The Union and State Governments have been endeavoring to expand the area under irrigation by executing major, medium, and minor irrigation projects and exploiting the ground water potential. Rural electrification programmes, to have been given importance so that they may help improve agricultural operations by facilitating the energisation of pump sets etc. these strategies brighten the prospects of industries which supply inputs for the development of irrigation infrastructure (like cement, steel etc,) electrification (aluminum cables, steel, etc.)

The introduction of high yielding varieties (HYV) of a number of field crops and hybrids of millets in particular led to agricultural development. These program covers major food crops namely, rice, maize, jowan, and bajara. The success of this program has revolutionized agriculture and brought about a phenomenal and rapid increase in food grains production in country. The HYV program is one of the most important phases of the new agriculture strategy. The increasing use of HYVs increases the demand for plant nutrients and protection like fertilizer insecticides and pesticides. The increase in the agricultural income normally increases the demand for a variety of goods and services.

The department of agricultural research and education, set up in 1973, is responsible for coordinating research, education and extension education in the field of agriculture, animal husbandry and fisheries in India. Steps have been taken for plant protection, soil conservation, drought prone area development etc. The Agro Service Center scheme was introduced in 1971 with the twin objectives of providing employment to trained enterprenuers and providing inputs to farmers at their doorsteps at a reasonable price.

INDIAN AGRICULTURAL POLICY

Land reforms–measures taken under this head includes

- abolition of intermediaries
- tenancy reforms to regulate rents paid by tenants to land lords
- provide security tenure to tenants
- Imposition of ceiling on the holdings in a bid to procure land for distribution among landless labourers and marginal farmers.

PROCUREMENT AND SUPPORT PRICES

Another policy measure of significant important is the announcement of procurement and support prices to ensure fair returns to the farmers so that even in years of surplus the prices do not tumble down and farmers do not suffer losses. This is necessary to ensure that farmers are not penalized for producing more. In fact the policy of commission for agricultural costs and prices in recent years has been to announce fairly high prices in a bid to provide incentive to the farmer to expand production.

OTHER MEASURES

- Improving the system of marketing through the establishment of regulated markets and introducing a variety of measures like standardization of weights and measures, grading and standardization of farm output, providing information regarding market prices to farmers etc, efforts have been made to strengthen the cooperative marketing structure.
- Initiation of steps to improve the economic conditions of agricultural workers. In this category covers measures to enforce minimum wages, abolition of bonded labour, grant of agricultural land to land less labourers, schemes for expanding rural employment etc.
- In recent years a number of policy changes have been introduced to make agricultural exports more viable. Most of the restrictions on agriculture exports have been removed. Export oriented units in the floriculture sector are being set up and import of capital goods, plants and machinery for establishing food processing units has been more liberalised.

AGRICULTURAL MARKETING

A suitable structure of support prices for various agricultural commodities adjusted from time to time in the light of the cost of production so as to ensure fair returns to the farmers. Adequate arrangements for the procurement of agricultural produce at support prices if the prices fall below that level, a well spread out and regulated infrastructure of marketing which will ensure fair price to the producer in open market conditions and help eliminate the non-functional marketing margins of intermediaries.

The union and state governments have taken a number of measures with the objective of ensuring that the above conditions are satisfied. Agricultural price policy seeks to achieve the first of the above mentioned objectives. The principal public agencies involved in support price operations on behalf of the Government to achieve the second objective are the Food Corporation of India, the Cotton Corporation of India, the Jute Corporation of India and the cooperatives with the National Agricultural Co-operative Federation of India (NAFED) as their apex organization.

Besides some state Governments have also been processing agricultural produce, particularly food grains, on support prices, either departmentally or through their own civil supplies corporation. To achieve the objective, a number of steps have been taken since the commencement of planning, aimed at regulating the marketing practices, standardizing weights and measures, developing sustainable infrastructure facilities in assembling markets, introducing quality standards through Agmark Certification.

REGULATING MARKETS

Over years, a number of regulated markets have been established to eliminate unhealthy marketing practices to reduce marketing charges and to ensure fair prices. The regulated market is administered by a committee which represents different interests like the state government, local institutions, traders, brokers, commission agents and farmers. The committee regulates the various activities connected with sales and purchases in the market.

CO-OPERATIVE MARKETING

It has been assigned an important role in agricultural marketing too. This co0operative movement has been promoted with the objective of the helping the small farmers. Co-operative agencies can play a vital role by arranging to collect the produce of the small farmers, grading and storing it, and helping them to sell at an advantageous price. In short co-operatives are expected to reduce market imperfections, render the required marketing services and to ensure fair prices. It should be noted that marketing is only one of the important functions of the co-operative sector.

Agricultural marketing infrastructure has not kept pace with the accelerated growth of production in the country. This has resulted in significant post harvest losses of agricultural produce. The Central Government has provided assistance for the creation of infrastructure facilities for marketing and for the setting up of rural godowns. The 9th plan has proposed to encourage Panchayats also to involve themselves actively in creating marketing infrastructure at the rural level.

26

INDUSTRIAL DEVELOPMENT AND ENVIRONMENTAL POLLUTION– A PERSPECTIVE

P. Narayana Reddy

INTRODUCTION

Industrialisation has contributed to the growth of economy of several countries it has improved the standard of living of its people and provided benefits to the society. It has also created in the process great environmental problems like climate change, forest destruction and denudation, soil erosion and desertification etc. Paul Hawkins in "Business and Environment" by Welford and Starkey observes that "100 years ago or even 50 years ago, it did not seem urgent that we understand the relationship between business and healthy environment. Till recently production and personnel pressures have been the deciding factors in corporate strategy. Of late information pressures are for corporate strategy. In the new millennium the corporate strategy will be driven by environmental problems."

With population over billion mark due to rapid population growth and subsequent industrial and economic growth to meet needs of this population, wastes and pollutants are released faster than the earth can absorb them and natural resources are consumed faster than they can be restored. With growing industrialization, problems of occupational healthy & safety also surfaced in India. Every year lakhs of accidents take place and thousands of workers die while working. Several categories of workers suffer from various types of diseases and health disorders which arise from dust, humidity temperature, noise, chemicals, postures, locomotion, radiation and other factors. Ensuring occupational health, safety and environment is not merely a technical question, but a political one as well, that it poses the question as to who decides and who suggest alternatives to the present day production process. Hence the workers need to have the knowledge of the risks and hazards at their work place, which also affect the surrounding and their living areas.

Industry in India has been diversifying into progressively more capital intensive and energy intensive are which degrading the quality of environment. It is generally perceived that environmental conservation is a stumbling block in the development of industrial activities. Recognizing the importance of E.A., procedure for environmental audit was first notified under the Environment (protection) Rules, 1986. Accordingly the industrial units are required to furnish the EA reports, By an amendment in 1993. The term for the document has been revised from "Environmental Audit Report" to "Environmental Statement".

Environmental statement has to be submitted by every Industry, requiring consent under section 25 of the Water Act of 1974 or under the section 21 of the Air (Prevention and Control of Pollution) Act of 1981 or both or authorization under the Hazardous Wastes (Management and Handling) Rules of 1989 issued under the Environment (Protection) Act of 1986. The statement has to be submitted to the concerned State Pollution Control Board for the period ending on 31st March in a prescribed format 30th September every year, beginning from 1993.

The Inter Governmental Panel on Climate Change (ICC) has predicted that we will see a doubling of pre-industrial levels of carbon dioxide in the atmosphere by 2050, raising global temperatures from one of three degrees Celsius by 2100.

Some commentators however ridicule the effect of such seemingly small temperature shifts. However even minute changes can be serious consequences. A Dutch study has visualized that by 2050, 24 percent of the World's parks and protected area could see major vegetation changes because of warming.

SUSTAINABLE DEVELOPMENT – RIO SUMMIT

The 1992 Rio Earth Summit produced several landmark agreements aimed at halting and reversing environmental destruction, poverty and inequality. Agenda 21 placed at center of the challenges facing humanity, the appropriate frame work for sustainable development. In accepting Agenda 21, we agreed to integrate social and economic developmental with environmental protection, in a manner that would ensure the sustainability of our planet and the prosperity of all humanity. These important decisions were reinforced by the conclusions ranched at a series of international conferences covering such important issues as gender equality, social and population development, children's rights, world trade, food security, health, habitat, racism and racial discrimination, financing for development, and the environment. The Rio decade has been successful in elevating the world's understanding that development must sustainable and that the three pillars of sustainable i.e. development: environmental protection, economic development and social development must go hand-in hand. Because of each pillar is internally linked to the others, effective pursuit of sustainable development requires a balanced approach that integrates all three components, Rio and post-Rio have no doubt established a frame work for addressing sustainable development.

PRESENT STATUS OF INDUSTRIAL POLLUTION IN INDIA

India is at present comparatively in the recent stages of industrialization, power generation, mechanized transportation, and urbanization we can expect the pollution to become uncontrollable as the present situation indicates, unless we take up some environmentally friendly strategies form now itself

Power plants, industries and vehicles are the biggest sources of pollution.

We can see that the Air pollution in our cities are growing in leaps and bounds, especially in the industrial cities. Central pollution Control Board released the air quality data for 70 cities in 1977, where the air was critically too disastrously polluted round the year for 33 cities. The industrialized cities like Kanpur, Surat, Agra, Patna, Faridabad. Jharia and Ankleshwar had alarming air quality with SPM ranging from 384 ug/cu to 412 ug/ sum. These were far more higher than Delhi which was referred to be the most polluted city in the country by WHO standards based on their assessment of 20 cities of the world with 340 macro-grammes/cubic metre, reaching the peak of 1055 on the worst day in 1997. While it was so for Delhi the recorded worst days for Cochin was 2506, Lucknow 2339, Kanpur 1385, Patna 1239, Agra 1222, and Ankleshwar 1198 ug/cum.

Industrial waste water treatment cannot realistically be separated from the larger problem of industrial waste management. Unlike the municipal sanitary official, the industrialist can exercise some degree of control over the quality and quality of this waste water flows by selection of alternate raw materials and/or manufacturing process.

The variation in consumption, concentration and flow of industrial waste waters from plants within the same plants with the same industrial category precludes defining rigid design parameters for industrial waste treatment facility. The most effective waste treatment systems are individually designed as apart of a total management programme and tailored to handle unavoidable pollution control of problems for a specific manufacturing facility. World Health Organization 2002 reports 40% of deaths each year occurs due to avoidable risk factors like malnutrition, smoking and poor sanitation etc., House wife's in Behala, Kolkata moved to court against various factories–chemical, plastic, paints, spray painting metal plating and plastic dusting responsible for water, air and noise pollution and also pose the danger of fire out break due to negligence and irresponsible functioning. Easter US,

Westerner and Southern Europe and Eastern China– some of the most industrialized regions in the world are also the most polluted areas.

INDUSTRIAL POLLUTION OF HIGHLY POLLUTING INDUSTRIES

Year wise progress in the implementation of pollution Control measures in the 17 categories of highly polluting industries is given in the table, on 30th September 2000 out of a total 1,551 large and medium industries, 1,326 industries have installed the requires pollution control facilities to comply with the prescribed environmental standards.

Statewise Summary Status of Polluting Control in 17 Categories of Industries

(A per information available with CPCB as on September 30th 1999)

		Status (No. of Units)		
State/Ut	*Total No. of Units*	*Closed*	*C*	*Defaulters*
Andhra Pradesh	173	29	142	02
Arunachal Pradesh	00	00	00	00
Assam	15	02	11	02
Bihar	62	17	35	10
Gujarat	177	07	168	02
Goa	06	00	06	00
Haryana	43	05	37	01
Himachal Pradesh	09	00	09	00
Jammu & Kashmir	08	03	05	00
Karnataka	85	09	72	04
Kerala	28	06	20	02
Madya Pradesh	78	11	60	07
Maharastra	335	24	302	09
Manipur	00	00	00	00
Meghalaya	01	00	01	00
Mizoram	00	00	00	00
Nagaland	00	00	00	00
Orrissa	23	01	15	07
Punjab	45	06	43	00
Rajasthan	49	06	30	00
Sikkim	01	00	01	00
Tamil Nadu	119	02	117	00
Tripura	00	00	00	00
Ut-Andaman & Nicobar Island	00	00	00	00

Contd.

State/Ut	Status (No. of Units) Total No. of Units	Closed	C	Defaulters
Ut-Chandigarh	01	00	01	00
Ut-Daman Daiu Dadra & Nagar Haveli	00	00	00	00
Ut-Delhi	05	01	04	00
Ut-Lakshadweep	00	00	00	00
Ut-Pondicherry	00	01	05	00
Uttar Pradesh	224	21	195	05
West Bengal	58	17	35	06
Total	1551	168	1326	57

Due to monitoring and follow up with the Central Pollution Control Board (CPCB) and the State Polluting Control Board (SPCBs) there has been an improvement in the installation of polluting control measures, which resulted in a decline in the number of defaulters during the year 1999-2000.

During 1997, the Ministry of Environment & Forests in coordination with the Central Polluting Control Board identified 851 industries along the major rivers and takes in the Courtney which were found discharging their untreated of partially treated effluents in the fresh water bodies. The recent monitoring report received from CPCB as on 30th September, 2000 indicates that 595 units were found to comply with prescribed standards.

SMALL SCALE INDUSTRIES AND ENVIRONMENTAL POLLUTION

The small scale sector is playing dominant role in Indian economy. But today they are caught in a double whammy. On one hand, they are hit by a plethora of court cases for widespread pollution. And on the other, this sector faces an existential dilemma. As the Government gradually withdraws its protection, and force to implement environmental regulations. In other words, on one side, small scale industries are badly needed and on the other they pollute the environment. The level of pollution caused by this sector in India per unit of output is higher than their counterparts in developed countries. The reasons are many.

Small Scale Industries and Industrial Pollution

Industry	*Cluster Regions*	*Wastewater Generated (Million litres per day)*
Engineering	Hands tools jalandhar and Nagaur Locks Aligrah Scientific Instruments Ambala, Ajmer Bicycle and parts Luchiana Brass parts Kohalpur, Agra, Rajkot, Coimbatore, Ghaziabad	2,125
Paper and Board Mills	Spread across the country	1,087
Textile Industries	Woolean and Cotton Hosiery Tripur, Ludhina, Kolkata, Delhi	450
Organic Chemicals	Gujarat	60
Tanneries	Leateher and Leather Products Chennai, Ambur and Vaniambadi (Tamil Nadu), Kolkata (West Bengal) and Agra and Kanpur (Uttar Pradesh)	50
Pharmacuticals	Gujarat and Maharashtra	40
Dye and dye intermediates	Gujarat	32
Soaps and detergents	Gujarat	10
Paints and varnishes		10
Petrochemicals		10
Edible oil and vanaspathi		7

(a) Continued usage of outdated and inefficient technologies that generate large amounts of water.

(b) Large and unplanned industrial conglomeration;

(c) Lack of resources for enforcement and implementation of pollution control programmes;

(d) Lack of public/market pressure for improving environmental performance; and,

(e) Lack of proper sitting thereby posing greater environmental risks.

IMPLEMENTATION

The recent Supreme Court order for imposition of fine on the Government of Delhi for damaging environment by its municipal effluent and other polluting industries, the industry and government bodies are in major shake-up. These orders have finally paved the way for people to seek compensation for land and water contamination by industrial and municipal wastes. These are live examples in India that era of "Polluters Pay Principle" has arrived. Now due to indifferent attitude of other systems towards environmental pollution. The judiciary is becoming more pro-active and its role is increasing day by day to provide better environment to citizen of India.

Lessions of the past have indicated that pollution grew very rapidly in Western countries with the economic boom during the II World War in early forties when the west created enormous economic wealth. This resulted in extreme pollutions of the air and water over London, Los Angeles, and Tokyo where it was impossible to breathe, while the rivers Thames and the Rhine became virtually sewers. Inspite of efforts the air pollution over these countries are unmanageable because of the industries, resulting in acid rain not only in the concerned countries, but beyond their frontiers into the neighboring countries as well.

STEPS INITIATED TO PREVENT AND CONTROL POLLUTION IN INDIA

A large number of initiatives have been taken and are begin taken by all concerned, still there exist a wide gap between existing condition of environment and desired one. The government regulation and judicial intervention is not the only solution to pollution. Due to inaccessibility of viable cleaner technologies. Indian industries are at crossroads.

GUIDELINES FOR NEW INDUSTRIES

1. Many of the environmental problems could be avoided if industries are located of the basis of environmental

Pollution Flashpoints

Place	*Problems*	*Status*
Delhi	More than 100,000 industries in residential areas. These include heavily polluting industries like electroplating, metal buffering, battery recycling, plastic, dyeing, powder coating and asbestos brake products.	Supreme Court's 1996 judgment ordered the government to relocate these industries. After four years of waiting, the court pulls up the authorities. A sealing drive takes place. Even today infrastructure to relocate the industries has not been developed.
Pali, Jodhpur and Balotra	More than 1,500 textiles dyeing and printing units releasing more than 50 million liters of wastewater into the luni river basin	Protects date back to early 1980s. Common effluent treatment plants (CETPs) set up in pali but not functioning satisfactorily, Jodhpur does not have a CETP.
Gujarat	More than 7,000 chemical industries manufacturing various industrial chemical including dyestuff, dyestuff intermediates and pesticides. Long history of pollution and protects. Today Gujrat is the most polluted state in India.	Various court cases filled by non-governmental organizations and local residents. Health problems rampant. Still, the Gujarat Government is busy setting up new industrial estates for chemical industries.

Contd.

Place	*Problems*	*Status*
Pimpri – Chinchwad Industrial area, Pune	More than 400 organised and unorganized electroplating units catering to the needs of the automobile industry. Severe water pollution problem.	Fish deaths reported in Mulamutha river several times. Villagers have protested. Nothing has been done till date.
Tirupur, Tamil Nadu	About 800 dyeing and bleaching units at this hosiery capital of India. Till a fe years ago, all the untreated effluents released into the river Noyyal. Reservoir at Orathupalayam dam filled with polluted wate rendering it unfits for any use.	CETPs and individual ETPs have been constructed but only a partial solution. Pollution still going on. Farmers filed a case to clean up the Orathupalayam dam. But industrialists haven't paid the cost, which is Rs.12.5 crore.
Kolkata	About 550 tanneries releasing more than 50 mid of effluents	A 1996 SC decision ordered them to shift. But no infrastructure has been developed to relocate them.

consideration, injudicious sitting of industry can seriously effect the environmental features. The entrepreneurs should be fully aware of these procedures and they should take necessary steps while setting up the industry so as to minimize the possible adverse effects on the environmental resources and quality of life.

2. On the basis of the industrial policy statement of July 1980, indiscriminate expansion of the existing industries and setting up of new industrial undertakings within the limits of metropolitan cities and the large towns should not be permitted.
3. To prevent air, water and soil pollution arising out of industrial projects, the industrial licensing procedure requires that the entrepreneurs before setting up the industry obtain clearance from Central/State Air and Water Pollution Control Boards.
4. In respect of certain industrial development projects it is not only necessary to install suitable pollution control equipment but also identify appropriate sites for their location.
5. According to the procedure for the select group of industries, the letters of intent should be converted to industrial licenses only after stipulated conditions have to be fulfilled including pollution abatement measures, comprehensive environmental impact assessment report and environment management plans, etc.
   - 24 critically polluted areas have been identified and Action Plans for have been prepared which are being implemented by CPCB/SPCBs.
   - Preparation of Zoning Atlas for silting of industries based on environmental consideration in various districts of the country has been taken up.
   - To check pollution in small scale industries, 40 waste minimization circles have been set up in various parts of the country.

- A scheme for setting up of common Effluent Treatment Plants (CETP) in clusters of small scale industrial unite has been taken for CETP projects have been approved which are various stages of implementation.
- The ministry has promoted environment management system (EMS) program by he industry for continual improvement of environmental performance and encouraging voluntary compliance of standards. More that 50 companies in India have acquired ISO 14000 certification.
  - Flexible Regulation
  - Eco-Labeling
  - Environmental Life
  - Environmental Life Cycle Assessment
  - Influence of Public Opinion
  - Promoting Self Regulatory Mechanism

ISO STANDARDS FOR ENVIRONMENTAL SAFETY

ISO 14000 signifies a new generation in environmental protection. This standard is directed at establishing a link between business and environmental management for all companies no matter their size purpose. ISO 14000 provides industry with a way to track, manage and improve environmental performance without conflicting with the business priorities of an operation.

ISO 14000 is a simplified environmental management standard which takes into account business and economic consideration while improving on already established environmental protection programs. ISO 14000 is not intended to supersede current state and federal regulations. Business consideration, flexibility and simplistic approach to environmental protection are the main differences between ISO 14000 and the old command and control system currently in place.

CONCLUSION

Industrial development significantly contributes towards economic development. Interestingly the industrial development brings a host of environmental problems too. It means on one side we need industrial development and on the other side we don't want the negative effects of it. In developing economies like India, we badly need industrial development to over come the problems of the society at the cost of environmental problems. However, now the issue is how to achieve the desired level of economic development with minimum or no environmental problems. This issue is more pertinent now because we re forced to integrate our economy into the world economy under the direction of World Trade Organization. Under the change international economic environment we have to produce goods and services according to the international standards with little environmental problems to the local people. As it is no doubt we have reasonably good environmental regulations, however, the implementation agencies and the entrepreneurs are not able to implement them. Therefore, there is a need to review the entire process of environmental issues and to evolve a new set of procedures suitable to the local entrepreneurs and economy.

REFERENCES

Dr. N.S. Raman & Er. Ajay Gupta (2000), 'Environmental Audit: An Eco-friendly Concept for Thermal Power Plants", Environment & People September.

Mahadevan (2000), "Environment, Development and Occupational Problems", Environment & People, October.

R.C. Vaishya and S.K. Gupta (2000), "Environment Management Approaches of Indian Industry", Environment & People July.

M. Kamal Naidu (2000), "Impact of Economic Reforms on Environment Protection", Environment & People August.

Thabo Mbeki (2002), "World Summit for Sustainable Development Opening Statement", Down to Earth September 6th.2002.

Dhurjati Mukherjee (2002), "Towards Sustainable Development", August 2,2001.

Dhurjati Mukherjee (2002), "Preventing An Environment Catastrophe", Young Indian September 20.

Kushal P.S. Yadav (2002), "The Small Big Polluter", Down to Earth, October.

R.C. Vaishya & R.A. Sharma (2000), "ISO 14000 STD. – Environmental Management Systems (Practical Tips), Environment & People, July.

27

ENVIRONMENTAL MANAGEMENT FOR ENVIRONMENTAL SAFETY

G. Manchala

The mad race among nations over the globe for development resulted into unlimited exploitation of every bit of natural resources and jeopardized the health and safety of mankind itself. This exploitation of nature by man disturbed the delicate ecological balance between living and non-living components of biosphere. Environmental sensitivity calls for an inter disciplinary approach. An integrated approach to environmental problems alone will help us to identify both curative and preventive aspects. Environmental issues were simple social issues as long as natural resources were abundantly available. In the name of development, governments are rolling out red carpet for big industrial homes to establish factories. Over the years Environment has been abused and plundered by man's greed. Defending and improving the environment for present and future generations has become an imperative goal for mankind. It is the imbalance of eco-systems referred to as the ecological imbalance that leads to an environmental crisis. Some of the present day concerns are Acid rain, deforestation, soil degradation, smog due to automobile and industrial pollution, depletion of Ozone layer, Green house effect, discharge of toxic wastes by industrial units into rivers, oceans etc., As Edmund Hillary said "Environmental problems begin with the people as the cause and end with people as victims".

There has been increasing International concern about environmental issues. In 1992 United Nations conducted a conference on "Environment and Development". Concern about global climatic change led representatives of 166 Nations to meet in Kyoto, Japan in December 1997 to negotiate a treaty to reduce emissions of carbon dioxide and other green house gases. Most of the industrialized nations agreed to reduce emissions by the year 2010. In addition to the above public interest litigations coupled with Judicial Activism has put the business in a tight spot. Driven against wall, businesses have stared recognizing their environmental responsibilities.

The problems of pollution were sidelined in order to promote rapid industrialization. As per the Environmental Protection Act - 1986. Industries have to take prior permission from Pollution Control Board specifying that the industry is well equipped to handle the effluents it generates. Though these sound effective on paper in reality political intervention and legal bottlenecks hinder their implementation. Pollution once caused is difficult, and in many cases impossible to cure. Studies indicated that water, and Air pollution is in dangerous proportions in industrialized cities in India. Industrial pollution in many developing countries including India is managed/controlled using end of pipe treatment. Using available evidence it is argued here that EOP treatment. Like Common Effluent Treatment Plant (CETP) dose not solve problem as many toxic metals remain into the treated water or in the sludge. Proactive approach "Pollution prevention should be the aim of any policy intervention. Environment management system is an attempt in this direction. Environment Management System is defined as the part of the overall management system that includes organizational structure, planning activities responsibilities, practices, procedures, processes and resources for developing, implementing, achieving, reviewing, and maintaining the environmental policy.

The subcommittee appointed by United Nations brought out what are known as ISO 14000 family standards. It is a certificate issued by International Standards Organization, Geneva. Specifications have been drafted to issue a uniform approach to environmental protection by al companies world wide. ISO 14000 set of standards or what are known as Environmental Management Systems Standards help the organizations to effectively tackle this environmental responsibilities is an evolving series of generic standards developed by the ISO. This can be used in manufacturing or processing industries, service industries like construction, architecture and engineering.

The basic philosophy for policy formulation under ISO 14000 is the concept of sustainable development. The definition by the World Commission on environment and development has been accepted by governments and Industrial Leaders. It requires that environmental resources for present requirements should be managed in such a way that these resources are preserved for future use. Application of the principle of sustainable development requires us to set a whole lot of new environmental standards and policies. Hence the ISO 14000 series. It provides businesses for managing environmental impact. The standards cover a broad range of functions measures to be taken in the spheres of basic management systems auditing, performance evaluations, labeling and life-cycle assessment.

COMPONENTS OF ISO 14000

There are six main areas in ISO 14000 broken down into various categories.

Environmental Management System Standard

This requires that company has a system that allows business units to meet environmental goals. A formal environmental policy and standards or specification are communicated and understood by all employees. Legal requirements and compliances are monitored.

Environmental Auditing Standards

This describes the general principles of environmental auditing.

Environmental Performance Evaluation Standards

This requires a company to evaluate its environmental management system and various operational systems that should be in place. Companies must develop measures and goals to asses environmental performance such as the percentage for reduction in air emissions, hazardous waste generated etc.

Environment Labeling Standards

It describes general requirements for various environmental seal and other label performance and deals with all environmental product claims, regardless of the media used.

Life Cycle Assessment

It describes the principles and guidelines used to determine the impact of a product on the environment from the design stage through to disposal. This implies that firms should implement design for the environment. This emphasizes that organizations have to use less pollutants, in other worlds cleaner production.

Environmental Aspects in Product Standards

Its purpose is to incorporate environmental training into the development of product standards to prevent adverse impact on the environment.

ISO Certification and India

The ISO 14000 certification has been acquired by about 200 Indian companies. One of the main reasons by organizations in India have not given serious thought to ISO 14000 due to

- Their irresponsible approach towards common environmental issues.

- Lack of corporate ethics.
- Laxity in implementation of pollution emission.

All the companies in Asia, to date, that have adopted and achieved ISO 14000 certification have already got ISO 9000 systems.

Many countries are now opting for more flexible and efficient regulation like pollution charges, community pressures, public disclosures etc., that provide strong incentives for polluters to change their ways. In this connection emphasis must be on cleaner production. There are a number of successful cases both in developing and developed countries where the production process has been altered so as not to use to toxic or problematic chemicals. An integrated systems where prevention along with cleaner production are more relevant in a fast growing economy like India. Collective Action combining regulation, direct control, government incentives, subsidies, voluntary organizations help etc., are required to protect our environment. Environment Management System is a right approach in this direction, as Mahatma Gandhi said there is enough in this World for everybody's needs, but not for everybody's needs, but not for everybody's greed.

REFERENCES

Ahluwalia J.S. (2000), "Total Quality Management", Tata Mc Graw Hill Publishing Company Ltd.

Karpagam M. (2002), "Environmental Economics", Sterling Pulishers.

Shridhara Bhat. K. (2002), "Total Quality Management", Himalaya Publishing House–Aug.

Ulaganathan Sankar (2001), "Environmental Economics"–Oxford India Paper Backs.

Indian Journal of Environmental Health (2002), Volume 44, No.:2, April.

Indian Journal of Environmental Health (2002), Volume 44, No.:2,3, April.

28

LARGE DAMS AND ENVIRONMENTAL SAFETY

P.L. Narasimha Rao

Water is vital for realising the full potential of the agriculture sector and country's development. Only when it is in short supply or of poor quality do we place water in its proper prospective. Perhaps its abundance (80 percent of the earth's surface is water) and inexpensiveness contributed to its casual treatment. Water has historically played an important role in economic development and continues to play vital role in Agriculture, Industry, and Urbanization. Perhaps no other substanceis is so versatile. Water is used in, irrigation, as source of power in transportation as an industrial product, and source of nutrition

India is one of the wettest countries in the world with average annual rainfall of 1100 mm. There is no accurate information about India's water resources. Narottam Shah of the Bombay based centre for monitoring Indian economy stated. "Unbelievable as it may seem, till now we have no arrangements in this country to compile and publish on an annual basis comprehensive data regarding various aspects of water which are important for policy analysis and programme formulation and for monitoring the efficiency of use of our scarce water resources"[1].

According to the ministry of Agriculture, Government of India, soil erosion and land degradation have assumed serious proportions. As per the data 174 million hectares of 53 percent of the total land area are India is suffering for serious degradation. Area subjected to water and wind erosion amounts to 144 million hectares and area degraded through special problems like ravines, salinity, water logging etc., accounted for another 34 million hectares.

Area degraded through special problems includes water logged area 8 million Hectares, alkaline soil 4 million hectares, saline soil 5.5 million hectares, etc., The Total flood prone area is 40 million hectares but the annual average area affected by floods is 7 million hectares and the annual average cropped area affected by floods is 4 million hectares.

WATER RESOURCES POTENTIAL

The average run-off in the river system of the country has been assessed as 1,869 km^2 (cubic kilometers). Of this, the utilisable portion by conventional storage and diversion is estimated as about 690 km^3. In addition, the replenishable ground water potential in the country is estimated at 432 km^3. The per-capita availability of water at national level has reduced from about 5,177 m^3 (cubic meters) in 1951 to an estimated level of 1,869 m^3 in 2001 with great variation in water availability in different river basins.

Even though water is plenty in India water is not being used properly. All the time we face paradoxical situations where the crops and other resources are damaged due to floods and lakhs of hectares of land and animals have insufficient water availability due to droughts.

Since water is not a central subject in the Constitution many problems and conflicts and disputes are cropping up. Various states have been entering into disputes because nd litigtion of water problem. All most all important rivers pass through many states and there is are no exemptions where there are no disputes between states. The conflict between Tamilnadu and Karnataka became a national Issue. For, the last two decades environmentalist have been disputing on the use of water through large dams. Infact, Governments also changed their policies and are undertaking up more medium and minor irrigation projects.

Multipurpose River Valley Projects: A Controversy

Soon after independance, multi-purpose River Valley Projects and other dams and canals were considered essential for meeting India's critical requirements Irrigation agriculture, electricity generation and flood control. Accordingly Construction of dams was given a top priority in our economic plans and over 15 percent of the total plan outlay was invested in dams and canals. India now ranks one among the more important dam building nations in the world. Dams were regarded as "The Temple of Modern India"- by Jawaharlal Nehru. Till now Irrigation and Hydro Power have been the major objectives of water resources development in India.

The Heavy Investments on major and medium irrigation projects have impressive results to show. The irrigation potential created by large and medium works has gone up from about 10 million hectares in 1950-51 to 33 million hectares in 1996-98. Irrigation is the single most important factor in achieving a successful break through in Agriculture and a measure of self-sufficiency in food production. Production of Hydro-electric energy capacity has risen smartly from 3 billion KWH in 1950-51 to 74.5 billion KWH in 1997-98- increase by 25 times.

By impounding a river's water so as to release it at a controlled rate, a dam acts as a buffer against floods. The so called multi-purpose river valley projects have been constructed to prevent floods in their respective regions. The National Flood Control Programme launched in 1954 has constructed many embankments, drainage channels and town and village protection schemes. In practice, flood control measures have failed miserably and over the years, the area affected by floods and the damage to crops, cattle and to human beings has increased sharply–despite the multipurpose projects.

A serious problem is the heavy siltation of the reservoirs of major dams. The rate of siltation is often much higher than originally estimated. Heavy siltation reduces the storage capacity and life span of many reservoirs which, as a result, are incapable of absorbing heavy floods. Often, panic discharges from these reservoirs have led to destructive flash floods in the stream.

Big dams and huge multi-purpose river valley projects have serious adverse environmental effects. A major environmental effect is the degradation of the soil in the command areas of irrigation projects due to water logging and soil salinity.

Further, the Environmentalists more particularly Ms. Metha Patkar, Sundar Lal Bahuguna, Ms. Arundhati Roy, and many others are opposing the large dams .

Discussions on the linkage of rivers has been going on for the last 50 years. In fact, the great irrigation engineer Dr. K.L. Rao gave fantastic plan decades ago but Central Govt. could not take interest and initiative due to political and economic conditions. Recently due to severe drought conditions, disputes between states and Supreme Court Insistences, the Govt. of India constituted a Task Force under the Chairman ship of Sri. Prabhu.

ENVIRONMENTAL PROTECTION AND DAMS

The environmentalists are opposing this plan of river linkages. It is true that there are certain problems and environment may also be effected to certain extent. But where is the solution ? They say the solutionlies in building minor irrigation projects.

But the experience shows that the minor irrigation projects are very uneconomical and practically impossible. More than economical reasons the political reasons will gain upper hand in managing these small projects. But in practice what we see is different . Even after 55 years of Independence more than 90 per cent of the village water tanks have become useless due to non-administration, owing to political reasons.

CONCLUSION

Finally, we can conclude that every body agrees on the need

for the use of water resources fully but the methods only differs. For faster economic development of India, only the way out is linkage of rivers and construct on of big reservoirs. The so called environmentalists have to take the practical aspects into account instead of living in a dream world. Displaced people are to be given proper compensation not only for the loss of land and assets but for their livelihood too. The Government and the persons benefited from major projects should contribute for paying adequate compensation to the displaced people.

29

NEED FOR USE OF SAFE DRINKING WATER FOR BETTER HEALTH AND ECONOMIC DEVELOPMENT IN INDIA

N. Sudhakara Rao, K. Vamsi Krishna

INTRODUCTION

The health status of an individual, or a community or a nation is determined by the Interplay and integration of two ecological universes-the internal environment of main himself and the external environment which surround him. Man has already controlled a number of factors in his environment, e.g., food, water, housing, clothing, sanitation. These controllable factors are those included in the "standard living". It is the control of these factors that has been responsible for Considerable improvement in the health of the people during the past century in the developed countries. However, man's mastery over his environment is not complete. As one problem is solved, other new problem is arising. India is still lagging far behind many countries in the field of environmental health. So there is need to make corrective efforts.

Health is wealth. Safe water is an important component in health. Safe water is required for many purposes. Such as: Domestic use, namely for drinking, cooking, washing and bathing, public use namely public cleaning, fire-fighting, maintenance of public gardens and swimming pools and numerous other civic purposes, industrial and agricultural purposes. Without water, there cannot be any industrial development. Some industries like the iron and steel and paper industry need quite a lot of water. The food and raw materials needed by the world cannot be raised without water. Water is therefore an essential factor in the economic, social and cultural development of community. It can eliminate waterborne diseases, promote rural development and improve the quality of life. From the standpoint of public health, water should be provided in adequate volume. A limited supply will be of very little benefit, however superior the quality of water may be. A daily supply of, 150 to 200 liters (35 - 40 gallons) per head is considered an adequate allowance. The consumption of water, however, depends upon climatic conditions standard of living and habits of the people. The larger the quantity and the better the quality of water, the more rapid and extensive is the advancement in public health.

Fresh water is crucial for any development in agriculture or industry and healthy life. With arise in population in India, the demand for water has grown. But, there was a reduction in availability by 25 per cent in the last 20 years and the picture remains gloomy in future. By the year 2050 AD, there would be a further steep fall in the availability of potable water to an extent of 35 to 40 per cent. This struggle would spread fast unless people are made aware of the imminent distressful years to come. So, planning and concrete actions are needed immediately to utilize this precious commodity carefully without waste with better allocation and distribution for various purposes and to harvest and recycle the water by appropriate methods for supplementing the fresh water. No country can afford overexploit its natural resources like Soil and Water. More sincere and disciplined affords are needed in these fronts. If the situation continuous like this it is difficult to survive as a Civilized Nation. We can witness battles the streets between good neighbors not necessarily for food but for this precious commodity namely water! In rural India especially in the drought prone areas, it could be a struggle to fetch a pet or two of water from distant places. Our Water Resources have to be augmented for agriculture industry and other domestic uses for our own survival in the globe. We need to plan for an immediate future! There is no time to waste whether we have funds or no funds. If you care for a peaceful living for now or for the generations to come, we have to contribute our sweat and also part of our earning for this noble cause. Environmental education perhaps may help us to live safely and preserve our water resources for all time to come ! Water use in India is currently apportioned into four major activities with agriculture taking the major share of 93.4 per cent, livestock of 1.1 per cent, industries and power generation of 1.3 per cent and municipal & rural water supplies of 3.7 per cent. We do not seem to have any control over this pattern of distribution. However in the near future, drinking water & domestic needs would increase sharply. Since the beginning of the century when international cooperation in public health began, safe water has been a major concern. A survey conducted by WHO in 1975 on community water supplies revealed the fact that in India while 80 percent of the population in urban areas had access to community water supplies, only 18 percent of the rural population, had reasonable access to safe water. The WHO attributes the slow pace of progress to shortage of funds and trained manpower, weakness in national programmes, difficulties in system operation and maintenance and insufficient involvement of potential users. The WHO today's committed to participating in the global effort to attain the target adopted by Habitat, the 1976 UN Conference on Human settlements, that is, to have "Water for All by 1990" itself.

Most of the people in the developed countries and elite of the developing countries, enjoy all the determinants of good health-adequate income, nutrition, education, sanitation, safe drinking water and comprehensive health care. In contrast only 10 to 20 per cent of the population of the developing countries enjoy ready access to health services of any kind. John Bryant in his book Health and the developing World presented a gloomy picture on health in system and felt that more than half of the world population don't have access to health care at all and there is need to reduce health gap between countries and among individuals in the same country. The World Health Assembly in its 34 world Health Assembly adopted global strategy for health for all. In 1981, it self WHO pledged for Health for all by 2000 A.D. that, permits all people to lead a socially and economically productive life. It implies health is to brought with in the reach of everybody and remove obstacles for health which means the elimination of malnutrition, ignorance, disease, contaminated water supply and hygienic housing etc. People are now demanding a better quality life. It is a composite summary measure of physical, mental and social well-being as perceived by an individual or society. Hereditary environment life style, socio-economic and health services, play a crucial role in improving quality of life in a society. It has to be noted that 75 percent of diseases are waterborne caused by bacteria and virus such as cholera, dysentery, typhoid, infectious hepatitis etc. The industrial effluents of chlorides and suspended solids and metals like zinc, nickel, iron, chromium and cadmium affect the quality of water.

OBJECTIVES AND SOURCE OF THE DATA

The main objective of the present paper is to examine the nature of drinking water sources of drinking water the relationship between the safe water health and economic development. The author also examines the quality of packaged drinking water and their standards in the country with special reference to Wisdom Packaged Water produced in Guntur. The required data for the present study is taken from secondary sources, medical reports and also data provided by the Wisdom Packaged Water. Guntur.

HEALTH AND DEVELOPMENT

The health is an essential component in socio-economic development package has gained increasing recognition now-a-days. During 1960s it was tough that socio-economic progress was not essential for improving the health status of the people in the developing countries and that substantial and rapid progress could made through introduction of public health measures alone and hence the role of human well being. The developing of this process was grossly under estimated. There are profound modifications in the economic theory during 1980s. It became increasingly clear that economic development alone cannot solve the major problems of poverty hunger, malnutrition and disease.

Human welfare emerged as a major objective of developing strategies. Since there is a close link between health and development. Health has become an integral part of development. All sectors of society have an effect on health. Health services are no longer considered merely as a complex of solely medical measures but a "sub-system" of an over all economic system. Human health and well being are the ultimate goal of development.

From data it is observed that disease rates are drastically cut down by an improvement in, the quality of public water supply. In Uttar Pradesh after waterworks sanitation, the cholera death rate decreased by 74.1 per cent, typhoid fever death rate by 63.6 per cent, the dysentery death rate by 23.1 per cent, and the rate for diarrhoeal diseases by 42.7 per cent. Money spent on supply schemes is a sound investment which will pay huge dividends in improved In short, the provision of safe community water supply is one of the most effective and health technologies for improving the health of people. Reports from several countries have shown an inverse statistical association between the hardness of drinking water and the death rate from cardiovascular diseases. Areas supplied with soft drinking water showed a significantly higher prevalence of either arteriosclerotic heart disease, or degenerative heart disease, hypertension, sudden deaths of cardiovascular origin, or a combination of these. The evidence is based solely on circumstantial evidence arid statistical association. Further studies are progress to establish a possible connection between certain water characteristics and the development of cardiovascular diseases.

The proportion of GNP spent on health services and related activities including water supply and sanitation, housing and nutrition, community development proportions spent on primary health played a crucial role for individual improvement. Provisioning of health care availability, accessibility, utilization and quality of care are important. An adequate supply of safe water basic sanitation, health education, environmental education, creating awareness on life styles is important for better life. Much of the ill health in the underdeveloped countries is largely due to lack of safe drinking water. No state in the country which can develop without community health development and safe drinking water supply.

SOURCES OF WATER

The selection of a source requires professional advice. In general, water sources must conform to two criteria, namely : the quality of water acceptable in value, and the quantity that can be sufficient to meet present and future requirements. There are three main sources of water are : Rain Water, Water, Surface Water (Impounding Reservoirs, Rivers and Streams, Tanks, Ponds and Lakes), and Ground Water, (Shallow wells, Deep wells and Springs).

Rain is the prime source of water. A part of the, rain water sinks into the ground to form ground water; part of it evaporates back into the atmosphere, and some runs off to form streams and rivers which flow ultimately into the sea. Source of water in the soil is taken up by the plants and is evaporated in turn by the leaves. These events are spoken of as "water cycle". Rain water is the purest water in nature. Physically, it is clear, bright and sparkling. Chemically, it is soft water containing only traces of dissolved solids (0.0005 per cent). Being soft, it has a corrosive action on lead pipes. Bacteriologically, rain water from clean districts is free from pathogenic agents. Rain water tends to become impure as it passes through the atnosphere. It picks lip suspended impurities from the atmosphere such as dust, soot and microorganisms and gases such as carbon dioxide, nitrogen, oxygen and ammonia.

Surface water originates mostly from rain water. The vast majority of Indian cities and town depend upon surface water such as Impounding Reservoirs, Rivers and Streams and Tanks, Ponds and Lakes. In surface water supplies possess a high probability of organic, bacterial and viral contamination.

Ground water is the cheapest and most practical means of providing water to small communities. Ground water is superior to surface water, because the ground itself provides an effective filtering medium. The groundwater is likely to be free from pathogernic agents. It usually no treatment and the supply are likely to be certain even during dry season. But, the problem is high in mineral content, e.g., salts of calcium and magnesium which render the water pumping or some arrangement to lift the water.

The usual ground water sources are wells and springs. Which are classified as shallow and deep wells, dug and tube wells. 'Wells are the main source of water supply in Indian villages and towns. A shallow well is one which taps the water from above the first impervious layer in the ground. The term "Shallow" has nothing to do with the depth of the well. A deep well is one which penetrates the first impervious layer in the ground and taps the water lying beneath the layer. Most of the wells in India are of the shallow type. Speaking generally, shallow wells are notoriously liable to pollution from neighbouring 'sources of contamination such as urinals, drains, cesspools, soakage pits and collections of manure.

A sanitary well is one which is properly located, well-constructed and, protected against nation with a: view to yield a supply of safer water. Tube wells are successful as a source of water in many parts of India. A spring is ground water which finds its way to the surface because of certain topographical characteristics of the land. Four kinds of springs are described-springs, deep springs, mineral springs and thermal springs.

RURAL WATER SUPPLY PROGRAMME IN INDIA

The provision of potable drinking water to all villages has been identified as one of the priority tasks of the Government. The National Water Supply and Sanitation Programme was launched in 1954 by the Govt. of India as part of the Health Plan to assist the States to provide adequate water supply and sanitation facilities in the entire country. Provision has been made in the successive 5-year plans to improve the water supply.The Accelerated Rural Water Supply-Programme (ARWSP), is implemented by the Department of Drinking Water Supply 1972-73 to assist the States and UTs to accelerate the pace of coverage of safe and adequate drinking water supply facilities to the rural population. The programme focuses on the coverage of all rural habitations specially the un-reached ones, to ensure susceptibility of the systems and sources, to tackle the problem of water quality and institutionalize water quality monitoring and surveillance through a "Catchment Area Approach". This programme has recently been revamped with an aim to usher in reforms by institutionalizing community participation in the rural water supply sector so as to gradually replace the government oriented, centralised, supply driven and non-people participating programme.

An area of concern is the reemergence of uncovered villages in view of poor quality of construction, non involvement of people in design/operation/maintenance of assets and fast depletions of ground water levels leading to problems of arsenic and fluoride content being enhanced. At the beginning of the Ninth Plan there were about 85,000 Not Covered (NC), 391,000 Partially Covered (PC) and 140,000 Quality Problem (QP) habitations in the country. The Ninth Plan seeks to cover all the NC, PC, QP habitations with safe drinking water facilities. In the first three years of the Ninth Plan, 62,000 NC and 242,000 PC habitations have been covered with water supply facilities. As on 1st February 2002, there are 1,257,532 Full Covered (FC) habitations, 147,241 Partially Covered (PC), with a balance of 17,891 habitations as Non-Covered (NC) ones.

The Pradhan Mantri Gramodaya Yojana (PMGY) Rural Drinking Water Programme is a specific component of the new initiative for achievement of sustainable human development at the village level, launched by the Government in 2000-01. A minimum of 25 per cent of the total allocation for the component is to be utilised by the respective States/UTs on projects for water conservation, water harvesting, water recharge and sustainability of drinking water source in respect of Desert Development Programme (DDP) / Drought Prone Areas Programme (DPAP) areas and other water stress / drought affected areas, and the balance 75 per cent utilised for tackling water quality and extension of coverage of habitations. During 2000 - 01. Rs. 513 crore was released to the States. In 2001 - 02 Rs. 636.7 crore has been allocated for this scheme and Rs. 355 crore released as the first installment. An amount of Rs. 1,637 crore has been released by the Centre and Rs. 1,496 crore separately by the States, upto end of January, 2002, under ARWSP. The number of habitations covered are 26,803 against a target of 45,527 and the population covered is 10.5 million as against a target of 21.6 million of the period. The programme achieved roughly 50 per cent success rate. This necessitates addressing of the problems of control on ground water withdrawal, water harvesting and soil and water conservation, and community participation for management of drinking water as an economic asset. Community participating is envisaged in implementation, managing and maintaining the rural drinking water supply system.

WATER POLLUTION

Water Pollution is the most distressing feature of modern days affecting the health and happiness of 60 to 75 percent of people in the "Developing" countries. As per World Health Organisation, 27,000 people die in these countries everyday for want of adequate water and sanitation. The Sources of water Pollution are : (1) the municipal effluents of biodegradable compounds and sewage; (2) industrial pollutants with organic effluents of pulp, synthetic compounds like paints, solvents, detergents, insecticides and inorganic sources of mineral acids, Salts, oils, sulphates, cyanamides and heavy metal like mercury, cadmium and lead; (3) agricultural run-off like nitrates, phosphates, pesticides and suspended sediments from soil erosion; and (4) radio active materials like uranium tailings from mining or processing, radio active materials and isotopes like Sr^{90}, P^{32}, and CO^{60}. What has to be noted is that there is an alarming increase in concentrations of these pollutants in various organisms as they pass up the food chain, which phenomenon is termed as Biological Magnification, DDT a chlorinated hydrocarbon is a classic example of this phenomenon. Algae assimilate DDT indiscriminately and the primary consumers take it in large quantities. With biological magnification, DDT concentration would raise from secondary (small fish) to tertiary (large fish) consumers and reach top consumers in toxic levels through this food chain.

POLLUTION OF RIVERS, LAKES, PONDS AND TANKS

Most of our rivers are highly polluted with domestic wastes, sewage and Industrial effluents at 30,000 million litters per day. Decomposition of organic wastes depletes the dissolved oxygen in water, which affects aquatic life. Thus, these are not healthy for human activities and as such they cannot sustain any form of healthy life. They also have a quota of fertilizers and pesticides washed down from the agricultural fields. Lakes, ponds and tanks have the same story to tell. Elaborate planned tanks in India catering to the drinking purposes deteriorated with no maintenance of these structures and with 30 to 40 percent of storage capacity lost due to sedimentation. Many have been destroyed due to negligence and urbanisation. Aquatic weels like Water hyacinth absorb heavy metals from sewage and industrial effluents. Nitrates and phosphates from the farms have lead to Eutrophication. Immersion of colorfully painted idols in water bodies release lead and mercury to these sources of water making way for slow poisoning. Sewage effluents and industrial wastes can add high concentrations of heavy metals. In the 10th Plan, the National River Action Plan is embarking on preventing pollution in 149 cities at a cost of Rs. 3000 crores!

GROUND WATER POLLUTION

Ground water pollution is increasing day by day. Wells all over were regarded as providing us pure water. It is no longer so. They have been observed to have nitrates in varying quantities (some beyond 50 mg per litre) and Fe contents of more than 10 mg per litre them unsafe for drinking. Some are possessing hard water with high salt and chlorine contents to make them unfit for drinking purposes. What is more is that this under-ground resource has been over-exploited resulting in high Flouride contents. Some wells have dried up even after digging to a depth of 200 meters. One of the reasons is that the catchment areas have intense activities urbanization disrupting the cyclic-management of tanks and wells; the tanks have been silted up and / or converted to housing colonies giving little scope either for water-storage or percolation into underground to recharge the reserves. Lechates from landfill sites can affect our ground-water resources. Without an impervious surface and without any measure to check leaching treatment, the land-fills mostly on the outskirts of the cities, release toxins such as lead, mercury, cyanide and arsenals into the ground-water. In the Seacoasts, coasts, sedimentation and erosion can affect sea-life reducing spawning areas and eggs of many species of fresh and marine orgnisms. Man's urban and agricultural activities notably of the draining of fertilizers and pesticides and coastal land-fills can carry these sediments to estuarine waters thus affecting the estuarine species.

POLLUTANTS IN OUR WATERS AND STANDARDISATION

The chlorinated Hydrocarbons like aldrin, dieldrin. BHC and the polychlorinated biphenyls (PCBS) also find their way into food chain similarly. Pesticides are ingested through food sources. Even polluted-water can be a source of many pesticides. They are toxic and affect our health. There is a great danger of nitrates to nitrite. When absorbed into the blood stream, nitrite binds with haemoglobin. This binding prevents haemoglobin from accepting the oxygen that is necessary for respiration. Thus, methoglobinemia disease can be fatal. Safe limit for drinking water is 10 mg of NO_3/litre. If in excess of 45 mg/litre, secondary and tertiary nitrosamines settled in the human bladder cannot be excreted out and can cause cancer. Heavy Metals like lead and mercury are dangerous and can reach water bodies. Lead is distributed widely in our environment and is found even in polar ice caps too. The concentration is increasing all over with industrialisation including the solder used to seal food cans. Lead gets into aquatic systems as particulate lead washed from atmosphere during rainfall. Lead poisoning leads to loss of appetite weakness, disorders in neuromuscular, brain and circulatory systems Lead poisoning could be observed with indication of 0.5 to 0.8 ppm in the blood. Lead is absorbed from air, water and food in cities, gasoline fumes are the main culprits. Mercury poisoning is due to exposure to methyl mercury, the organic form being continuously released from metal mercury through bacterial conversion. Those on fish diet mainly, are prone to mercury exposure. Mercury poisoning could be from as low as 0.2 ppm level. Symptoms include deafness, loss of coordination, insanity and death. Copper, cadmium, chromium, cobalt and nickel have also been found in the water bodies and may enter food chain through lobsters and oysters. Even lethal radio-active wastes may find their way in the food-chain, if adequate precautions are not taken in transpiration, storage and disposal.

HAZARDS OF WATER POLLUTION

Man's health may be affected by the ingestion of contaminated water either directly or through food; and by the use of contaminated water for purposes of personal hygiene and recreation. Many people consume unsafe water since it is a free good and purchase diseases. Even the richest people in the country who can afford to buy safe drinking water think that purchasing and drinking water is a waste of money. But they are not aware safe water is cost effective and give benefits 10 times more than the cost. In terms of health and wealth. It is an investment in the future health of an individual in the society. The hazards of water pollution may be classified into two broad groups - biological and chemical. Biological Hazards comprise the classical water-borne diseases caused by the presence of an infective agent or an aquatic host in water. Such as Viral (Viral hepatitis, Poliomyelitis), Bacterial (Choiera, typhoid, paratyphoid, bacillary dysentery Esch coli diarrhoea, Rota virus diarrhoea in infants), Protozoal (Amoebiasis, giardiasis), Helminthic (Roundworm, whipworm, threadworm, hydatid disease), Leptospiral (Well's disease), Cyclops (guinea worm), and Snail (Schistosomiasis). Chemical Hazards are caused by Chemical pollutants of diverse nature derived from industrial and agricultural wastes are increasingly finding their way into public water supplies. These pollutants include detergent solvents, cyanides, heavy metals, minerals and organic acids, nitrogenous substances, bleaching agents, dyes, pigments, sulfides, ammonia, toxic and biocidal organic compounds of great variety. Chemical pollutants may affect man's health not only directly, but also indirectly by accumulating in aquatic life (eg. fish) used as human food. The present concern about chemical pollutants in water relates not so much as to their acute toxic effects on human health as to the possible long-term effects of low level exposure, which are often nonspecific and difficult to detect. Further, some of the new pollutants are not easily removed by conventional water treatment or purification processes. In many developed countries where water-borne communicable diseases have virtually disappeared, more attention is now being paid to chemical pollution. While pollution seems to be an inevitable consequence of modern industrial technology, the problem, now is to determine the level of pollution that permits economic and social development without presenting hazards to health. The evaluation of the health effects of environmental pollutants is currently being carried out as part of the WHO Environmental Health Criteria Programme.

WATER QUALITY STANDARDS

The quest for pure water dates back to antiquity. In modern times, it has led to the formulation of specific standards to provide a basis for judging the quality of water. These standards are exposure limits for bacteriological, viral, chemical and physical agents that have been adopted by governments or appropriate authorities and therefore have legal force. The purpose of standards is to minimise all the known health hazards, since it's obviously impossible to prevent all pollution. The WHO has published two sets of standards for drinking water. The International Standards and the European Standards. The International Standards set out the minimal water quality requirements that are consistent with health protection and attainable by every country at present. The European Standards are higher than the minimal ones specified in International Standards. The recommended standards in India are those set out by the Indian Council of Medical Research based on International Standards. The standards of water quality are by no means static; they are constantly under review in the light of new knowledge. The WHO 'International Standards for Drinking Water' (1971) relate to 5 water quality variables : (a) Microbiological pollutants (b) Toxic substances (c) Specific substances that may affect health (d) Characteristics affecting the acceptability of water (e) Radioactive substances.

In recent times there was discussion with regard to pesticide recedure in the mineral water. T he current standards prescribed by PAS for packaged drinking water arid natural water covered under the relevant prevention of food and adulteration act. These standards simply say that the pesticide recedure should be below dectable limits when tested in accordance with relevant methods. These standards are only qualitative and not precise. In the recent survey it was found that the pesticide recedures are high in the processed mineral water in India. So, it is felt that there is need for use capillary method to detect pesticide recedures. There is need to adopt European standards which more stringent. The individual pesticide recedure should now not exceed 0.1 micron (i.e. one part of a billion) and total pesticide recedure should not be beyond 0.5 microns (i.e. five parts in a billion) The Indian Council for Agricultural Research represented O.B.Dubey declared that pesticides were not poisoners. However the BIS has decided to adopt new guidelines covering five out of the ten pesticides tests of the European norms.

Water intended for human consumption should be not only "safe" but also "wholesome". A safe water is one that cannot harm the consumer, even when ingested over prolonged periods. Water may be safe, but if it has an unpleasant taste or appearance, it may drive the consumer to other, less safe, sources. Drinking water therefore should be not only completely safe but agreeable to use or wholesome, such a supply may be termed "acceptable" or "portable". Safe and Wholesome water is defined as water that is: (1) free from pathogenic agents; (2) free from harmful chemical sustenance; (3) pleasant to the taste.; and (4) usable for domestic purposes. Water is said to be contaminated when it contains infective and parasitic agents, poisonous chemical substances, industrial or other wastes or sewage. The term polluted water is synonymous with contaminated water. Pollution and contamination are the result of human activity.

Water is never "pure" in a chemical sense. It contains impurities of various kinds - both - dissolved and suspended impurities. These comprise dissolved gases (e.g., hydrogen sulfide, carbon dioxide, ammonia, nitrogen); dissolved minerals (e.g., salts of calcium, magnesium, sodium); suspended impurities (eg; clay, silt, sand, mud) and microscopic plants and animals. These are "natural" impurities derived from the atmosphere, catchment area and the soil. A more serious aspect of water pollution is that caused by human activity - urbanization and industrialization. The sources of pollution resulting from these are :(a) sewage, decomposable organic matter and pa pathogenic agents (b) industrial and trade wastes, which contain toxic agents ranging from metal salts to complex synthetic organic chemicals (c) agricultural pollutants, which comprise fertilizers and pesticides, and (d) physical pollutants, viz heat (thermal pollution)) arid radioactive substances.

In India, water pollution is becoming a serious problem. To protect water from being contaminated, Parliament in 1974 passed the Water (Prevention and Control of Pollution) Act. The Act seeks to provide legal deterrent against the spread of water pollution. The Act is a comprehensive piece of legislation. It provides for the constitutions of Central and State Water Boards and Joint Water Boards endowed with wide powers for controlling pollution. Hardness may be defined as the soap-destroying power of water. The consumer considers water hard if large amounts of soap are required to produce a lather. The hardness in water is caused such as Calcium bicarbonate, Magnesium bicarbonate, Calcium sulfate and Magnesium sulfate. The presence of any one of these compounds produces hardness. There are others which are of less importance. Chlorides and nitrates of calcium and magnesium can also cause hardness but they occur generally in small amounts. Iron, manganese and aluminum compounds also cause hardness, but as they generally are present in such small amounts, it is Customary not to consider them in connection with hardness. Hardness in water presents several disadvantages both to the domestic and industrial consumer. They are : hardness in water consumes more soap and detergents; when hard water is heated, the carbonates are precipitated and bring bout, furring or scaling of boilers and leads to greater fuel consumption; loss of efficiency and may some-times cause boiler explosions; hard water adversely affects cooking; food cooked in soft water retains its natural colour and appearance; fabrics washed with soap in hard water do not have a long life; there are many industrial processes in which hard water is unsuited and gives rise to economic losses and hardness shortens the life of pipes and fixtures.

Purification of water is of great importance in community medicine. It may be Purification of water on a large scale or Purification of water on a small scale. Water on large scale, (such as an urban water supply), is purified in 3 main stages: (1) Storage (2) Filtration Chlorination. Physically: by mere storage, the quality of water will improve. About 90 per cent of the suspended impurities settle down in 24 hours by gravity. The water becomes clearer. This allows penetration of light, and reduces the work of the filters, Chemically : certain chemical changes also take place during storage. The aerobic bacteria oxidize the organic matter present in the water with the aid of dissolved oxygen. As a result, the content of free ammonia is reduced and a rise in nitrates occurs. Biologically: a tremendous drop takes place in bacterial count during storage. The pathogenic organisms gradually die out. Filtration is the second stage in the purification of water, and quite an important stage because 98-99 per cent of the bacteria are removed by filtration, apart from other impurities. Chlorination is one of the greatest advances in controlling water pollution. It is supplement, not a substitute to sand filtration. Chlorine kills pathogenic bacteria, but it has no effect on spores and certain viruses leg, polio, viral hepatitis) except in high doses. Apart from its germicidal effect, chlorine has several important secondary properties of value in water treatment: it oxidizes iron, manganese and hydrogen sulphide; it destroys some taste and odor-producing constituents; it controls algae and slime organisms, and aids coagulation.

The ordinary consumer judges the water quality by its physical characteristics. These are Turbidity Colour, Odor and Taste. One cannot judge the quality of drinking water by physical characteristics alone. A detailed chemical and microbiological examination are also needed for complete assessment. Chemical Qualities are important. All waters including rain water contain chlorides. In the neighborhood of the sea, the salinity of water tends to be high Since the chloride content of water varies from place to place, it is necessary first of all, to determine the normal range of chlorides of the unpolluted surface and ground water in the given locality. Bacteriological Indicators. These are based on organisms indicative of faecal pollution, such as Escherichia coil and the colifrom group as a whole, Faecal streptococci and Clostridium perfringens. Furthermore, examination for protozoa and other organisms (parasitic. worms and larvae) is also recommended. Ozone is a relatively unstable gas. It is a powerful oxidizing agent. It eliminates undesirable odor, taste and colour, and removes all chlorine demand from the water. Most importantly, ozone has a strong virucide effect. It inactivates viruses in a matter of seconds, whereas minutes are required to inactivate them with either chlorine or iodine. Germicidal property of UV rays were recognised for many years. UV irradiation is effective against most microorganisms known to contaminate water supplies including viruses.

WISDOM PACKAGED AND PROCESSED WATER

Wisdom Packaged and Processed Water project is one of the biggest establishment in the state, located near Guntur. The source of the water is ground water is taken from a drilled bore exclusively meant for the purpose with hygienic precautions. The composition of the water is superior having total dissolvable solids in far better ranges, paving way for the best quality treated water. Our water clearly distinguishable from ordinary drinking water fulfilling the BUREAU OF INDIAN STANDARDS criteria in respect of (a) Source-obtained from directly from drilled source from under ground water for which all possible precautions to avoid pollution and external influence. (b) Presence of trace elements and certain mineral salts. (c) Microbiological purity and chemical composition of essential components. (d) Packaging close to the point of emergence of source and (e) Treatment permitted by the BIS. The processing for manufacture of WISDOM Processed Water include fifteen stages of most sophisticated systems, such as Chlorination, Sandfiltratilon, Carbon filtration, Cataion ionisation, Anion ionisation. Blending, Micron filtration, UV sterilization, Micron filtration, UV sterilization, Silver ionisation, UV sterilisation, Ozonation and Packaging. The treatment is carried out without any modifications in the mineral content with regards to their essential constituents. Also the disinfection will be done to the extent required as per the BIS standards.

HYGIENIC CONDITIONS

The more Hygienic practices are followed while processing the water. The Hygienic practices cover appropriate general techniques for collecting water, its treatment, bottling, packaging, storage, transport, distribution so as to guarantee a safe, healthy and wholesome product. Adequate precautions would be taken with the protected parameters to avoid any pollution of, or external influence on, the chemical and physical qualities of mineral water. The equipments, pipes, pumps and other possible devices coming into contact with natural mineral water be made of such material as to guarantee that original quality of water is not changed. Buildings and facilities are of sound construction in accordance with the provisions of Indian Standards and maintain in good condition. Rooms for storing, packaging, cleaning of containers is provided. Adequate working space is provided to allow for satisfactory performance of all operations. Floors, walls, ceilings, windows, doors, auxiliary structures, piping, drainage lines and fuel storage area received importance as per requirements mentioned in Indian Standards. All necessary steps were taken to maintain personal cleanliness by giving hygiene training for the staff working with the plant. Necessary medical examination for communicable diseases would be done for every individual.

PHYSICAL PARAMETERS / MICRO ORGANISM

Conforming to the Indian Standards the TOTAL DISSOLVED SOLIDS mg/l and PH are maintained at less than at 76 and 7.2 PH respectively. 'Taste and odor are maintained in agreeable ranges. Water is clear and colorless. The turbidity (NTUS) is colourless. Nitrate ($N0_3$) is 1.0, Nitrite (NO_2) is nil, Fluoride (F) is 0.1, Chloride (Cl) 8, Sulphate (SO_4) nil, Calcium (Ca) is 8, Sodium (Na) nil, Alkalinity copper (Cu), Zinc (Zn) etc., are at reasonable levels which in excessive amounts cause harm to the human body are put well in control as per the requirements furnished by the Indian Standards. Toxic substances such as Arsenic (As), cyanide (CN), Mercury (Hg), Lead (Pb) and radioactive residues such as alpha emitters and beta emitters are completely processed to bring about to normal limits as per the BIS standards. We have taken utmost care to avoid all sorts of micro flora such as clostridia group, pseudomonas form the mineral water. Regular samples are drawn in original sealed bottles and sent samples are sent for ascertaining the conformity of the material to the requirements of the specification. Recording will be done for each generation of mineral water. We have facilities to test the samples to the extent desirable at plant level as indicated by BIS. E. Coli, Coliforms, Salmonella, Yeast, Moulds are absent in the Wisdom

Processed Water. The total plate count is less than 1x10′. The State Food Laboratory, Hyderabad certified the water is not adulterated. The Regional Laboratory, Guntur given the certificate Wisdom Processed Water parameters are with in the permissible limits for drinking purpose as per BIS standards. Thus, Wisdom Processed Water is one of the safest water certified by the Health labs at the state level and safe to drink.

POLICIES AND PROGRAMMES

Safe drinking water is one of the indicators of health and highly inter related with economic development in the country. In the advanced countries almost all the people take only Mineral Water and the use of the mineral water is a common habit to every body. But, unfortunately in the developing countries such as India even elite of the society who can afford to buy safe drinking water do not do so as they feel that water is a free good and there is no, need to buy it. Unsafe drinking water is associate with ill health and many other health problems. Hence there is every need to educate people the need to use the portable drinking water. Since is cost effective in terms of health. In recent times in India also the use of safe water has increased and there is some awareness among the public for use of processed water. However the coverage is so small and there is every need to improve the coverage to the nook and the corners of the country. In the recent times there is lot of heats as far as mineral water process and standards are concerned. It observed that processed water in the country contain pesticide recedures and hence there is need for pesticide recedure test also in the BIS standards. Some experts pesticide recedure are not harmful to the health of the individual. However the BIS is going make pesticide recedure test also as mandatory and going to adopt European standards (International Standards) for Indian processed water. There are different ways and means of providing safe water to the people those who can not afford to use processed water. Watershed development and tank rehabilitation could be one answer in this direction. It is the primary unit of integrated development and conservation of soil; water, agriculture and other productive activities including improvements in power, social and economic resources. Besides long term development goals, the existing tanks have to be restored to collect and store the rainwater within the watershed to provide drinking water to men and animals and for protective irrigation to crops. HUDCO is also coming up to help improve tanks and also to recharge the ground water. De-silting, maintenance of structures and distribution of water should be managed by the Water-Users themselves.

When people wash cloths, utensils, animal and take bath or exceretia. Water in rivers, wells which are open access will be contaminated. If people by chance use these water they are -throne to cholera, typhoid, jaidences and diarrhea etc. There is a need to avoid such human consumption. You must always collect drinking water from protected source only. Hand pump water is always better. We should always collect in clean vessels. The vessels should be kept clean and neat. It is better to take out water through a mug instead of taking water by dipping the hands in the pots. We always take care that water is not stagnated near by borewells. The entire surface near by the borewell should be dry only and if necessary cemented. Environmental sanitation is important. High priority must be given to observe the basic principles of sanitary disposal of human waste. What we should aim at is prevention by safe water supply and disposal of human waste. Chlorination is the method of choice for making water safe for drinking. There must be free residual chlorine in the water to ensure safety. Water can be safe by boiling. It must be kept boiling for at least one minute. This is effective but expensive, especially when fuel is in short supply. Another way is to add a chlorine releasing chemical. Among the products available for chlorination are calcium or sodium hypochlorite or bleaching power.

Availability of safe drinking water and clean water for other purposes such as personal hygiene is a basic requirement for health. Unfortunately this basic need is neglected. There is lack of awareness among the people. There is apathy among policy and decision-makers. All efforts must be made to ensure enough safe water for drinking, preparation of food and personal hygiene. Properly-treated drinking water should be made available to the entire population of towns and cities through a piped system. It is the responsibility of the Municipalities and the Government. If a piped system is not possible, good quality drinking water should be available at stand points (kept clean) and from tanker trucks. In the rural areas, it may not be feasible to have piped supply. Enough water must be made available from tube wells and protected wells.

Roof-top rainwater harvesting is not new especially in desert areas of Rajasthan and Gujarat where people through this ingenuity have managed to survive worst famine-situations with only 150 mm rainfall in some years! There is absolutely no way to augment our water resources other than effecting all round savings, capturing every drop of rain that falls on the soil and on our roof tops i.e. It is emphasized that not a drop of this precious water goes out of the compound to join the drainage system finally getting mixed with effluents and sewage. In apartments and multi-storey buildings, sumps of suitable dimensions can be constructed in the parking lots while constructing them. Even in the existing buildings, a small tank of 500 to 1000 liters can he used to collect the harvested water from roof-top, filter it and pass on this filtered water to the existing sump/well as and when the rain occurs. Such modifications would cost Rs. 6000 to 8000. This aspect of creating Water-Resources should be suitably incorporated in the by-laws of Town Planning.

There is also need to improve sanitary measures to protect the water from pollution. The recommended area is 2.2 sq.m. (24 sq.ft) per swimmer. Rules and regulations governing the use of the swimming pools should be posted in a conspicuous place for the information of the Users. Persons suffering from skin diseases, sore eyes, cold, nasal or ear discharge or any communicable disease should not be allowed into the swimming pool. All bathers are strictly instructed to empty the bladder, and if necessary use the toilet. A cleansing shower bath in the made with soap and water is required before entering the pool. Spitting, spouting of water, blowing the nose, etc. are prohibited. The environment of the swimming pool including the shower rooms, walk ways and pool decks should receive proper disinfection to destroy bacterial, viral and fungal agents. Swimming pools are equipped with rapid sand filters. The filtering is continuous such that all the water is refiltered in less than 6 hours. Part of the water, up to 15 per cent, should be replaced by fresh water. The function of water replacement is to remove solutes consisting of ammonia, albuminoid, organic arid nitrate, nitrogen derived from the bathers. These solutes have the capacity to reduce the bactericidal activity of chlorine. Chlorination is the most widely used method of pool disinfection. Various workers have stated that a continuous maintenance of 1.0 mg/litre (1 ppm) of free chlorine residual provides adequate protection against bacterial and viral agents. The PH of water is kept between 7.4 - 7.8. The bacteriological quality of water should reach as nearly as possible the standards prescribed for drinking wafer. Recharging borewells either by percolation method through a pit of 10 ft to 12 ft with stones, piebalds etc., or through direct recharge of the borewell by removing the casing at desired depth and linking it to the pipe from rain water system would be essential. Over exploitation of ground water for irrigation or for drinking is dangerous affecting the food chain with toxins. We have not been examining the cost of water and consequently Water Use Efficiency is at the lowest. Water should be metered out and the most suited and economically. No legislation appears to be feasible in this regard. Though India's average rainfall is 1200 mm per year, there is wide variation in the onset of monsoons, distribution and the amount received. Floods and droughts are common features in one part or the other, bringing great stress in the livelihood of hundreds of thousands of people. Flood control, Grid to link major rivers and creating greater numbers of dams in future remain either as dreams or unremunerative with sinking of huge capital under borrowed loans. They would be attendant with ecological disasters too. It is therefore, imperative that our water resources be managed by the people at the local levels apart from whatever major interventions that the Governments could make.

The provision of merely good water supply does not in itself secure freedom form water-borne diseases. People must recognise safe water as a "felt" health need and give up their old, unhygienic habits of polluting water supplies. In these circumstances, health education emerges as an important weapon in creating among people a desire for higher standards of life.

REFERENCES

Bolly J. (1976), Water and Sweage Works, 123, pp. 66-67.

Fish N.A. (1969), Canadian Journal of Public Health, 60. p.279.

Hussain L. and Wood W.E. (1974), Slow and Sand Filteration. WHO, Geneva.

Indian Council of Medical Research (1975), Manual of Standards of Quality Drinking Water, Spl. Rpt. Ser. 44, quoted in Park and Park op.cit.

India, 1993-94. Bombay, Popular Prakasam, 1994.

Kohan. R.C. (1976), JAWWA, 68, pp. 302.

Morely David Ital (1()S4), Practising Health for All, Oxford University Press.

ORS (1994), The Life Saving Solution. Health Action, Vol. No. 5, May.

Planning Commission (2001-2002), Government of India, Economic Survey.

Park J. E. and K. Park (1991), Preventive and Social Medicine, Jabalpur Banarsidas Bhanot, Thirteenth Edition.

Siva Shankar K. Water Value, Rain Water Club, Bangalore.

WHO-UNICEF (1978), Health for All. Serial Number 1.

WHO (1964) (1968) (1972) (1976), World Health Statistics.

SECTION - III

Urbanisation and Environment

30

URBAN SOLID WASTE MANAGEMENT : PRACTICAL PROBLEMS

K.B. Reddy

INTRODUCTION

In exercise of the powers conferred by Sections 3,6 and 25 of the Environment (Protection) Act, 1996 the Ministry of Environment & Forests, Government of India issued the Municipal Solid Waste (Management & Handling) Rules 2000 Notification on 25-09-2000. The A.P. State Pollution Control Board (APPCB) through its letter no.142/PCB/MSW/VC/ 2002, Dt.16-10-2002, apart from directing the Municipalities to develop landfill facilities has also specified the sitting and design criteria for landfill sites. Further, the municipalities have been reminded of their responsibilities of identification and development of landfill sites within the time frame.

In this context, a quick estimate of the population growth, life-styles, solid waste generation and the extent of urban lands required for landfill sites reveal that it is almost impossible for any Municipality to dispose off its solid waste in accordance with the MSW (M & H) Rules, 2000.

The Supreme Court has granted four weeks time on 14-01-2003 to the Government of India to file its comprehensive response on solid waste management in major cities in the country and for marketing urban compost as an alternative to chemical fertilizers.

PRACTICAL IMPLICATIONS OF IPLEMENTATION OF MSW RULES

1. Most municipalities in India as well as in Andhra Pradesh could not initiate and implement any action programme for solid waste management in accordance with the time schedule as notified in Schedule I of MSW rules - 2000.
2. Many municipalities have not even acquired sufficient and suitable land for landfills. Some municipalities do not have at least 10% of the land required. Acquisition and development of land and treatment and disposal of MSW in accordance with rules may be beyond the capacity of several municipalities which do not have resources even to maintain essential services.
3. In accordance with Schedule II of MSW rules - 2000, some municipalities have streamlined the collection and transport of solid waste but they are unable to segregate, treat and dispose properly.
4. In defiance of the compliance criteria VII of Schedule II, the solid waste is burnt openly on road sides as wall as in the landfills. In this connection, a mention may be made that burning of biomass in open places is a cognizable offence in many parts of Europe.
5. Disposal facilities for biomedical wastes have been created only in some cities and in certain clusters of towns. But many nursing homes continue to dump their biomedical wastes in the garbage bins.
6. Segregation of MSW is yet to be streamlined.
7. MSW is not processed in accordance with point No.6 of Schedule II. Accordingly, only insert and non-degradable waste is to be sent to a landfill. All biodegradable organic wastes should be used for production of organic fertilizers by composting or vermin-composting and or production of fuels like biogas by fermentation. All the reusable and recycle materials have to be segregated and put back into

the solid waste cycle. Unless, municipalities and the government encourage the production and usage of organic fertilizers, segregation and recycling will continue to be unattractive.

SPECIFICATIONS OF LANDFILL SITES

Biomedical wastes and Hazardous wastes have to be disposed off in accordance with the Biomedical Waste (M & H) Rules, 1998 and Hazardous Waste (M & H) rules, 1989 respectively. Only the inert, non-degradable solid waste is expected to go to a landfill. In such cases, a secure landfill with clay lining of 90 cm underneath a HDPE liner of 1.5 mm, covering the solid waste with a minimum of 10 cm thick soil at the end of each day; capping with clay (60 cm), drainage layer 10 cm and top drainage layer of 4.5 cm may be desirable as a matter of abundant caution but it is certainly beyond our budget and resources. Hence, we have to have a need-based and affordable design which varies depending upon the quality of waste and solid characteristics. implementation of the MSW (M & H) rules, 2000 will have serious implications as stated under:

HOW MUCH AREA IS REQUIRED FOR LAND FILLS?

For the total urban population of nearly 300 million in India, about 45 thousand hectares of urban lands are required at the rate of 1.5 m^2 for the next 25 years. For a city like Delhi, about 1950 ha is needed for landfills. Similarly, the Municipalities in Andhra Pradesh require as much as 3150 ha for disposal of solid waste. Hyderabad alone needs six hundred hectares. For a projected population of 13,600,000 in 2020, Hyderabad requires atleast two thousand hectares in 2020. Will it be possible for us to have so much land around our cities and towns for disposal of solid waste within reasonable distance from the municipal limits and in suitable localities in accordance with the sitting norms?

Can we divert the productive agricultural lands for landfills without risking our food security? How many municipalities in the state can acquire the required land and how many of them can make heavy investments in non-productive programmes? In most of the delta areas, with wetlands around the towns and cities, with very high water table, is it possible to get a landfill site which meets atleast the main sitting criteria?

Apart from it, around each of the landfill sites, a buffer zone of no development must be maintained and construction of residential houses should not be permitted within a distance of 1 km from the boundaries of landfill sites. If this buffer zone is also included in the total area required for landfill sites, it is going to put tremendous pressure on our land resources. The MSW (M & H) rules 2000 require that all degradable waste should be used in an appropriate manner and only the non-degradable and non-reusable/non-recyclable inert waste should go to a landfill. Do we require a very expensive secure landfill for dumping inert waste? Can't we think of a better strategy for disposal of such wastage? Can't we use it for filling stinking ditches and low-lying areas wherever possible?

We don't really need such expensive landfills for disposal of Municipal Solid Waste after salvaging the organic materials as well as the recyclable materials. Do we need to monitor the ambient air and ground water quality around the landfills at frequent intervals? It is always desirable to monitor the environmental impact of each of these units at internals of six months or one year depending on population in accordance with the MSW, (M & H) Rules 2000. But the monitoring of the chemical parameters require sophisticated laboratories, expensive instruments like AAS GC and HPLC and trained man power. Either the municipalities have to acquire these facilities or get their samples analysed in any standard laboratory by paying heavy user charges. Since, the Municipal Solid Waste does not contain biomedical waste, industrial waste, or other hazardous waste it may not vary qualitatively from place to place and hence it is highly desirable to develop models for prediction of impacts on air and water depending upon the quantity of waste generated.

IMPACT OF MSW TRANSPORT AND DISPOSAL ON ATMOSPHERE

What would be the impact of the envisaged methods of disposal of MSW on the air quality? Development of such huge landfill sites with a buffer zone around can only be done at a minimum distance of one km from the periphery of the town or city. Depending upon the area of the city and the location of landfills, each of the tractor trailors/trucks require a minimum of 5 litres of diesel for each trip in both the directions, produces about 500 tonnes of solid waste per day and if each truck requires 1 litres of consumption would come to about 625 litres. It ends up in producing almost 1875 tonnes of Green house gases (GHG) per day. Development of such large landfills with a buffer zone around can rapidly expand the radai of towns and cities which further enhances the distances of travel and transport. Thus, overall impact on atmosphere may be more than the unscientific methods currently under vogue.

Will it be possible for our municipalities to collect the leachates, treat them, and monitor their quality before they are discharged into sewers or drains? Do we need to strictly monitor the quality of compost and the leachates before they are disposed off on land? Can we really afford to do it? It is necessary to cover the landfill with a 10 Cm thick layer of soil or inert debris? If a layer of 10 Cm soil cover is used every day, how soon the landfill gets filled up?

With only 2.5% of the total geographical surface of earth, with about 17% of global population, can we blindly follow the models developed by the affluent Nations? A city in North America with a population of 650,000 has an urban expanse of about 30,000 km^2 of land for its domestic needs but it is just 2,900 km^2 in India. By 2006 half of the population of the world is going to live in towns and cities. The Hyderabad Urban Development Authority (HUDA) master plan for Hyderabad metropolitan area - 2020 predicts a population of 13,600,000 in 2020. During the next 30 years, two billion people are expected to join the urban experience. Will it be possible for us to deal with the mountains of garbage without monetary and land resources ?

Needless to add that it will not be possible for us to fully implement or enforce the MSW (M & H) Rules, 2000. We need to look for alternative strategies and down to earth solutions which are suitable to our specific conditions. Not only the characteristics of our solid waste are different from that of the industrialised nations with specific reference to degradability and toxicity, the rates of decomposition and degradation are much faster in India because of tropical climate. Further, we have large work force which should be properly exploited. Hence, we need to act in a area-specific and problem-specific manner.

MSW MANAGEMENT STRATEGIES

Most of the biodegradable organic solid waste produced in towns and cities comes from Villages through food, fruits and vegetables. Hence, it should be returned to the villages. But it should be transformed into organic fertilizers by composting and vermicomposting before it is returned to the villages. (Fig.1) Application of organic fertilizers, improves soil erosion and enhances groundwater recharge. Farming communities around towns and cities, as well as the self-help groups may be involved in the transformation of solid organic materials

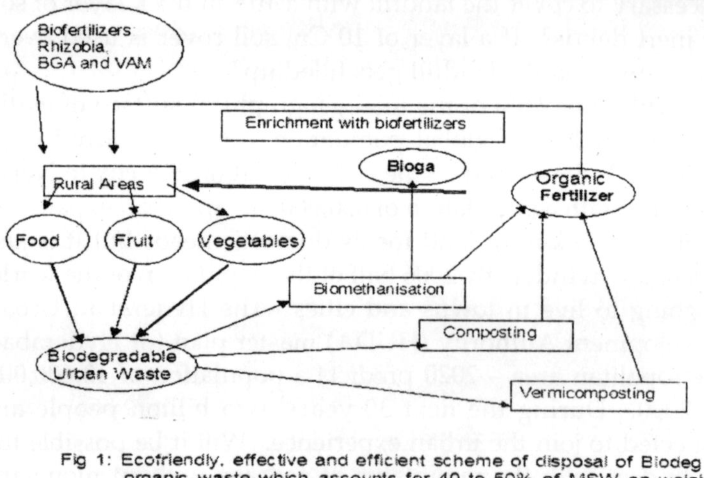

Fig 1: Ecofriendly, effective and efficient scheme of disposal of Biodeg organic waste which accounts for 40 to 50% of MSW on weigi and 60 to 75% on volume basis.

so that over 70% of the volume of solid waste can be reduced. There are a number of programmes such as KVIC, Rural Employment Guarantee Programme etc., which can provide necessary financial assistance for people to start composting and vermicomposting units. For instance, the Pune Municipal Corporation (PMC) is producing 700 tonnes of organic fertilizer everyday from about 1000 tonnes of solid organic waste by making use of EM (effective nucriirgabusns) developed in 1982 by Teruo Higa from the University of the Ryukyus, Japan. One litre of the EM solution is now available at Rs.115/- which can be mixed with three litres of molasses and 100 litres of chlorine free water. This solution is fermented in air-tight containers for one week under anaerobic conditions during which the microbes multiply by 100 times. This solution is further diluted and sprayed on the garbage. The bacterial inoculums containing about 80 strains of naturally occurring microbes such as LACTOBACILLUS and ACTINOMYCETEScan convert the waste into compost in 45 days. The cost of production of 700 tonnes of compost is only about Rs.15,000/-. Similarly, vermi-compost can also be produced very rapidly by making use of the most efficient earthworm varieties. If the subsidy on chemical fertilizers is withdrawn and if the same amount is spent on creation of infrastructure for transformation of solid organic waste, we can solve the problems of garbage, soil

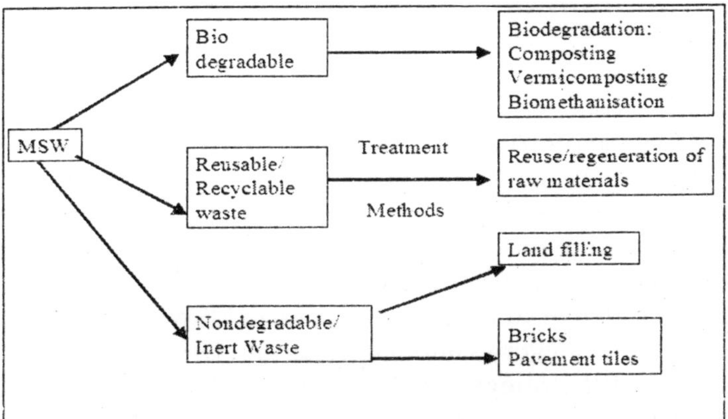

Fig. 2: Segregation and disposal of MSW

erosion and ground water recharge in a sustainable manner. If properly implemented, atleast 10 billion man-days of work can also be created to benefit the unemployed.

All reusable and recyclable materials should be segregated and reused or recycled. The inert and inorganic waste, a low volume, high density material can go for land filling (Fig.2). All housing colonies and multi-staired residential complexes be encouraged to have their own segregation and treatment facilities (Fig.3). All the biomedical waste be sent to the biomedical waste disposal facilities. Solid waste from commercial establishments should be segregated at source. Industries should be directed to take care of any hazardous waste that they produce. Industrial waste should not be mixed with the MSW.

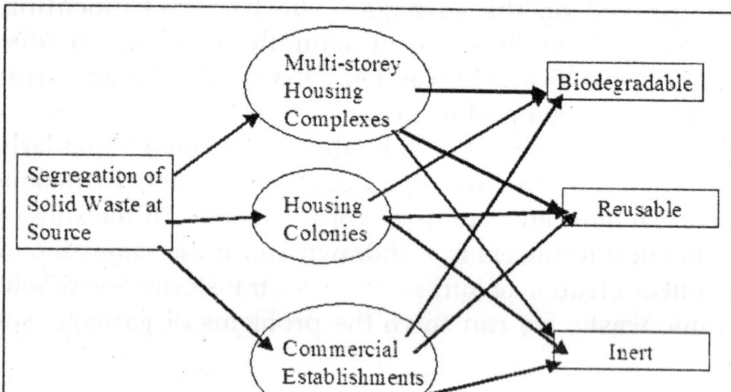

Fig. 3: Segregation of solid waste at source by bulk producers

Thus the problems of collection, disposal, development of landfills can be handled in an integrated manner. The garbage should in fact be treated as a resource and wealth should be generated from this waste. That is how we can generate cash from trash and wealth from waste.

The different strategies for disposal of MSW can be clubbed under three categories and named as $-R^3$, D^3 and C^3.

The RRR strategy involves waste reduction, reuse and recycling. The DDD strategy is disposal by dilution and dispersion. The CCC strategy involves control by concentration and confinement. We need to evolve a RDC strategy which includes an appropriate combination of the R^3, D^3 and C^3.

We need to understand why the theoretically sound organic waste utilisation/treatment systems are not economically viable and see that they are sustainable. As far as the biodegradable waste is concerned, we have to evolve and implement DDD strategies. The RRR strategy can be further promoted by encouraging and organizing rag pickers. The CCC strategy is required to deal with the hazardous waste which is not supposed to be a part of MSW.

Table 1
Land Required for Disposal of Municipal Solid Waste
(in accordance with msw (m & h) rules, 2000)

Place	*Urban Population (2001)*	*Land Required* (in Hectares)*
India	300,000,000	45,000
Delhi	13,000,000	1,950
Andhra Pradesh	21,000,000	3,150
Hyderabad	4,000,000	600
Hyderabad in 2020	13,600,000	2,040

* Exclusive of buffer zone. The area will increase by 4 to 5 times if buffer zone of 1 km in all directions is also included.

Table 2
Estimates of Municipal Solid Waste Production (tonnes/day)

Place	*MSW (TPD)*	*(TPY)*	*No. of Truck Loads (PA)*
India @ 0.4 kg	120,000	43,800,000	10,50,000
Delhi @ 0.5 kg	6,500	2,372,500	593,125
Andhra Pradesh @ 0.4 kg	8,400	3,066,000	7,665,000
Hyderabad @ 0.5 kg	2,000	730,000	182,500
Hyderabad in 2020	6,800	2,482,000	620,500

(TPD = Tonnes per day; TPY = Tonnes per year and PA = Per Annum)

In stead of covering the landfill after each day of dumping with 10 cm thick layer of earth, it can be covered with a 5 cm layer of well-decomposed compost obtained from the old landfill of the same site. This process can speed up the process of degradation besides making room for reuse of the old landfill. In order to avoid and eliminate monitoring of air and

Table 3
Impact fo MSW Transportation of Fossil Fuels and Atmosphere

Place	*Diesel Oil Consumption (KLPA)*	*CO_2 Emissions TPA*
India	54,750	164,250
Delhi	2,966	8,897
Andhra Pradesh	38,325	114,975
Hyderabad	913	2,739
Hyderabad in 2020	3,103	9,308

(KLPA = Kilo-litres per annum
TPA = Tonnes per annum)

Table 4
Demand, Supply and Importance of Organic Fertilizers (in million tonnes = MT)

Total Organic Fertilizer required	=	1500 MT
Supply (Availability)		
Farm yard manure & rural compost	=	600 MT
Urban Compost	=	15 MT
Green Manure	=	30 MT
TOTAL	=	645 MT
Production potentials of organic fertilizer by		
Composting of biodegradable MSW	=	1200 MT
Realization of 60% of potential	=	720 MT
Grand Total Production	=	1365 MT

Note : ICAR proved that use of recommended dose of NPK combined with 10 to 15 tonnes of organic manure per hectare can increase yields by 3 times compared to the yields obtained by use of nitrogenous fertilizers (urea) only.

Table 5
Enrichment of Compost with Bio-fertilizers

Fertile soils contain 4,000 kg of live microbes in the upper 15 cm of soil in every hectare.
There are over 100 million bacteria and 10,000 eukaryotes in every gram of fertile soil.
Enrichment of compsot/vermicrompost with Rhizobia/blue green algae/VAM fungi can enhance the value and utility.
Every hectare of land could be a home for over 2.5 million earthworms.
They convert about 25 tonnes of leaves, dead roots and debris into vermicompost in about 100 tonnes of soil.
All these biological activities are supported only by the organic matter.
Since, the reates of decomposition are higher in India because of the tropical climate, production of compost, vermicompost from MSW for use in Agriculture is the best strategy for India.

water quality by every municipality, region-specific predictable models have to be developed taking into account the characteristics of hydrology, geology and climate.

BENEFITS OF IMPLEMENTATION OF MSW RULES

Cleanliness is considered next only to Godliness. If properly collected and treated, all the plant nutrients can be effectively recycled and dependence on chemical fertilizers reduced. If all our biodegradable solid waste is converted into organic fertilizer and if these organic fertilizers are properly amended and enriched with bio-fertilizers, we don't require chemical fertilizers in agriculture. Fertility of soils can be improved and infiltration of rain water and groundwater recharge can also be enhanced. Further, a large number of poor people who are willing to work can be provided gainful work.

MUNCIPAL SOLD WASTE (MANAGEMENT & HANDLING) RULES, 2000

- Whether these rules can be implemented in India?
- Whether these rules are in consistence with the concepts of sustainable development?
- Whether they are suitable to our local needs?
- Do they reflect the aspirations of the people?
- Can we blindly adopt the strategies and management practices of the developed world?
- Do we have equally good options and alternatives, if not better?
- Do we have effective indigenous, area-specific solutions?
- Can they remove poverty and solve the problem of population explosion?
- Can they prevent migration of people from rural to urban areas?
- How can we integrate and solve simultaneously the problems of poverty, population explosion, pollution and solid waste management?

MSW (M&H) Rules-2000 have to be carefully reexamined and modified suitably so that they can be implemented practically.

31

ENVIRONMENTAL SANITATION AND ECONOMIC DEVELOPMENT IN INDIA

K. Narasimhulu

INTRODUCTION

The World Bank estimates that more than one billion urban dwellers or 65 per cent of the total urban population in Developing Countries breath unhealthy air. At least 170 million people in these areas lack sources of drinking water near their homes, while 350 million city residents lack adequate sanitation. The urban population of the developing world is growing at an annual average rate of 3.8 per cent and will increase from 1.4 billion to 2.2. Billion by 2020[1]. There is an urgent need for industrial and agricultural development on account of growing need for food, shelter, clothing, and health and for a better standard of living. "What is needed now is a new era of economic growth-growth that is forceful and at the same time socially and environmentally sustainable[2].

It is no doubt that the pattern of economic development about by revolution in the scientific and technological fields substantially attested man's relationship with nature in a country like India. Most of our environmental difficulties originate from man's ecological misbehaviour. Increasingly, we consider ourselves not as lodgers on the earth, but as its landlords. We identify progress with the conquest of the external world even if this means destruction of those parts of nature, which we assume often erroneously, to be irrelevant to our welfare.

To some extent environmental pollution is an escapable by-product of industrial development. This means that man must accept responsibility for the stewardship of the earth, a place suitable for human life not only now but also for future generations.

At the turn of the 20th century environmental issues have emerged as a major concern for the survival and welfare of the mankind. Modern civilization armed with rapidly advancing technology and fast growing economic system, is under increasing threat from its own activities, causing pollution of air, water and soil. Rapid industrialization has accelerated he environmental pollution problem in its most dramatic form. More and more of the world's people live in cities. At the beginning of the Industrial Revolution only about three people out of every hundred lived in urban areas. By the year 2000, about half of the world's population lived in urban areas.

Despite the frequent recurrence of environmental problems throughout the world, widespread concern about environmental quality in the late 1960s was largely confined to the United States and few other economically advanced countries. But now most of the developing countries with all their natural resources of soil, water, plant and animal life face the destruction of their natural resources, base that provides the very foundation of sustainable development.

MAGNITUDE OF THE PROBLEM

Environmental pollution is global in nature and afflicts all countries, whether rich or poor developing or developed. However, the poorer and developing countries have to be more careful and realistic with respect to environmental matters, since they can not afford to waste time and money by ways of delay and wrong approaches.

The most alarming problem is man's assault on the environment by contaminating the air, earth and water with dangerous and even lethal materials. This pollution is, for the most part, irrecoverable. Man has failed to imagine of a time, when the air and water would lose their sparkling quality, when each man's living space would itself begin to shrink and the pressure of growing population, when the beauty of life on our planet would be marred by offensive rights and sounds and odours. In the words of Albert Schweitzer, man has hardly even recognized the devils of his own creation[3].

Environmental pollution is, in essence, the unfavourable alteration of our surroundings, wholly or largely as a by-product of man's action, through direct or indirect effects of changes in energy patterns, radiation levels, chemical and physical constitution and abundance of organisms. These changes may affect man directly or through his supplies of water and agricultural and other biological products, his physical objects or possessions, or his opportunities for recreation and appreciation of nature[4].

There is no doubt that there has been substantial environmental degradation in recent times. People live with plenty of hazards created by air pollution generated by motor vehicles. These induce a wide range of respiratory diseases. Air pollutants are known to cause a wide variety of diseases, including lung cancer, bronchitis and mental depression.

The crux of the problem is that very few people are using too many resources, too wastefully, resulting in rapid degradation of environment. Modern ecologists have averted that many factors, such as human population explosion, unplanned urbanization and deforestation. Profit oriented capitalism and technological advancement are responsible for the origin of pollution crisis. In fact, countries with technological advancement are responsible for the origin of pollution crisis. In short, the worst pollution occurs in countries with greatest technological advances. In these countries, whether capitalist, socialist or communist, there is greater emphasis on growth and what W.G. Rosen (1970) has called frontier or flat earth concept of the world, instead of a spaceship or round-world view. In nations well developed on a per capita basis, citizens consume more food; use more pesticides, fertilizers, fuel, minerals and other manufactured products all of which, in turn, exacerbate the pollution problem.

ENVIRONMENT AND DEVELOPMENT

The nexus between environment and development is being critically examined to answer question on whether environmental constraints will limit development and whether development will cause serious environmental constraints that will limit development and whether development in turn would impair the quality of life of presence and future generations. The World Development Report (1992) explored the two-way relationship between environment and development. It described how environmental problems undermine the goals of development. The report also explored the impact of good and bad economic growth on the environment.

Studies on development that examined its impact on environment have noted that development has been effete at tremendous environmental costs. The renowned scientist M.S.Swaminathan observed: "Both globally and nationally, the life support systems upon which prospects for sustained economic development and the livelihood security of millions of poor people depend are being damaged by the very process of development".

Realizing the deleterious impact of development on environment several analysts have argued that reckless approaches of development have depleted the exhaustible and non-renewable natural resources and have invariably degraded the environment. It is in this backdrop that the Brundtland Commission (1987), the World Bank and the United Nations Environmental Programme emphasized the idea of "Sustainable Development", a development which is 'environmentally responsible', 'environmentally benign' and 'eco-friendly'.

The current concern for sustainable development suggests that the bounties of nature are drying up and there is going to be an acute scarcity of basic resources. The rampage of technology has killed the feeling of continued abundance of natural resources. While sounding a caution, the World Bank emphasized the complimentarity of economic development and sound environmental management. It said that both form part of the agenda. World Development Report (1992) concerned with the World Bank view. It said that, "Good economic policies are good environmental policies and vice-versa". Economic growth, said World Bank, need not be an enemy of environment and the best policies for environmental protection will help, not hurt, economic development.

ENVIRONMENTAL SANITATION

The environmental sanitation is an integral component of environment and also an essential ingredient of development.

SANITATION AS AN ENVIRONMENTAL AND DEVELOPMENT PRIORITY

The concern for both environmental protection and development is basically for improving the quality of life and good sanitation system is one of its important indicators. But regrettably enough, sanitation rarely figures in different kinds of debates on both environment and development. This I think is to miss the very essence and purpose of environmental protection and development, since both aim at improving the quality of life. The World Development Report (1992) mentions sanitation as an important item of developmental agenda. The Report says:

– "Potential health benefits from improved sanitation serves are huge"
– "The ill-effects of poor environmental sanitation are greatest in high density urban settlements".
– "Investments in sanitation offer high economic, social and environmental returns".

Having said that the Report says, "The one-third of the world's population has inadequate sanitation, and that 1.7 billion people in developing countries lack access to sanitation. The effects on health are shocking; they are the major contributors to 900 million cases of diarrhoeal diseases which cause deaths of more than three million children; two million of these could be prevented if adequate sanitation and clean water were available. The Report concluded by saying that "The current environmental debate has paid two little attention to the problems of sanitation". The Report, therefore, advised substantial investments in better sanitation as a measure of improving environment, health and hygienic of the people.

The problem of environmental sanitation has assumed considerable importance only, recently. In fact, the realization of the damages caused by environmental pollution led to the acceptance of the need and significance of environmental sanitation. The awesome scenario of environmental insanitation, especially in bigger cities and towns, has led to a nation-wide concerns for presenting and promoting a holistic plan of environmental sanitation. As a result of this, the genesis of the idea of environmental sanitation has taken place.

Until the present decay, 'sanitation' has never been a major investment priority in India although it is well known that protected water supply and sanitary waste disposal are vital for the health and well being of a nation like India. The impetus for the improvement of sanitation scenario has been provided by the United Nations all for designating the current decade as the International Drinking Water Supply and Sanitation Decade. The Government of India started the National Water Supply and Sanitation Decade Programme from April 1, 1981. The Ministry of Works and Housing, Government of India had addressed the State Governments to provide funds in the Sixth Five Year Plan (1980-85) and in the Seventh Five Year Plan (1985-90) to achieve the decade's targets. Subsequently, these targets were scaled down, since adequate resources were not available to meet the targets by March 31, 1991.

In 1995, roughly half of the urban population of India had no sanitation facilities at all, a quarter had dry latrines and the rest had sewerage or septic tank system. Despite the plans of leaders like Mahatma Gandhi, demanding sanitation to be accorded a high priority, successive Governments at both national and state levels ignored this basic need for more than five decades.

The rationale for including sanitation as an investment in plan allocation is not merely for improving civic services. In fact, the purpose is that of waste disposal and eliminating the spread of diseases, particularly waterborne diseases. In such a scheme of things, sanitation has been viewed as a public health measure, which can effect an improvement in the status of the community. Investment in sanitation is economically justified as a means of preventing the spread of many diseases that are widely prevalent in India.

INDIA'S SANITATION SCENARIO

Viewed in the context of international development in the field of environmental sanitation, India's sanitation scenario is too given. The severity of the problem would be judged on the basis of facts regarding the existence of sanitation facilities in India's cities/towns and villages.

1. Out of 3245 cities/towns, only 217 have sewerage system, and that too partially and not for entire city/town.
2. The septic tank system is not extensive enough in Indian cities/towns in spite of its 200 year old history in the country and most of the urban population can not afford the system. Hardly 20 per cent urban households have septic and toilets.
3. According to the national statistics, almost the entire rural population barring less than 10 per cent defecates in the open of the households, which have latrines, only 3 per cent have sanitary latrines.
4. Nearly 48 per cent of the urban households had sanitation facility by March, 1995, while another 22 per cent have bucket privies cleaned manually by scavengers and the remaining 30 per cent have no latrines at all, they mostly defecate in the open.
5. It is estimated by the Planning Commission that there are over 76 lakhs dry/bucket latrines in the country, of which 54 lakhs are in the urban areas employing about 4,00,000 scavengers in 1995.

6. Approximately three-fourths of the population in the country has no latrines for their daily use.
7. These figures, frightening and demoralizing as they are also refer to the magnitude of the problem of scavenging that has to be done by 4,00,000 scavengers.

Safe disposal of human excreta is the most challenging problem, both in rural and urban areas. The lack of modern sanitary system (The non-availability of toilet facilities with in-built system for the disposal of human excreta), health hazard free drainage system, lack of garbage disposal facilities and the scarcity/unavailability of safe drinking water continue to be the most pressing problems. Amongst these, the problem of open-air defecation in both valleys and cities is the most serious and challenging one. Attached to this is the problem of bucket latrines that are to be cleaned manually by a section of people. The excreta from bucket privies often spill over during its transportation to the disposal site. Due to the cleaning of the privy chambers by pouring water through the squatting holes, excreta flows into drains running along the houses and, thus exposing the entire locality to health hazards and foul environment.

CONCLUSION

Human excreta are the cause of many enteric diseases such as cholera, dysentery, and typhoid, look worm, etc., and over 50 types of infection can be transferred from a diseased person to a health one by various direct or indirect routes from excreta. Therefore, safe disposal of human excreta is considered to be the primary objective of improved sanitation in order to build a healthier nation and provide a cleaner environment.

32

URBANIZATION AND ENVIRONMENT

T. Sivalingam, M. Sekar

INTRODUCTION

The general consensus all over the world is that the quality of urban environment is deteriorating at a rapid rate. The United Nations assessed that two out of every three persons in the world would live in urban centers by 2025. In the developing world where the rate of urbanization is still low, this rapid growth of urbanization is likely to put severe pressure on the capacity of the environment to sustain it. For example, in India, according to 2001 census–approximately one out of every four persons live in urban areas. If this increases to two out of three, the urban population would jump from 285 million people in 2001 to more than 1100 million within the next twenty-five years. This illustrates the serious danger that urban areas are likely to face in order to accommodate four times the present population within a short period of time. All urban settlements are net consumers of environmental resources. The environmental resources available within the urban areas are inadequate to meet all the demands of a growing population. Therefore, there has to be certain amount of import of resources from its hinterland at the cost of environmental protection.

LIVING SPACES

Man needs shelter. It is one of his earliest demands from the environment that he constantly struggles with. No wonder each and every traditional house type reflects this bond. Then over time this relationship grew like an organism into an intricate meshwork of cultures, religions and customs that determined how a man built his living space.

Research on this aspect is so captivating that it opens newer vistas of knowledge unendingly. However before embarking on this concept-journey let us inform you that we are just presenting the lip of the iceberg. There is a whole lot more waiting to be discovered.

WHERE SHOULD MAN BUILD HIS HOME?

That depends on who poses the question. If you were the early man who has just begun to feel the need for habitation, then you would be looking for a dry and warm place within natural formations, such as a cave. Here you would be relatively safe from the chilling cold, incessant wet rain and scorching sunny days. Moreover wild animals can't get you so easily! Here your settlement would be for your own protection.

But as you got bolder and more clannish you might dare to make a leafy home, or even one from the skin of dead animals but locating that home will depend on many factors.

First is the need for water. Take a cut into the past. You and your friends and relatives liked the cave but found it very difficult to carry water up the slope. So when the weather was good, you all decided to locate yourself next to the river, spring or lake that beckoned below. Huddled together in little hatchments life was easier. There were more plants and berries here, fish too could be caught easily and land all around could be easily inundated once you learnt how to grow crops.

A wet point settlement now would be our shelter. As the cycle of life went on, the population of your tiny hamlet grew. Now you had more crops, surpluses, traders, soldiers and kings. Water was no more the sole requirement of a happy life. Requirements grew enormous. You wanted land and more land. Rolling fields and plains were on your most wanted list. Thus settlements now changed location and you now built your home in the middle of large agricultural tracts.

Only then man required space to settle and develop himself, that would be beginning of urbanization. The growth in towns and cities across the world be it developed or developing, industrialized or pre-industrial, has always fuelled man's appetite to be informed about the spatial aspects of cities-their location, growth and relationship both one with another and with their surrounding regions. However, the recurrent pattern of urban land use has to be formulated and for that a fair knowledge and understanding of laws and theories is the primary requirements.

UNDERSTANDING THE URBAN

The word urban underlies a basic theme. First that its population size is larger than its rural counterpart, second that its size is definitely larger and three that its functions are varied. Function is probably the most important criterion to define a town. The other criteria are population size and population density. Different countries have different parameters to explain an urban space. India has one too.

In India the criteria for identifying urban places kept changing with time. The frequent changes in the criteria reflected the basic problem of identifying urban places and the issue could not be settled till 1981.

In India urban areas are given different administrative status by different state governments. The conferring of this status depends on the state-level Municipal and local bodies acts. A place has to satisfy all the three Census criteria in order to be designated as an urban place even if some to be vague, rigid and conservative criticizes the requirements.

THEORIES OF URBAN STRUCTURE

Concentric Zone Theory

This theory based on hypothetical pattern of urban growth was first postulated in 1923 by an urban sociologist, E.W. Burgess, while studying the urban morphology of the city of Chicago, the USA. Through this model Burgess stated that the development of a city place from its central commercials core takes place in a series of concentric circles. He identified five zones in concentric pattern expanding outward from the city core.

Zone No. 1: This is the CBD (Central Business District), the heart of the city. It has shops, offices, banks, theatres and hotels. It has multi story skyscrapers, transport lines, etc. converging in this zone. The CBD draws its business from all other encircling zones.

Zone No. 2: Surrounding the CBD, lies a traditional area, a zone of residential deterioration, marked also by the encroachment of business and light manufacturing. This is a zone of urban plight of tenements and slums and inadequate services.

Zone No. 3: This is the Zone of working men's houses.

Zone No. 4: This consists of middle class residence, a suburban area that is characterized by greater affluence and spaciousness.

Zone No. 5: This is the Urban Fringe consisting of communities that are in effete dormitories of the CBD, where most of the economically active residents go to work. Here lies some of the highest quality residential houses.

The Sector Theory

Homer Hoyt and M.R.Davie proposed this theory in 1939. According to this theory, the arranged routes radiating from the city center creating a sectoral pattern of land and rental value influencing the urban land use pattern condition patterns of urban land use.

Sectors

- The CBD
- Wholesaling and light manufacturing
- Low class Residential Area
- Medium class Residential Area.
- High class Residential Area.

Sinclair's Model

Sinclair propounded a ring type model in 1967. The progression of intensity of his ring's is directly proportional to the degree of urban influence in forms of high urban taxes, constrained zoning and disturbances in the vicinity of urban areas. Two British writers, Best and Gosson, also support this theory. They believe there is a shift supported by cause i.e., increasing competition from distant areas with better production facilities, and loss of casual labour to city jobs by rural-urban fringe farmers.

Sinclair's Pattern of Land use around an expanding metropolitan area composes follows:-

- Urban Farming close to the city
- Vacant and grazing land
- Field crop and grazing land
- Dairying and field crop land
- Specialized food grain livestock

DEVELOPMENT AND CONSERVATION OF ENVIRONMENT

Environment is where we live and development is what we do to improve that living. Therefore development and conservation of the environment are not mutually exclusive, but are interdependent sides of the same coin. The question is how to achieve these from diversified objectives of sustainable development. Environmental conservation and improvement in the quality of life and ensuring a rising standard of living for everybody on a equitable basis is a major concern for sustainability. Can we achieve through the process of physical development or does it need a multi-dimensional approach? It was thought that the development plans provide the physical matrix for urban activities to take place and could be used to encourage development in other sectors, such as economy, society, education, recreation and health, whose actors would be able to find a place in the urban scheme of events. Unfortunately, the agenda for all these sectors may not be same as the agenda for urban planning. Earlier urban development projects were considered to be environmentally benign, on the presumption that urban development was meant to improve the urban environment for living. The main culprits for degradation of urban areas were identified as the industries, traffic, poor municipal services, etc., which if correctly located and managed, would automatically improve the quality of the environment. Unfortunately, evidence suggests that all forms of development have some impact on environment and it is necessary to evaluate the impact of all urban development proposals on the environment.

STUDYING ENVIRONMENTAL IMPACT

The main steps of studying the environmental impact can be divided into the following:-

- Preliminary Environmental Assessment i.e., assessing the nature and intensity of adverse effect of it is not very serious, then further examinations are unnecessary.
- Environmental Impact Statement, i.e., it records the likely adverse effect and identifies mitigative methods.
- Environmental Impact Statement, i.e., in case of a substantial impact, a detailed study is called for.
- Mitigation Measures, i.e., measures to reduce or eliminate the adverse effects.
- Environmental Audit, i.e., to keep track of effects over a period of time, and
- Environmental Management, i.e., to continuously manage and monitor development to ensure environmentally satisfying development.

ENVIRONMENTAL IMPACT STATEMENT (EIS)

This is a simplistic approach to complex issues relating neither to the regulatory nor the planning process, incapable of estimating the cumulative impact on multiple actions or the probability of a impact on site or the possibility of impact off site. They do not distinguish clearly between the identification and evaluation of impacts or satisfying different levels of alternatives at site, in the design and so forth. ESI is seen as only an incremental perspective, rather than sequential comprehensive viewpoints.

ENVIRONMENTAL IMPACT ASSESSMENT (EIA)

The objective of the ELA can be enumerated as the follows:

- EIA is the study of proposed action on the environment, which includes all aspects of natural and built environment.
- EIA seeks to compare various alternatives to achieve the same objectives for any project and programme. Each alternative is assessed against economic costs and benefits.
- EIA makes predictions. The technical work involved in estimating the changes is an environmental quality, which may result due to proposed action is a complex method.
- EIA assesses environmental effects on a common basis with economic costs and benefits, which require sophisticated economic modeling.
- EIA is a decision making tool. Its ultimate objectives to aid decision by providing decision choice of alternatives.

The urban project Environmental Impact Assessment is a reiterative process, designed to reduce in negative adverse impact of urban development projects.

CONCLUSION

Urban centers are said to play lead roles in offering avenues for employment and at the same time act as centers of cultural synthesis. This synthesis brings together forces that assimilate us into a single body. Urbanization also has a significant positive relationship with economic development. Urban India's contribution to the GDP of the country is estimated at 50-60 percent. In addition to facilitating industrial development the process of urbanization in the country has also contributed towards development in other sectors including agriculture, industry etc., Urbanization has also led to improved availability of superior quality of services and amenities for an increasing number of people. However juxtaposed to such benefits is the increasingly degraded urban environment continually pulling in cheap workforce from rural areas but remaining unable to extended required essential services. The dichotomy that exists in a city is indeed astonishing with peaks of prosperity and affluence on one end of the spectrum and dark depths of misery on the other. Yes, the poverty levels in urban areas are the direct outcome of rapid urban growth. And coupled with the lack of basic services the result is gruesome.

What then is the future? Perhaps the answer lies in recognizing the role of Good Urban Policies so that our cities may be ensured a sustainable environment through consensus strategies and participatory solutions.

REFERENCES

"Geography and You".

Publication on Ecology Impact Assessment Series by (CPCB).

Publication on Control of Urban Pollution Series by (CPCB).

Indian Infrastructure Report.

Publication on Environmental Mapping and Planning Series (CPCB).

Programmes Objective Series (CPCB).

33

URBANIZATION AND ENVIRONMENT

Jameelunnisa Begam

Environmental education is the process of recognizing values and clarifying concepts in order to develop skills and attitudes necessary to understand and appreciate the interrelatedness among man, his culture and his biophysical surroundings. Environmental education involves teaching about value judgments and the ability to think clearly about complex problems about the environment, which are political, economic and philosophical as they are technical. Urbanization is a process of migration of people from rural areas for better living which leads to population explosion in urban areas, which in turn affects environment.

Apart from industrial development, urbanization is also causing a number of problems. In India urbanization has become a phenomenon of this century. Many cities face problems such as deteriorating infrastructure, environmental degradation inner-city decay and neighborhood collapse. Yet comparably, the physical environment in many cities of the industrial world has improved substantially over the past two decades. Garbage and auto emissions, including noise pollution, now greatly influence environmental conditions in these cities. In contrast industrial growth and employment is the powerful stimuli for the rapid urbanization of developing countries. Lack of planning and collapse of infrastructure due to rapid migration frayed urban fabric putting enormous pressure on shelter and services. Air, water, noise and solid waste pollution problems have increased rapidly with consequential impacts on the life and health of city and suburban inhabitants and their economy. A growing number of urban poor suffer from a high incidence if diseases linked to poor sanitation and contaminated drinking water (Diarrheaea, Dysentery, Hepatitis and Typhoid are usually endemic). It is interesting to note that 60% of Kolkata population suffers from pneumonia; bronchitis and other respiratory diseases related to pollution. It is no wonder as Calcutta is the most polluted city in India. The Hooghly estuary near Calcutta is choked with untreated industrial wastes from more than 150 major factories. Out of India's 3,119 towns and cities only 209 had partial and only 8 had full sewage treatment facilities. Unguided industrial growth and uncontrolled physical expansion of cities are two factors which played havoc on the most productive agricultural land and on the health and economy of neighboring villages of an urban area. Further this increased inter regional disparities are creating social and economic imbalances.

The Thane region near Mumbai is a revealing example of urban decay due to improper planning, haphazard construction, poor sanitation, large-scale health problems, lack of proper financial structure with in civic bodies and gross mismanagement. Industrial effluents of a factory near Thanjavur in Tamilnadu, affected the neighboring villages like Gopalnagar, Kurungulam, Thuvalagiripalli and Nagappudaiyanpalli. 2,00,000 Liters Effluents, per day degraded agricultural fields and water sources. Cattle die after consuming the effluent water. Health problems due to effluents are gradually surfacing. Despite representations administration and the concerned industry remain unmoved.

Total urban population in India is 217 millions; accounting for one fourth of the countries population. About 25 per cent urban population lives in slums and under conditions of severe deprivation, illegal land tenure, deficient environment and services. Through housing has been recognized as a basic need, so far a comprehensive national housing policy is yet to be put in to place.

The national commission on urbanization had noted that urban land records are in helpless disarray and observed that the census of 1981 collected less information on urban issues than the census of 1971. It suggested a modification in the course of urbanization with this objective in mind the commission had prepared a preliminary list of about 600 cities and towns most of which recorded high rates of population growth and expanding economic activity. These cities and towns, which were identified as Generators of Economic Momentum (GEM) were further screened from the point of view of physical locations, availability of water, power, transport links and the facilities and a final list of 329 GEMS was prepared. They were further defined into Spatial Priority Urbanization Regions (SPUR) taking into account the 15 agro climate regions in context of overall development.

Andhra Pradesh is one of the five big states in India. With three district natural regions, it houses a large variety of natural resources. Prior to 1980 its economy was considered to be predominantly, agriculture based. In the past two decades. The state has continuously and deliberately forced to move away from the agriculture economy. From a modest beginning during independence with only 45 large and medium industries and with an investment of Rs. 63 crores this state has emerged as one of the major industrialized states in the country. By 1992 it had 828 large ands medium industries with a total investment of Rs. 11.772 Crores providing employment to nearly 5 Lakhs persons. This pace of industrialization was particularly rapid between 1985-1995. However, industrialization was tended to be clustered in the capital city and one or two others centers with concomitant socio economic problems.

Intensive location of cement industries in Wadapalli, Kodad of Nalgonda District and Near Vijayawada has spread pollutant particles across surrounding areas. Villages like Ramapuram, Dospeta, Malkapuram, Madhupuram,

Metlacheruvu, Bajinepalli, Mallareddy Gudem, Kadi Banda, Lakshmipuram, Ganapavaram, Kuchipudi, Kapugallu, Togari Gudibanda, Yerravaram and Nallabandagudem and now Wadapalli are affected by the cement dust settling their crops to people residing near cement industries, generally are plagued by lung disorders, and others bronchial aliments.

Visakhapatnam is considered as one of the Asiaest fast growing industrial cities. Hills on three sides and ocean on the other side surrounds this city. It houses several major industries including an oil refinery, two fertilizer plants, one zinc smelter, two petrochemical industries, one cement factory and a numerous small scale units. Apart from these, there are plans to establish four more industries in the petrochemical sector, by the central government. Several ancillary industries are also on the anvil. Vizag steel plant is the biggest industry in the city.

Waste asthma, bronchitis and lung related problems are rampant in areas of excessive pollution. There have been reports of miscarriages of pregnant women and delivery of still born babies.

Most industrial areas lack proper infrastructure facilities like water supply, roads and sewer lines, which have not been developed properly. Much of the water needs are met by individual bore wells. Sewer lines are almost absent. Many units also depend on the tanker supply of water. Roads are improperly developed. Effluents of these industries are released into the open, which collect on roadside drains and pits. As a result ground water with in industrial area is polluted and is unfit for consumption The best example is Patancheruvu Industrial area.

The commissions employed by government should complete their mission by collecting adequate data on urbanization and industrialization and strictly caution the concerned authorities who are responible for polluting the environment. This is the area where Indians are failing in spite of having the legal powers.

It is only due to careless attitude of man towards the environment; the environmental degradation is taking place.

If environmental degradation is not checked in time, it will endanger the very existence of human species itself. The need of present time is environmentally conscious citizens who will save the environment from disaster.

34

SAFE AND WHOLESOME WATER: SOME PRACTICAL MEANS OF PROVIDING WATER TO SMALL COMMUNITY

P. Ravindranath

After air water is the second most vital need to sustain life on Earth. In Yazurved water has been described as 'Elixir' of life. It is the factor and source of energy that governs the evolution and functioning of life on Earth. Though a man may live without food for several weeks, he can go without water only a few days. In fact physical discomfort begins with in a few hours and grows steadily, worse as time passes. Water is nature's free bounty to man kind. Safe and clean drinking water enhances life expectancy, but ever increasing population, reckless deforestation and rapid growth in Industrial sector and Urbanization has led to depleted and polluted water resources, thereby making drinking water, a scarce commodity.

Of the Global water resources about 97.2% is salt water, which mainly occurs in Oceans and only 2.8% is available as fresh water. Out of this 2.8% about 0.6% water is available as Ground water and about 2.2% as surface water. Even out of this, most fresh water is locked in Glaciers and Ice caps.

Water to day contaminated by visible and invisible impurities. The visible impurities are found in the shape of suspended particulate, dirt etc. The invisible impurities include bacteria and virus that causes diseases like jaundice, cholera etc. When we drink water, we are drinking more than just water. As a result of Industrial waste, break down of water means, herbicide and pesticide use, acid rains and oil spills, the water may be contaminated with hazardous substances. Even ground water has undesirable concentration of minerals and dissolved salts adding bad taste to water as well as harmful effects due to them.

It is in this context, to day's health conscious Society people are searching for safety, healthy purified water and at the same time it should be easy to operative and less expensive.

Water intended for human consumption should be not only safe but also wholesome. Such supply of water may be termed as 'acceptable' or potable. This water is to be free from pathogenic agents, free harmful chemical substances, pleasant to taste and usable for domestic purpose.

SOURCE OF WATER SUPPLY

There are three main sources of water : a) Rain b) Surface water (Impounding reservoirs, Rivers and Streams, Tanks, Ponds and lakes) Ground Water (Shallow wells, Deep wells, Springs).

Rain is the prime source of all water. Surface water originates mostly from rain water. The vast majority of Indian cities and Towns depends upon surface water source only. In general surface water supplies posses a high probability of Organic, bacterial and viral contamination. Ground water is the cheapest and most practical means of providing water to small communities. Ground water is superior to surface water, because the Ground it self provides an effective filtering medium. The advantages of Ground water are 1) It is likely to be free from pathogenic agents 2) It usually requires no treatment. The disadvantages are high in mineral content, which render the water hard and in some areas excess fluorides in Groundwater, may give rise to dental fluorosis and skeletal deformation.

PURIFICATION OF WATER

It may be considered under two headings, I) purification of water on a small scale ii) purification of water on a large scale.

Purification of Water on a Small Scale

Household purification of water : *Three methods* are generally available for purifying water on an individual or domestic scale. These methods can be used singly or in combination.

(a) *Boiling:* Boiling is a satisfactory method of purifying water for household purposes. Water must be brought to boil for 5 or 10 minutes. It kills all bacteria, spores, cysts and ova and gives sterilized water. The taste of water is altered, but this is harm less.

(b) *Chemical Disinfecting:* Chlorine solution may be prepared from bleaching powder. If 4 kgs of bleaching powder with 25% available chlorine is mixed with 20 liters of water, it gives a 5% solution of Chlorine. Ready made chlorine solutions in different strengths are also available in the market. The principle in chlorination is to ensure a free residual chlorine of 0.5 mg/litre at the end of one hour contact. Highly polluted and turbid waters are not suited for direct chlorination.

(c) *Filtration:* Water can be purified on small scale by filtration through Ceramic filters. The essential part of the filtration is the candle with surface coated with silver catalyst so that bacteria coming in contact with the surface are killed by the "Oligodynamic" action of silver ions. Filter candles of fine type usually remove bacteria found in drinking water, but not the filter passing viruses. Filter candles are liable to be clogged with impurities and bacteria. They should be cleaned by scrubbing with a hard brush under running water and boiled at once a week.

Disinfecting of Wells: Wells are the main sources of water supply in the rural areas. The need often arises to disinfect them. Some times on mass scale during epidemics of Cholera and Gastroenteritis. The most effective and cheapest method of disinfecting wells, is by bleaching powder. The following formulla is to be followed for well disinfection.

Find volume of water in well by the following method

- Measure the depth of water column ...... h meters
- Measure the diameter of well ....d meters
- Substitute h and d in volume of water (liters)

Volume of Water (Liters) $(3.14 \times d^2 \times h)/ 4 \times 1000$

(Once cubic meter = 1000 liters)

Find out the amount of bleaching powder required for disinfection. Roughly 2.5 grams of good quality bleaching powder would be required to disinfect 1000 liters of water. This will give an approximate dose of 0.7 mg of applied chlorine per liter of water.

The bleaching powder required is placed in a bucket (not more than 100 gr in one bucket of water) and made in to a thin paste. More water is added till the bucket is nearly three fourths full. The contents are stirred well and allowed is transferred to well as it increases the hardness of well water. This bucket containing the chlorine is lowered some distance below the watch surface and the well water is agitated by moving the bucket violently both vertically and laterally. This should be done several times until the required dose of Chlorine mixes intimately with water inside. A contact period of one hour is allowed before the water is drawn for use.

Defluoridation of Water: Fluorine is often called a two edged sword. Ingestion of large amounts is associated with Dental and Skeletal fluorosis and inadequate amounts with Dental caries.

Prevention & Control: A simple technique known as *Nalgonda Technique* or defluoridation of water is suggested. It involves addition of lime and Alum in sequence followed by flocculation, sedimentation and filtration. Lime powder is added first (30 mg/liter) and mixed well with water. Generally the lime dose is 1/20 of the alum dose. Alum (500 mg/liter) is added and then the water is stirred for 10 minutes. The contents are allowed to settle for an hour. The settle water will contain fluorides within permissible limit. This technique is suitable for both domestic and community water treatment.

Purification of Water on Large Scale: Water on large scale such as Urban water supply is purified by three main stages 1) Storage 2) Filtration 3) Chlorination of Ozonation or Ultraviolet irradiation. Germicidal property of UV irradiation were recognised for many years, but the process is generally more expensive than Chemical treatment. A further disadvantage is that colour and turbidity reduce the disinfection potential of UV rays irradiation and is presently used on small scale household purification of water.

Water fit for human consumption should satisfy the following requirements.

- The water should be clean odorless and colour less.
- It should have turbidity less than 10 ppm
- The pH of water should be in the range of 6 to 9
- It should be soft in nature
- The total concentration of dissolved solids should be less than 500 ppm.
- The water should be free from harmful bacteria, toxic materials.

Much of the ill health in the under developed countries is largely due to lack of safe drinking water. The provision of safe community water supply is one of the most effective and permanent health technologies for improving the health of the people. An attempt is made to provide some information regarding the practical means of getting safe drinking water so that the measures can be taken at individual or at small community level.

REFERENCES

Nawlakha. W.G. et.al. (1975), Ind. J.Enu.Hlth., 17.26.

Hoehn. R.C. (1976), Jaww, 68, 302-308.

Text Book of Environmental Chemistry, A.K. De, Fifth Edition, New Age International Publisher–New Delhi-2003.

Text Book of Preventive and Social Medicine, J.E. Park and K. Park, Eleventh Edition, B.B. Publishers–Jabalpur–1986.

35

POVERTY REDUCTION – ENVIRONMENTAL SAFETY

M. Tirupalaiah

INTRODUCTION

Poverty and Environmental Safety are mutually interrelated. They influence each other inversely. Poverty reduction contributes to environmental safety in many ways. Similarly, environmental protection leads to poverty reduction and human development. Poverty monitoring in India since the 1960s has been mainly based on the National Sample Survey (NSS). State – level projections up to 1999 – 2000 suggest that the incidence of poverty has been falling in India. The overall rate of poverty reduction implied by these results is 0.8 percentage points per year for the period since 1993 – 94[1].

POVERTY REDUCTION – ANTI-POVERTY POLICIES: IMPLICATIONS FOR ENVIRONMENT:

India is a low income country, with a GDP per Capita in 1996 of $380 (1580 at purchasing power party). About 35% of the total population fall below the official poverty line, which is lower than the $ 1 a day bench mark. Majority of the poor people live in rural areas, where the incidence of poverty is (37%) slightly higher than in urban areas (31%). Rates of poverty vary widely between states, from 12% below the poverty line is Punjab to 55% is Bihar. For most states, however, the figure is 12–45%[2]. Their living conditions are deplorable. They do not have adequate drinking water, housing and sanitation. They utilise the local natural resources which are commercially exploited by the urban rich. They are victims of environmental depletion and degradation.

INTERNATIONAL TARGETS

The targets are designed to provide milestones against which progress towards the goal of poverty elimination can be measured.

(a) Economic Well-Being

- A reduction by one-half in the proportion of people living in extreme poverty by 2015.

(b) Human Development

- Universal primary education in all countries by 2015.
- Demonstrated process towards gender equality and the empowerment of women by eliminating gender disparity in primary and secondary education by 2005.
- A reduction by two-thirds in the mortality rates for infants and children under age five and a reduction by three-quarters in national mortality by 2015.
- Access through the primary health care system to reproductive health services for all individuals of appropriate ages as soon as possible and no later than the year 2015.

(c) Environmental sustainability and Regeneration:

- The implementation of national strategies for sustainable development in all countries by 2005, so as to ensure that current trends in the loss of environmental resources are effectively reversed at both global and national levels by 2015[3].

INDIA'S RECORD

The World Bank Report(1998) titled "Reducing Poverty in India" deals with anti – poverty policies of the Government. It concludes that during the fifty years since Independence, India has secured many notable social and economic achievements including the eradication of famine, a reduction in population growth and significant reduction in levels of poverty. The government has implemented a large number of Pro-poor policies and programmes. These include reservation policies for scheduled castes and tribes, legislative measures, and a wide range of employment and subsidy programmes for the poor. The world bank report states, however, that many policies and schemes have been only partially effective and targeting at the poor has generally been weak. Rural public works have generally been the most successful, providing out-of-season employment to large numbers of poor people, but have not involved any upgrading of skills. Credit schemes have also benefited both poor and non-poor groups, and have not been linked to training. Recent government evaluations have recommended measures to rationalise the multiplicity of schemes and improve their effectiveness; these are currently under consideration. Government at both national and state levels has shown inadequate attention to longer term investments in basic health and education, despite their importance in poverty reduction, largely because they have focussed attention on subsidy and safety net programmes. The present government's national agenda seeks to promote growth with social justice and equity. It gives priority to agricultural and rural development to generate sufficient employment in order to eradicate income poverty. The adverse affects of environmental destruction are increasing felt. An environment friendly development strategy for poverty reduction is being evolved in most parts of the world.

The picture of poverty, illiteracy and ill-health as measured by infant mortality rate are still alarming and have a damaging effect on the physical and social environment. Therefore, they have to be tackled as early as possible.

The message and a lesson of Gandhi on "Protecting and Conserving Environment along with the Development process", not only for Indians, but also for the world to follow at large[4]. Amidst all sorts of problems such as rapid population growth, production and consumption pattern causing stress and strain on natural systems, degradation and depletion of natural resources affecting the life-support-system (air, water, soil and bio-diversity), unpredictable global-climatic-change. Ozone-layer depletion and sea-level-rise, unemployment poverty, economic inequality, social injustice, poor conditions of villages, big polluted cities, rivers and polluting Industries. In the course of development, we have to think of these problems and try to find out the solution best suited to our needs. Self-sufficiency of villages, promotion of small and cottage Industries, control on the import of consumption goods, improved agriculture, etc. are some of the ways. Importance should be given to the qualitative improvement of human resources-education and health[5].

OVERVIEW OF RICE POLICIES IN DIFFERENT COUNTRIES – ENVIRONMENTAL SAFETY

Ever since the Uruguay Round Agreement on Agriculture (URAA), there has been considerable concern in developing countries about its implications for poverty. This is particularly true of rice, which is the life line of almost 70 percent of the world's poor residing in Asia. Asia alone accounts for more than 90 percent of world rice production of 397 million tonnes in 2001 (FAOSTAT 2002) and an overwhelming share of world consumption rice trade liberalisation therefore has tremendous implications for poverty[6] especially under the WTO.

Rice sectors across the world attract high level of government intervention. This is true of both developed and developing countries in liberalising rice trade for the sake of food security. It leads to environmental security. Indeed, rice is regarded as a strategic commodity in many of these countries and differs in a fundamental way. While the farmers have high producer prices to maintain farmer incomes, Govts have tended to tax producers to ensure the availability of cheap staples for the mass of poor consumers.

IMPLICATIONS OF RICE TRADE LIBERALISATION FOR POVERTY AND ENVIRONMENTAL SAFETY

How do rice trade liberalisation and the consequent predicted changes in trade flows affect poverty in developing countries? To answer this question, it is important to recognise that the link between incomes and rice trade flows operates at different levels and in complex ways. The immediate effect is through change in price levels. In a competitive market, trade liberalisation would trigger exports and domestic prices would rise to equalise with world prices. This would benefit the net sellers of rice, while net buyers of rice face higher prices. More recently, Minto and Goletti (1999) predicted, using a spatial equilibrium multi market model, that the elimination of the rice export quota in Vietnam would raise prices by 14 to 22 per cent on average and can be expected to reduce both the incidence and depth of poverty[7]. In the poorer countries, imports have always been viewed with some misgivings since they are feared to be a threat to domestic food security and livelihoods. It creates some environmental pollution in such countries. However, contrary to popular opinion that trade liberalisation would be inimical to food security and poverty alleviation, some research shows that trade liberalisation in importing countries, by providing a 'low cost rapid response mechanism' to increase domestic supply and stabilize prices, can help enhance food security. For instance, following Bangladesh's poor harvest of rice in 1997, and floods the following year, trade liberalisation measures in rice both in Bangladesh itself and in neighboring India made possible imports from India by private traders, which contributed significantly (Dorosh 2001)[8].

INCREASING HEALTH–POVERTY REDUCTION

Health is basic to national progress and in terms of resources for economic development nothing could be of greater significance than the health of the people. People with sound health can accelerate the pace of economic, industrial and social development. The National Health policy, announced recently aims at reviving the ailing health system and increasing the primary health sector outlay to ensure a more equitable access to health services across the social and geographical expanse of the country. The govt plans to increase its contribution to the healthy sector from 0.9 per cent of the GDP over the next eight years. By 2010, the policy envisages an increase in aggregate expenditure on the health sector from 5.2 percent to 6 per cent. It has also been recommended to the states to increase expenditure from 5.5 per cent to 7 per cent of their budget by 2005 and further to 8 per cent by 2010[9]. Funds thus raised can be used for meeting the services. Some amount can be set a part for extending free medical facilities to the poor without imposing any burden on the government. Kerala has made notable achievements in health and these are reflected in the attainment of low infant mortality rate, low death rate and high expectancy of life. The decadal growth rate (1981– 91) in population was 14.32%. Kerala stands apart from the rest of the states in the achievement of health standards, and the standards attained all comparable to those of the developed countries. These achievements have been made possible through a network of health infrastructure, general health consciousness and clean health habit of the people, combined with virtually total literacy among not only men but also women of Kerala.

Data also throws some light on the incidents of poverty, infant mortality and health expenditure across a group of developed and developing countries. Poverty reduction in an environment-friendly way is important for protecting the natural environment from further degradation.

CONCLUDING REMARKS

Issues of poverty reduction, development and environmental are the once that are widely discussed and debated all over the world. Poverty in all its dimensions poses a threat to prosperity and the sustainability of our environment. Some times, a clash of issues is involved between poverty reduction and environmental safety. Provided a forward looking people-oriented employment-augmenting, resource conserving strategy of development is evolved the apparent clash will disappear. Poverty reduction and environmental safety can go together at the local, national and global level. It will lead to real peace and Human welfare in the true sense. But wisdom should down on the leaders of society and government. Let the stakeholders work for it.

36

ENVIRONMENTAL POLLUTION-AFFECTS-REMEDIAL MEASURES

M.S.N. Reddy, A.G. Prasad, V. Narender

United Nations Conference on Human Environment held in 1972 at Stockholm and creation of United Nations Environment Programme (UNEP) have given a big boost towards the awareness of environmental pollution and the need for protection and conservation of the environment. The observance of the world environment day on the June 5th of every year is the sign of people's concern to keep the environment free from pollution.

Pollution is the unfavourable alteration of the surroundings largely as a by-product of man's action, through direct or indirect effects of change in energy pattern, radiation levels, chemical and physical constitution and abundance of organism. These changes affect the quality of air, water, and agricultural and other biological products. Pollution is an undesirable change in the physical, chemical or biological characteristics of air, water and soil that may be harmful and affect the life or create potential health hazard to any living organism. Pollution thus is undesirable for humans and harmful for living components.

This paper makes an attempt to list various types of pollution, sources of pollution, and remedial measures taken to prevent the same.

KINDS OF POLLUTION

Pollutions are classified in different ways. On the basis of the type of environment being polluted, we may have sulphur dioxide pollution, fluoride pollution, lead pollution, mercury pollution, solid waste pollution, radioactive pollution, noise pollution, etc. All the above pollutants are categorized into two types non-degradable pollutants and biodegradable pollutant.

Non-degradable Pollutants

These are the materials and poisonous substances like aluminum cans, mercuric salts, long chain phenolics, DDT etc. that either do not degrade or degrade only very slowly in nature. They are not cycled in eco-system naturally. They not only accumulate but also are often biologically magnified with their subsequent movement in food chains and biochemical cycles.

Biodegradable Pollutants

These are the domestic wastes that can rapidly be decomposed under natural conditions. They may create problems if their input into the environment exceeds their decomposition.

The atmosphere is an insulating blanket around the earth. It is the source of essential gases ad maintains a narrow difference of day and night temperatures and provides a medium for long distance radio communication. It also acts as a shield around the earth against the lethal UV radiations and meteors. Without atmosphere there will be no lightening.

AIR POLLUTION

The normal composition of clean air Nitrogen 78.08%, Oxygen 20.95%, Argon 0.93%, Carbondioxide 0.03%.

Sources of Air Pollution

The main sources of air pollution come from motor vehicles, industries, particularly their chimney wastes, and fossil fuels based plants as thermal power plants.

Remedial Measures and Steps to be taken to Control Air Pollution

The steps that have to be taken to control and prevent the air pollution at source as well as after the release of pollutants in to the atmosphere are to

- Check the pollution emission from vehicular exhaust;
- Control the evaporation from fuel tanks;
- Use of filters and Carburetors;
- Make laws to banish polluting vehicles.
- Use of devices like Electrostatic Precipitators and cyclone Collectors, to prevent industrial pollution.

WATER POLLUTION

It can be defined as *"The addition of any substance to water or changing of water's physical and chemical characteristics in any way, which interferes with its use for legitimate purposes"*. In general water is never pure in a chemical sense. It contains impurities of various kinds dissolved as well as suspended. These include dissolved gases, dissolved minerals, suspended matter, and even microbes. These are natural impurities derived from atmosphere, catchment areas and the soils. They are in very low amounts and normally do not pollute water and it is potable. Polluted waters, however, is turbid, unpleasant, bad smelling, unfit for drinking, bathing, and washing. It is harmful and are is the vehicle of many diseases like cholera, dysentery and typhoid.

Sources of Water Pollution

The chief sources of water pollution are

- Sewage and other wastes;
- Industrial effluents;
- Agricultural discharges;

— Industrial wastes from chemical industries, , thermal power plants and nuclear power plants.

Remedial Measures for Control and Prevention

- Setting up of processing plants for drinking water.
- Not lenthing in the industrial effluents into water ponds or rivers.
- Industrial effluents have to be processed before they are let out on to the soil.
- Processing the industrial wastes before they are let out.

SOUND POLLUTION

The human ear is constantly being assailed by man-made sounds The word "noise" is an unwanted and unpleasant sound that causes discomfort.

Sources of Sound Pollution

The main contributors to noise pollution are factories and industries, Aeroplanes, trains, cars, automobiles, and pneumatic drills, radio television etc. Sound has become a permanent part of our lives these days. Sound not only the body and mind it indirectly forces our heart to work faster. Formerly noise was only restricted to industries. With modernization, globalisation. Due to population explosion particularly in urban areas, heavy traffic, electric equipment, vehicles have all added to noise pollution.

Remedial Measures and Steps to Control Sound Pollution

Sound pollution can be controlled but cannot be prevented. Total prevention is highly impossible because of the industrial development all over the country.

CONCLUSION

Nature is full of different types of ecosystems. Plants are the basis for life and provide oxygen for living organisms, without which living beings cannot exist. In the developed or developing countries, it is a must for all of us to trees for controlling environmental pollution and provide fresh air for good health and long life of human beings. The trees prevent global warming by reducing carbondioxide in the atmosphere.

Measures to prevent and control environmental pollution.

- Reforestisation has to be taken up on a large scale.
- Felling of trees should be avoided.
- Overgrazing should be avoided.
- Forests should be protected.
- Inter cropping and multiple cropping must be encouraged.
- Governments should educate the farmers, and the illiterate about the importance of trees and their protection.
- Schools should have curriculum, to educate the children about the importance of the trees.
- Laws should be made and strictly enforced control air pollution and sound pollution.

37

IMPROPER TOWN PLANNING–EFFECTS ON ENVIRONMENT

P. Venu Gopal

INTORDUCTION

People around the world, particularly those living in the developing countries, are beginning to ask whether the developing costs are not too a price to pay for the promised benefits. India had centuries of history of the conservation ethic and simple life style where nothing is wasted and the earth is nourished with only what it helps to produce. This perfect balance in nature came to be slowly destroyed, partly due to development itself, partly because of the acquisitive mind of the man and senseless copying of the life styles of western countries, which ahs been consuming an inordinate share of the world's resources, creating in the process, unmanageable proportions of affluents, wastes and what not.

For the last few decades, urban areas have become hellholes with industrial pollution, water pollution, air pollution and noise pollution, all put together. The World Commission on Environment and Development(WCED) warned, as far back as in 1987, about the problem of industrial waste management challenging us, as a society, and wanted as much care to be taken for present and succeeding generations as for those in the distant future. Governments have failed to cope up with these challenges. Environmental Ministries and agencies of the government, with their narrow mandates, did not respond adequately to these challenges.

On the other hand, in Indian economy we can predominantly observe the rural nature and most of our population is concentrated in rural areas. After independence and because of the industrialisation most of the rural population is moving to urban areas to earn their livelihood. It caused the uneven growth of the metropolitan cities. Most of the researchers in India argue that because of the unplanned or improper town planning, it has reduced vast swathes of our cities into cesspools. In this connection an attempt is made in this paper to examine the effects of improper planning on environment with special reference to Municipalities and Municipal Corporations.

GROWTH OF TOWNS IN INDIA

Sixty years since India's attaining republic status, the potential of those Asian focal points lies in latters, victims years of depredation by blinked local administrators, their cityscapes blighted forever by run away growth. Civic disorder become institutionalized and the municipalities and municipal corporations have to make a proper planning for reducing its effect on environment.

Data shows the growth of population in India for the last 100 years by rural urban breakup, the percentage of population in urban areas has been increasing compared to rural areas. The urban population increased by 12 times in the 100 years and rural population increased only at around three times. Recent census data reveals that almost one third of the population are living in urban areas and it is revealed in a number of studies that the percentage of urban population will reach to 42 per cent by 2010. Hence Municipalities and Municipal Corporations must change their town planning procedure to meet the future requirements.

Regarding urbanisation in India for the last 50 years data reveals that Class I cities are those with a population of 1,00,000 and above, Class II: 50,000 to 99,999; Class III: 20,000 to 49,999; Class IV: 10,000 to 19,999; Class V: 5,000 to 9,9999 and Class VI: less than 5,000 population. It can be observed from the table that the percentage of Class I towns have been increasing and Class V and Class VI have been decreasing for the last few years. However, we can observe small decrease in the percentage of Class IV towns between 1981 and 1991.

Regarding percentage of urban population, it also depicts the same trends. About 20 per cent change can be observed in case of Class I towns. In 1951, Class IV,V and VI towns, together have about 30 per cent of the total urban population and it decreased to 10 per cent by 1991. It shows that the towns with less than 10,000 population have been decreasing rapidly. In case of Class III towns also we can observe decreasing trends. However Class II towns increased only about one per cent during the study period.

Decennial growth rate of Principal Cities in India can be observed from various census reports. Particularly in the cities like Agra, Aligarh, Allahabad, Amaravati, Asansol, Bikaner, Gorakhpur, Hyderabad, Kozhikode, Lucknow, Ludhina, Nashik, Thiruvananthapuram, the growth rate netweem 1981-2001. In the cities like Bereilly, Kanpur, Mangalore, Moradabad, Mysore, Pune, Rajkot, Vijayawada it is almost stable with a small variation. In the remaining cities the growth in 1991-01 is less than 1971-81.

EFFECTS OF IMPROPER TOWN PLANNING

In India all the towns and cities are planned before fifties and they are developed according to the requirements at that particular time. Because of the urbanisation most of the rural population has migrated to the cities. Growing destitution in our countryside has engendered an out-migration of economic refugees to our cities. These municipalities run into a brick well of reality once they arrive with their raggedy belongings and glowing dreams and are soon forced into a peripheral existence where they gravitate into slums. Because of urbanisation there is change in the boundaries of town and they have extended. As the cities extended the outlying rural areas have been included in urban areas. Most of the agricultural lands have been changed into house sites. It has effected even the agriculture sector. As there is growth of the cities the industries located in the city outskirts are known located in the middle of the cities. So the dangerous effluents released from these industries effect the environment of the cities and it causes both sound and air pollution.

The another aspect is because of urbanisation and unplanned town development the municipalities are not able to provide sufficient drinking water and unable to provide proper sanitation. The solid waste disposals in urban areas are left to decompose and putrefy on road sites and in the vicinity of houses. Quite a substantial portion of this waste flows into the drains, choking them and spawning breeding grounds for pests.

It is also observed that most of the municipalities are unable to provide the power supply to all the areas in the cities. They are constructing roads and again they are digging for the telephone and water connections and also to provide the drainage facilities. The another aspect is because of growing commercial areas it is becoming difficult to park the vehicles near commercial complexes. It is creating disturbances in the traffic and which in turn causes air pollution and sound pollution. The another aspect is because of unplanned road constructions and buildings and growing commercial areas it is becoming difficult to manage the traffic which lead to frequent traffic jams and road accidents. When we are planning for the development of a town we have live one-thirds of the area for construction of the roads. We have to estimate the total number of houses, their water requirements, drinage facilities, and sources for releasing the wastes, recreation parks, schools and libraries. These aspects have not taken into consideration by the municipalities.

The another aspect is the municipalities are not in a position to provide safe drinking water to the growing population. Only about 60 per cent of the population receive organized pipe water supply and remaining rests on surface or ground water. But the domestic waste water and industrial waste water are released into water bodies open dumps and poorly designed landfills which causes surface water and ground water contaminated.

SUGGESTIONS

All these problems are causing because of the improper planning techniques adopted by the municipalities. Hence the municipalities have to make certain changes in their attitudes and methods in planning and management of the infrastructural facilities. An attempt is made here to suggest some remedial measures to overcome the problems of the improper planning by the local governments.

- Roads have to be expanded to control the traffic and in some areas, if it requires, huge investments for expanding roads the traffic rules have to be changed by introducing one-ways and fly-overs which controls the traffic directly and controls the air pollution and sound pollution indirectly.
- Municipalities should go for better urban design to avoid congestion and reduce transport needs.
- The municipalities must impose strict restrictions for releasing the dangerous effluents by the industries located in the center of the cities. It should design industrial estates faraway from the cities. So it can reduce pollution effect on environment.
- The wastewater released from the domestic and industrial usage should be treated and then only it should be released into water bodies and open dumps.
- They should develop under drainage facilities in all the areas.
- They should collect the solid waste released from both domestic and industrial estates and treat them in a better way. And the solid waste may be utilised for energy generation.

- The garbage dumpsites should be given initial treatment to reduce bad odor and health risk emanating from them.
- They should provide housing facilities to the people living in the slum areas and should also provide safe drinking water and good health measures, which will not effect the entire environment.
- They should develop greenery on the roadsides, which will protect the environment from air pollution.
- They should continuously conduct pollution control check for automobile vehicles.
- While giving permission to newly constructed apartments it should approve only if it satisfies all the needs like sufficient area, growing of trees and building of sumps for collecting the rainwater and providing parking space.
- More Sulabh type of toilets should be built.
- Public awareness should be developed about sanitation and its impact on their health should be promoted.

CONCLUSION

In conclusion, it can be said that government's response has been inadequate towards problems caused by environmental pollution. At the policy level, it consistently refuses to recognise the human suffering caused by pollution resources. All its mechanisms favored the protection of industry, and property; irrespective of the costs of the people, environment and ecology. Politics of survival dominates the thought process of conventional articulating structures like political parties and interest groups. Only genuine people's movement could alter this situation.

38

URBANISATION AND ENVIRONMENT

T. Jayakumar

"Urbanization now has for grater influence than ever before. A world process its impact may be found almost everywhere".

INTRODUCTION

Urbanisation means the redistribution of population and a change in the demographic balance between rural and urban areas. Urbanisation is sometimes referred to as ",Location revolution" because it shifts people from smaller communities to large communities. It has been said that the world, which was 29% in urban in 1950 and 39% in 1995 will be half urban and half rural by the coming years.

REASON FOR URBANISATION

It is brought about by four factors:

- Natural growth induced by increase in urban population,
- Migration of people from rural to urban areas,
- Reclassification of towns by which some large village as they grow come under the classification of urban area,
- Some sporadic factors like wars, partition families and floods which results in massive migration

By and large people move to urban areas for higher income better job opportunities and better standard of living.

URBANISATION AND ENVIRONMENT

The growing concern is that as cities grow larger environmental stress multiplied. The unprecedented growths in world population, accompanied by technological and economic growth have enhanced Urbanisation. This increases the pressure on existing facilities of housing and infrastructure facilities leading to congestion.

IMPACT ON ENVIRONMENT

One of the impacts of urban growth is the transformation of the natural environment. Forests and other natural vegetation have row been replaced by infrastructure, residential homes, office space, industries and other commercial buildings. Too often not enough provisions are made for open space and green areas, and this had lead to depletion of green areas.

URBANISATION AND ITS IMPACT ON ENVIRONMENT

- Air pollution and Acid rain
- Water Pollution
- Natural environment is Polluted
- Deforestation
- Proliferation of slums
- Noise pollution

Air Pollution

Air pollution, particularly in urban areas, important because it can cause a wide variety of negative health effects ranging from eye irritation, to heart and lung diseases, to death. It can also impair visibility and reduce crop production, as well as damage ecosystems, wilderness areas, parks, and bodies of water.

Where Air Pollution can Originate

- Factories that emit smokes
- Power plants

- Smelter
- Automobiles such as cars, buses, Two and Three wheelers
- Jets
- Trucks, Firewood burning, burning of waste, and burning the tyre.

Causes of Air Pollution

Pollution is changing the earth's atmosphere so that it leads in more harmful radiation from the sun. At the same time, our polluted atmosphere is becoming a better insulator, preventing heat from escaping back into space and leading to rise in global average temperature. Scientists predict that the temperature increase, referred to as global warming, will affect world food supply, alter sea level, make whether more extreme, and increase the spread of tropical disease. Warmer temperatures are expected to partially melt the polar ice caps, leading to a projected sea level rise of 50 cm (20in) by the year 2050. A sea level rise of this magnitude would flood coastal cities, free people to abandon low laying islands, and completely inundate coastal wetlands.

Each year the U.S. discharges into the atmosphere :

15 Million tonnes sulfur dioxide

70 % from power plants burning coal or oil

30 % from smelters and refineries

For sulfur dioxide, the U.S. is the greatest contributing nation. But the emission rates are increasing so fast in Asia that this region has now replaced Europe and U.S. as the major emitter:

Countries	*1980*	*1990*	*1995*	*2000*	*2010*
Europe	59	42	31	26	18
U.S.	24	20	16	15	14
Asia	15	34	40	53	79

WATER POLLUTION

The National Water Policy, adopted in September, 1987 stress that ", Water is a prime natural resource, a basic human need and a precious national asset. Planning and development of water resources need to be governed by national perspectives". Rapid growth has resulted in higher demands from commercial and industrial sectors. We are all aware of importance of the environment and water issues. Water is necessary to life on earth. All organisms contain it. Some live in it. Some drink in it. Plants and animals require water that is moderately pure, and they can't survive if their water is loaded with toxic chemicals or harmful microorganisms.

One sixth of the world's population has no access to fresh drinking water, what is even more drastic is that there are fears of war over water in the coming year of the situation remain the same. Essential suggest that nearly 1.5 billion people lack safe drinking water and that at least 5 million deaths per year can be attributed to waterborne diseases.

How Water is Polluted

Petroleum products, Pesticides, herbicides, Heavy metals, Hazardous wastes, organic matter sediments, Thermal pollution and also major source of pollution coming agro-based industries, manufacturing, livestock farming and domestic waters.

NATURAL ENVIRONMENT

The impact of urban growth on the natural environment is also manifest by changes in climatic conditions and increased levels of background method of solid waste disposal which has raised fears of ground-water contamination as well as problems related to vector borne diseases, airborne dusts and odors.

DEFORESTATION

The adverse impact of urbanization on ecological balance is mainly reflected through deforestation. An increase in urban population increases the demand for firewood because of the rise in the price of kerosene. The consumption of firewood is high in many cities because of poverty and proliferation of slums resulting from Urbanisation. Urbanisation depletes both renewable and non-renewable resources faster because of the excess energy requirement.

With urbanization even the simple matter of waste disposal becomes a problem. The 'throw away' societies of cities generate the most trash disposal, which poses a major threat today. The overloading of the environment with noxious substance contained in our daily consumption causes the worlds leading cities. Discarded in the air, land and water they become the wrong thing in the wrong place at the wrong time.

Deforestation Techniques

The deforestation technique of slash and burn, utilized extensive to clear large areas of forest for agricultural and other purposes, causes an enormous amount of environment damage. The large amount of carbon dioxide given off into the atmosphere during burning adds to the greenhouse effect. The removal of all trees and groundcover destroys animal habitats and greatly accelerates erosion, adding to the sediment loads of rivers and making seasonal flooding much more severe.

PROLIFERATION OF SLUMS

One most impact of urbanization in developing economies, is the proliferation of slums. This is chiefly a problem of the third world countries. The environment in the cities of the third world countries are affected not so much by industrial or automobile exhausts than by poverty and the inability of the government to tackle the problem. Housing is a prominent problem in all the third world countries leading to extension of slums

NOISE POLLUTION

Noise pollution or sound pollution, exposure of people or animals to levels of sound that are annoying, stressful, or damaging to the ears. Although loud and frightening sounds are part of nature, only in recent centuries has much of the world become urban, industrial, and chronically noisy.

Sound intensity is measured in units called decibels. The decibel scale is logarithmic and climbs steeply: An increase of about three decibels is doubling of sound volume. In the wilderness, a typical sound level would be 35 decibels. Speech runs 65 to 70 decibels, heavy traffic generates 90 decibels. By 140 decibels, sound becomes painful to the human ear, but ill effects, including hearing loss, set in at much lower levels.

Most noise pollution comes from machines, especially automobiles, trucks, and aircraft. Construction equipment, farm machines, and the din of machinery inside factories can be dangerously loud. Some home appliances, shop tools, lawnmowers, and leaf blowers can also be noisy, as are guns, firecrackers, and some toys. Even music, when played at very high volume, particularly through personal headphones, is as damaging to the ears as a roaring chain saw.

Even oceans are increasingly noisy. The engines of ships, especially large vessels and supertankers, produce a lot of sound, and traffic is increasing. Offshore oil exploration and drilling are also noisy. And more recently, very loud, very low-frequency sonar signals are being sent through the seas to detect submarines and to gain information about water temperatures global warming.

Cause of Noise Pollution

The most significant health problem caused by noise pollution is hearing loss (Deafness). Ten million Americans have some hearing loss due partly or wholly to exposure to loud sounds, and 20 million are at risk. In addition to deafness, many people with damaged ears are affected with ringing in the ears.

Most hearing loss occurs in workplace, where workers may be unable to avoid unhealthy noise, and where exposure may continue for years. Factory workers, construction workers, farmers, military personnel, police officers, firefighters, and musicians all have reason to be concerned about their occupational to noise.

Even at levels below those that cause hearing loss, noise pollution produce problems. Noise pollution makes conversation difficult and disturbs sleep. As a source of stress, it can promote high blood pressure and other cardiovascular problems, as well as nervous disorders. According to National Institute of Health, 65 million Americans are exposed to noise levels that can hamper their work or disrupt their sleep, and 25 million risk health problems due to noise. Noise also puts stress on domestic animals and wildlife. In remote areas, helicopters and military aircraft often frighten animals. Aircraft noise in Alaska, for example, has been shown to reduce the survival rate of caribou claves. There is concern that increasing noise levels in the oceans may confuse the natural sonar that whales use to navigate, communicate, and locate food.

Remedies for Noise Pollution

- Noise pollution is not a necessary price to pay for living in an industrial society. Much can be done to reduce the severity of the problem. For example, Vehicles and other machines can be built to reduce less noise.
- Even after noise is generated, steps can be taken to reduce human exposure to it. At homes or in office, insulation of walls and double-glazing of windows can muffle sound from traffic, neighbors and other sources from the outside world.
- Individuals can protect themselves with earplugs or muff like ear protectors, particularly when noise levels exceed 85 decibels.
- In the industrial nations, government have laws and policies to counter noise pollution.

REMEDIAL MEASURES

(1) Population growth is also one of the cause for environment. Population growth should be controlled.

(2) Air pollution: In Asia air is highly polluted by industrial units and vehicles, so proper rules should be enforced based future.

(3) Water Pollution: About the importance of water, should create awareness among the public.

(4) Deforestation: Deforestation is happening in the name of infrastructure for home, dam and other reasons with any reason should not allow them to even cut a small tree than only possible to save the forest.

(5) Proliferation of Slums: Air, water and natural pollution is happening because of the slums. Poverty should eradicate than only possible to safe guard nature.

CONCLUSION

Environmental pollution can be controllable in two ways:

- Comprehensive approach i.e. implementing laws, penalties and punishment.
- Public interest litigation i.e. public interest litigation has really played in the pollution management regime in India.

The urban environment depends on age of the building, function of the city, availability of adequate finance, maintenance of sound infrastructure and transportation. Over urbanization has to-day necessitated most of the cities to unrealistic renewal schemes. The British Government set a comprehensive approach to urban environment problem. It created the world's first department of environment, at full ministerial level. Similarly legal measures have been taken in Japan and USA to improve the quality of urban environment.

As the urban man satisfied his needs and desires, he spoils the environment. The trend towards urbanization has led to the neglect of the countryside, in addition to the evils like deforestation, soil erosion, and pollution in all forms. There should be a balance between the rural urban distribution of people and economic activity.

REFERENCES

Viegas, Philp and Menon, Geeta (1989), "The Impact of Environmental Degradation on People", Indian Social Institute, New Delhi.

Khoshoo T.N. (1986), "Environmental Priorities in India and Sustainable Development", Presidential Address 73rd Session, Indian Science Courses Association, New Delhi.

Mishra, R. (1991), "Planning for Environmentally Sustainable Development" in Ecology and Sustainable Development, (ed. B. Gopal), pp. 1-8, National Institute of Ecology, New Delhi.

39

URBAN MIGRANTS – A THREAT TO ENVIRONMENT ?

H. Sadasiva Rao, A. Abhishikth Sandeep

The urban areas are today an enigma, an oxymoron of advantages and disadvantages, of good and bad, of happy and sad things.... On one hand, it is seen as a settlement of choice for an increasing number of the world's populace, but this is difficult to reconcile with the huge amounts of resources consumed and wastes generated.

"Posh areas choke on automobile fumes. Good roads offset heavy traffic"
– Hindu, 17/1/2003.

"Growing construction activity is leading to rapid depletion of ground water resources and additional burden on sewage lines."
– The Hindu

"Insanitary conditions upset C M"
– Hindu, Feb 5, 2003.

Scream the Headlines of most newspapers in cities all over the world.

The reasons are not difficult to fathom.

Cities today are already bulging to the seams with a lower burden population, which is invariably leading to large-scale environmental degradation.

Indian Cities represent 27.8% (285 Million) of total population and is continuing to grow at an alarming rate of

2.1% per decade. (1991–2001 census). This is primarily due to two reasons.

REASONS FOR INCREASING URBAN POPULATION

- Natural growth rate of urban population
- Net migration from rural to urban

The natural growth of population of residents in cities is a natural phenomenon, the second being migrants from rural areas and the country side into cities in search of jobs and livelihood as they are being threading by both nature and man in their natural habited.

> *"Where drought threatens very survival–clouds of starvation deaths loom large over poverty stricken drought hit areas of Mahaboobnagar."*
>
> *– Hindu, Feb. 3.*

Today the twin cities of Hyderabad and Secunderabad are playing host to large number of migrants. On an average a thousand people are entering the city not only from surrounding districts such as Mahaboobnagar, Nalgonda, Medak, etc. but as far as from Aurangabad and Ahmadabad in Gujarat. This is causing a heavy burden on the already over strained infrastructural facilities such as water supply, sewage, roads, apart from contributing to pollution of land, water, and air.

Today 48% of the world's population lives in urban areas (UN report 1998). UN projections estimate that the world's population will grow from 5.7 billion (1997) to 10 billion between 2150 (UN report 1999) while the corresponding increase in urban areas will be from 2.5 billion to 6 billion i.e. by 2020 the world's population will reach 57% urbanization level, of which 80 percent of urban increase in the next 20 years will occur in developing countries. The population will have changed from a predominantly rural scenario to an urban one. Urban population around the world is growing at the rate of 4% p.a. at this rate over the next 20 years developing countries must absorb nearly a billion additional urban residents.

	Urban	*Population %*	*Annual Growth*	*Rates (%)*
	1960	*1992*	*1960 –1992*	*1992-2008*
India	18	26	3.4	3.0
World	34	44	2.7	2.6

A major trend in rural to urban migration has been the increasing migration of women. In Asia, women are traveling in hundreds of thousands from rural areas of Asia to cities in search of work In India there has been an increase in the share of women in the rural to urban migration flow. The reason being the availability of lower economic opportunity /markets in rural areas. On the other hand the urban areas offer a plethora of attractions in the form of several job avenues, higher income, improved standard of living, health care etc.

PROBLEMS OF INCREASING URBAN POLLUTION

1. The rate of influx of rural folk into urban areas is very high, more than that the urban infrastructure can support
   (a) *Drinking Water Supply:* Cities are being threatened by a severe shortage of drinking water, due to increased requirements. Hyderabad has water sufficient for just a month's requirement. Drinking water after that depends on the monsoon. Due to unplanned construction and vested interests of a few persons the ground water level has fallen alarmingly to a depth of 15-20 meters below ground level. Hyderabad has around 250 lakes. Most of which have been converted into garbage dumping grounds or are being encroached upon by the burgeoning population. Most lakes are on the verge of vanishing.
   (b) *Vehicular Pollution:* According to a Report of the regional Road Transport Authority, one lakhs vehicles are being added to the city roads every year, most of them are auto's, tempo's, etc. which are being driven by migrants who migrated to the city in search of livelihood (in Hyderabad 20000 auto rickshaws are plying.) Most of them use adulterated fuel and don't maintain their vehicles in condition. Thus bulging poisonous fumes causing noise and air pollution, forcing residents to keep awake all night.
   (c) *Land Pollution:* Increased influx of migrants' calls for increased usage of land resources, which leads to increased pollution. Growing construction activity is

leading to rapid depletion of ground water resources and additional burden on sewage lines. Apart from which it generates tones of garbage, the disposal of which is a problem and a headache for civic authorities. The authorized dumping grounds of the city at Auto Nagar, Gandham Guda, and Hakeem Pet, are over flowing and today there is a urgent need for scouting additional places for dumping of garbage. Excessive garbage, most of which is not degradable (plastics, bottles etc.) Pollutes the soil, prevents recharging of ground water and is a health hazards to surrounding residential areas.

Most of the migrants either camp in the cities peripheries or in the existing slums. Unofficially the number of slums in Hyderabad number 100 approximately. Most slums are over crowded where people live in unhygienic conditions, which pose a health hazard (due to ground water contamination, contaminated drinking water supply, low nutrition, and unhygienic surroundings. According to estimates every other person in the world today lives in a city of these 1/3rd lives in slums (UN Report June 2001) Urban Population in Asia is expected to surge from 35% to 50% over the next 30 years. Every day on an average 1,80,000 people are added to cities. Thus making cities across the globe virtually sit on a time bomb (environmental disaster).

Out of the total of 20,503,597 persons living in urban areas of India Hyderabad hosts 3,686,480 spread over 225 square kilometers (16,384.35 persons per sq. km.) which by any yardstick is over crowded. To accommodate the ever-growing population and their necessities trees are being mercilessly hacked and numerous rocks are broken/defaced, making the surroundings an eyesore.

(d) *Air Pollution:* Highly polluting industries coupled with heavy vehicular traffic, use of chullas and low quality coal by households below the poverty line and migrants is polluting the air. According the State Pollution Control Board the resituate particulate matter (R P M) is 60% more than normal limits, emissions of Carbon Monoxide is on an average 20% above normal limits. In 1999 India emitted 0.25 metric tons of carbon per person.

Urbanization has resulted in a profound deterioration of India's air quality. Of the 3 million premature deaths in the world that occur each year due to outdoors and indoors air pollution. Energy related carbon emissions have grown nine fold over the past four decades. With increased migration into cities meeting energy requirements in a sustainable manner continues to be one of India's main challenges.

2. The urban sector is predominantly automated thus causing unemployment leading to poverty and environmental degradation.

The Haris and Tadaro model suggest that for every new job created in the urban sector, 3 or 4 workers who were productively occupied in rural areas may come to urban areas, setup their dwellings in open areas in the country side or camp in slums thus causing a burden on the already over strained infrastructure. Thus increasing land, water and air pollution levels.

CONCLUSION

Studies show that the informal sector is full of hidden but creative entrepreneurial talents, which offers lot of employment opportunities, which is taken advantage of by migrants in urban areas. The same may be encouraged in the rural areas through the development of necessary infrastructure such as road linkages between urban and rural areas, transportation facilities (buses, minivans, tempo's etc.) and make available the necessary raw materials and other inputs necessary for producing finished goods and indulging in other productive activities. Also required is the provision of adequate credit facilities to promote the growth and expansion of the rural sector

It is necessary that policy makers give an impetus to the rural informal sector so that the potential migrants may find employment preventing their migration to urban areas. Nature's gifts are being plundered and subject to sacrilegious acts, little realizing the fact that these resources are not to be frittered away and exhausted by one generation. It is high time we realized that every generation owes a duty to all succeeding generations to develop and conserve natural resources and the environment. It is not only in the interest of the nation but also in the interest of mankind.

The Ancient Roman Empire developed legal theory known as the "doctrine of Public Trust" - This primarily rests on the principle that resources like air, water, sea, forests, are for the common benefit of mankind and it enjoys the government to protect the resources for the enjoyment of the general public. In pursuit of this policy and the urgent need to conserve natural resources and preserve the environment and to arrest the outflow of rural folk from their villages the government should adopt a pro active approach comprising of a *two-pronged strategy*.

Development of Rural Areas and Rural Employment Generation

This includes:

- Aggressive adoption of rural development programs, which include a) Drought Prone areas Programs, b) Desert Development Program, c) construction of Check dams.
- Watershed Development Programs.
- Encourage fisheries and forestry programs witch active participation of NGO's, SHG's, and user groups.
- Adopt a single window approach by banks/ government agencies for financing and granting pollution for commencing and operating infrastructural projects for ensuring speedy growth of rural economy, connectivity with cities besides boosting employment.
- Check spiraling population growth by providing healthcare, education and promoting contraceptive awareness.

Environmental Conservation Programmes

This should encompass

- Encouragement of tree plantation (including continued care). This is necessary as in the last year over 2000 saplings were planted in peripheral areas but most perished due to lack of care. To prevent recurrence of such instances tree growers co-operative societies should be formed, also the "Tree Patta Scheme" is to be streamlined and implemented with active participation of SHGs.
- Check rampant haphazard construction policy through effective town planning policies.
- Ensure recharge of ground water resources through water harvesting. There is a need for adopting an aggressive water conservation mission to put an end to commercial exploitation of ground water resources. Under the Green Hyderabad Environment Programme, funded by Royal Netherlands Embassy, HUDA has proposed the conservation of 87 lakes, which are on the verge of drying up. The same may be extended to cover other lakes.
- Develop awareness and educate the masses (especially in cities) on issues related to environment.
- Facilitate research, monitoring and evaluation of environmental programmes on a sustained basis.
- Promote "Green Corps" policy aggressively to protect and nurture the environment

In the bleak scenario of rapid urbanization can Andhra Pradesh with a population of 66,508,008 (in 1991) (7.86% of All India Population) of which 20,503,597, live in urban areas transform itself into a Clean, Green and Pure "Swarnandhra Pradesh" is a big question which only time can tell .

40

ENVIRONMENTAL EFFECTS OF STONE CRUSHING: A STUDY

B. Srinivasa Rao

INTRODUCTION

The exploitation of mineral resources through opencast and underground mining has caused wide ranging environmental problem such as air, water, and noise pollution. All methods of surface and underground mining results in the generation of wastes that can affect surface water quality. The erosion of dumps and its flow can give rise to silting and choking of existing natural water courses. It affects ground water quality too. The magnitude of air pollution in mining areas varies with methods of mining, type of minerals and level of mechanization. Open cast and underground mining often exposes large amounts of pyrite and other sulphide minerals to the air, which accelerates their oxidation. Once oxidized to sulphates, they form an acid in water that can severely damage plant and animal life it leaks from the mine. In the mining area biodiversity is at a low level. Mining especially opencast mining would disturb the land mass. Slope stability problems give rise to landslides and rapid soil erosion. Blanketing of top soil in the nearly agricultural grazing land results in poor yield. Due to open cast mining forest land and consequently flora and fauna would get disturbed. Extensive damage to the national wealth without any compensatory a forestation disturb the ecosystem greatly. Unsound blasting operation results in vibration and damages houses and other surface structures due to blast vibration. Private contractors illegally mine a lot of land. Further disposal of mining debris creates pollution.

Mineral deposits are to be mined where they are. While the developed countries are in what might be called "recycling phase" waging war with dirty air, polluted water noise, congestion, energy shortage, etc., the developing countries, primarily of agriculture or mineral based are accelerating their pace of industrialization and exploitation of resources in the footstep of the former. Thus, the richer tends to be cleaner and poorer continues to be dirtier in the same parody of the technological exploitation in the present system.

One of the visible expressions of mining activities on earth is its affects on health. Occupational diseases like Silicosis, flurosis, asbestosis, manganism, plumbirm, itai-itai etc., have been well known to be associated with mining societies world over. Open Cast Mining activity has played havoc with the environment and is killing workers slowly 25% of the workers suffer from silicosis, bronchitis, asthma and tuberculosis and 50% from malaria, which has spread as a result of mosquitoes breeding in the open pits. Noise levels touch 96-125 decibels way above the permissible limit of 75 decibels causing stress and affecting the mental health of workers.

The impact of Mining on environment would be widespread and manifold. Mining could lead to irreversible damages. There are a number of ways to reduce the damage. They include collection of environmental cess, issuing of safety bonds or deposits, which can be issued for the purpose of reclamation, etc. This would escalate the initial costs of production and may deter competition. In such an event imposition of environmental tax on value basis would facilitate the distribution of the burden. The amount from this cess could be deposited in a separate account for usage at a later stage. The privatization of mining would also cause social problems like displacement of local populations. Any conflict would adversely affect the developmental efforts.

Pollution is a clear case of policy failure. Both policy makers and implementing agencies are aware of the mess and appropriate measures are in place to tackle the market failure situations. But nothing concrete is being done about it. Compliance is the major problem at industry level. The problem could be solved only through awareness building and promoting environment friendly technologies. In the short-run, planning the location of the industries will solve the problem to a large extent.

Awareness and involvement of the civil society is a precondition for checking environmental degradation. Environmental protests and movements would have a discerning effect in this regard. Environmental protests may not on their own, solve the problems but they are instrumental in bringing awareness among policy makers and the civil society. This would put pressure on the polity to have a full-fledged environmental policy rather than having an adhoc approach. Although there is no dearth of policies the crux of the problem lies with implementation. Compliance to rules and regulations can be achieved only through strengthening the hands of the implementing agencies and tightening the environmental legislation. In this connection an attempt is made in this paper to examine the effects of stone crushing on environment and to suggest appropriate measures.

STONE CRUSHING INDUSTRY

Stone Crushing Industry is an important industrial sector in the country engaged in producing crushed stone used as raw material for various construction activities such as construction of roads, bridges, buildings and canals. The stone crushing units can be seen in the vicinity of almost all major cities towns through out the country in all the states. During the stone crushing operations such as crushing, screening. conveying etc., substantial quantity of fine fugitive dust is emitted which has negative impact on the health and well being of human beings and also affects visibility in the vicinity and affects vegetation etc. The emissions are further added due to usage of outdated equipments without enclosures, unmetalled approach roads etc., and prevailing wind.

Stone crushing industry in India is an unorganized small-scale industry sector. Most of the plant and machinery has been conventional in nature and fabricated locally and has lacunae in its design, layout &operation etc., which results in excessive dust generation at source leading to fugitive emissions. There are hardly any reputed manufacturers of the crushing equipments or dust control equipment's in the country. Some crushers have tried to install some dust control systems but due to lack of proper technical assistance and inappropriate designs, the systems installed are not satisfactory.

The Indian stone crushing units (SCUs) can be categorized into three types-small, medium and large scale. Most of these SCUs operate for about 12 hours a day and some operate round the clock in shifts. In most cases the stone crushers come up in clusters of number of units ranging from five to fifty in one cluster. The crushers are located nearer to the source of raw materials such as stone mines, river beds etc., Most of the laborers who work in stone crusher units are from rural and economically backward areas where employment opportunities are limited and therefore it carries greater significance in terms of social importance in rural areas. It is a source of earning for the uneducated poor unskilled rural people.

Large SCUs generally have their own open cast stone mines. The units are situated within 0 to 5 kilometer distance from the mines. Mining is generally done using explosives and mechanical equipment. Most of the medium and small scale SCUs mine stones from nearby hillocks or riverbeds. These smaller units mostly use a combination of local explosives, mechanical and manual breaking of large stones. The mine stones are transported to the crusher sites besides road through tractor trolleys or pay-loaders. The pay-loaders unload the mined stones into materials such as stone mines, river beds etc.

The conversion of naturally occurring rock into crushed and broken stone products involves a series of distinct yet interdependent physical operations. These include both quarrying and mining operations (drilling, blasting, loading and hauling) and plant process operations (crushing, screening, conveying and other material handling and transfer operations). All are potentially significant sources of particulate emissions. Emission sources may be categorized as either process sources (primary sources) or fugitive dust sources(secondary sources).

STONE CRUSHING UNIT –STANDARDS FOR SUSPENDED PARTICULATE MATTER

The standards under the EP Act, rules,1986:

The standards consist of two parts:

1. Implementation of the following pollution control measures:

   Dust containment cum suppression system for the equipment.

   Construction of wind breaking walls

   Construction of the metalled roads within the premises

   Regular cleaning and wetting of the ground within the premises.

   Growing of a green belt along the periphery.

2. Quantitative standard for the SPM

The suspended particulate mate measured between 3 to 10 meters from any process equipment of a stone-crushing unit shall not exceed 600ug/m3.

AIR (PREVENTION AND CONTROL OF POLLUTION) ACT, 1981

The Air(prevention and control of pollution)Act,1981, was very innovative in its approach. The air act empowers the state board to lay down the standards for emission of air pollutants into the atmosphere from industrial plants, automobiles or from any other source, having in view the standards laid down by the central board. The state boards are empowered to inspect any factory premises, to check any control equipment, or the manufacturing process so as to take necessary steps for the prevention, control or abatement of air pollution. Under section 21 of the act, no person can operate any industrial plant without prior consent of the state board. If an industry is already in operation it should have applied for consent to the board within a period of three months from the date the area is declared as air pollution control are under section 19 of the act.

THE ENVIRONMENT(PROTECTION) ACT, 1986

This is a landmark legislation to provide a single focus in the country for the protection of environment and to plug the loopholes in earlier laws. It is a comprehensive act. It contains a stringent mechanism to control environmental pollution.

PROCESS DESCRIPTION

The mined stone is transported to the crusher sites by road through tractor trolleys or pay loaders. The pay-loader unload the mined stones into storage hoppers, located at elevated levels of the crusher sites. These stones are crushed in a primary crusher and sent to a vibratory screen. The oversize from the screen is sent for further size reduction in secondary and tertiary crushers. From the secondary and tertiary crushers, the crushed stones are sent for screening. In the Screen, products of various sizes get separated which are stored in heaps. Movement of stones from crusher to screen to product piles is done through belt conveyors. The product is generally stored in open areas.

ENVIRONMENTAL PROBLEMS ASSOCIATED WITH STONE CRUSHERS

These stone crushers though socially and economically an important sector, create substantial amount of environmental pollution by way of the fugitive emissions from various sources and adversely affect the ambient air quality and thereby affect the human health etc.,

VARIOUS SOURCES OF DUST GENERATION

1. *Emissions during Mining:* The stone is mined from stone mines with the help of blasting and breaking by mechanical means or manually. During blasting and other operations substantial amount of fugitive dust emission occur intermittently.
2. *Emission during Unloading of Mind Stones at Crusher Site:* At the time of unloading of mine stones into the storage hopper, large amount of fine dust is emitted, which appears like dust cloud. These emissions are intermittent and last for about a couple of minutes during every unloading. Generally there could be two to six unloading per hour. These emissions occur at an elevated levels and the dust is carried by wind currents to long distances.
3. *Emissions during Crushing Operations:* During the crushing operation size reduction takes place bigger stones are broken into smaller sizes and in the process some stone pieces get excessively crushed which, results into formation of stone dust. The finer dust gets airborne and escapes as fugitive emissions. The emissions occur at the inlet chute, from the crushers body and from the discharge chutes. These emissions occur at all types of crushers such as primary, secondary, and tertiary crushers in varying degrees.
4. *Emissions during Material Movement and Transfer:* The crushed stone is moved from one place to the other such as crusher to vibratory screen , screen to crusher, and again to storage piles, and between conveyor belts. During the movement and free fall during transfer of crushed stone, fine dust particles get airborne as fugitive dust emissions.
5. *Emissions during Vibratory Screening Operation:* During vibratory screening of crushed stones and due to vigorous movement of the stones, the fine dust particles get loose and airborne and fugitive emissions occur. These emissions escape from the openings around the screen as well as at the bottom of discharge location.

6. *Emissions during Transportation:* During transportation of the mined stones as well as the crushed stone products, due to vehicular movement on non-metalled roads, fine dust settled on the ground gets airborne.
7. Secondary emission from stockpiles: Generally the crushed stone is stored in open in heaps/piles. At times, when the wind sped is higher, the fine dust adhered to the stones is blown away from the stockpiles and gets airborne.
8. Emissions during loading of crushed stone products: The crushed stone products from the stockpiles are loaded into trucks or trolleys for dispatch. The loading is done either manually or with the help of conveyor belt. During loading, due to the movement of stones, the fine dust adhered to stone gets loosened up and gets airborne.

DUST GENERATION PATERN AT VARIOUS PROCESS STAGES

Starting from unloading of mined stones at the crusher site up to finished product, the stone either crushed or screened or transferred from one place to the other. During these operation substantial quantity of dust is generated at various stages. The results of a sieve analysis are as follows

- After primary crushing about 2% of the stone crushed is dust of size less than 150u, fine part of this dust can get airborne during material movement or transfer.

FACTORS THAT INFLUENCES EMISSIONS

Factors affecting emissions that are common to most operations include moisture content of the rock, type of rock processed, type of equipment, and operating practices employed. These factors apply to both process (primary) sources and fugitive (secondary)dust in quarry and plant operations.

Depending on geographic and climatic conditions, the inherent moisture content or wetness of quarried rock may range from nearly zero percent to several percent. The effect of moisture content is especially important during quarrying, material handling, and initial plant process operations such as primary crushing. Surface wetness causes fine particles to agglomerate or adhere to the faces of larger stones, resulting in a dust suppression effect. However, as new fine particles are created by crushing and attrition and moisture content is reduced by evaporation , this suppressive effect diminishes and may even insignificant.

The type of rock processed is also important. Soft rock produces a higher percentage of fines than do hard rocks because they are more friable. Therefore, processing of soft rocks has greater potential for emissions. The type of equipment and operating practices employed also affect uncontrolled emissions. Equipment selection is based on a variety of parameters, including quarry characteristics, rock type processed, and desired and products. Emissions from process equipment such as crushers, screens, and conveyors are generally a function of the size distribution of the material, and the amount of mechanically induced velocity imparted to it.

The crushing operation is similar in almost all the units except the variation in the type of crushers, their capacity and number. Most units predominantly use Jaw Crushers as primary, secondary or tertiary crushers. Very few units employ high production rate crushers such as Rotopoctors, Impactors, etc., to achieve highest production rates or to met specific shape/size requirements.

ADVERSE IMPACTS DUE TO DUST EMISSIONS

Some percentage of the fugitive dust emissions may get settled down within the unit's premises itself, but a substantial percentage of airborne emissions are carried away to the surrounding places by wind currents. Dust settled within the plant gets airborne again due to vehicular movement or by wind and acts as a secondary emission source. Dust settled over the equipment may cause rapid wear and tear of the rotating parts and may lead to frequent breakdowns and highest maintenance costs.

The work environment in some selected industries like Jute processing and Stone-Crushing units clearly indicate continuous violating of prescribed norms. The high concentration of dust in jute processing units continue to pose health hazards specially lung ailments of the workers. The death of workers in stone crusher units in Medinipur and subsequent ruling of the Supreme Court had led the State Pollution Control Board to issue a 9 point directive to all units in West Bengal to guarantee health safety to the workers. A first hand study during the present project in 25 units in Mallarpur in Birbhum district showed total violation of the directives without any penalty or closure notice. (Status of Environment in West Bengal (September 1998) env.information system dept. of env., W.bengal)

Environmental Protection, Training, Research Institute (EPTRI), Hyderabad Study reveals that the farmers in and around stone crushers at Srikalahasti in Chittoor district are afraid to work on their own fields because of flying stone missiles from the blasting. The crusher owners do not follow any timings in resorting to blasting neither do they announce in advance. There are schools nearby. But no precaution is taken. Children are scared to go to school. There are many people and animals in this area have been severely injured by these flying stones. There are cases of people losing their limbs. There are also cases of animal mortality because of this blasting. Once a mine of stone is closed it ought to be filled up. But that is not taking place. This is leading to many accidents animals and people die when they fall in to these mined pits, either in search of water or by accident. Blasting in the mines is one of the sources of these accidents. But they are not reported.

Centre for Resources and Environment (CRE) study finds that Rock quarrying and stone crushing is a global phenomenon, and has been the cause of concern everywhere, including in countries like Singapore, Lebanon, united states, Pakistan and Israel. Frequent blasting is causing noise problems as well as vibrations resulting in damages the houses and other structures nearby. Dust emissions affect the climate; damage the material, human health, and vegetation.

The physical properties of atmospheric particulates affect human health either by allowing penetration of the lung and causing irritation to the internal membrane, or by transporting absorbed toxic gases and vapors deeper into the lung than they would normally travel. The work place environment at stone crushers sites contain millions of suspended mineral particles of respirable size that get deposited in lungs following inhalation.

National Institute of Occupational Health (NIOH) study explains that Silicosis is the commonest and one of the most serious occupational diseases. It is irreversible fibrosis of the lungs caused by inhalation of free silica dust. It is estimated that about 3 million people working in various types of mines, ceramics, potteries, foundries, metal grinding, Stone Crushing, agate grinding, slate pencil industry etc., are occupationally exposed to free silica dust and are at potential risk of developing silicosis. Silica exposure also predisposes to development of pulmonary tuberculosis, which is an important public health problem in the country. Some of the landmark studies carried out by NIOH are as follows.

An environmental and epidemiological survey carried out in stone quarry workers revealed evidence of silicosis in 22.4% workers. About 32% workers showed radiological evidence of tuberculosis. Most of the cases of silicosis were found in the workers who had worked for over 10 years.

TB Control And Training Centre, Nagpur study reveals that Stone quarry workers from an unorganized sector of industry scattered all over India. Various procedures and operations are involved in the work viz. stone cutting, loading and crushing. Based on these operations, the workers are employed at different places as per the nature of work and are exposed to silica dust of different concentrations. The health impact of the working conditions and environmental factors in stone quarry industry have been well documented and therefore, a very high degree of respiratory morbidity is associated with this industry. Moreover as the workers are exposed to silica dust over a long term, a considerable lung function impairment in this group of workers is reported in the literature. The present study was therefore, designed to evaluate the respiratory effects of occupational exposure t silica dust in stone quarry workers. A very large extent of respiratory morbidity and lung function impairment is observed in this group of employees. It can be concluded from this study that even low dust level exposure for longer duration can result in lung and lung function involvement. Hence stone quarry workers, because of their occupational exposure to silica dust, are at increased risk of lung and lung function involvement.

National Environmental Engineering Research Institute (NEERI), Nagpur in an interesting observation found that India is a source of high levels of dust generation in the vicinity of the stone crushers and in the communities surrounding them. Ambient air quality network consisting of 26 sampling locations were operated to continuously monitor the total and respirable particulate matter concentrations. Both ambient concentrations and occupational exposure levels exceeded the Indian national standards at most of the locations. Pulmonary function tests performed on workers showed that the average values of pulmonary function in these workers are significantly lower than the average values reported for normal south Indian healthy males.

Stone crushing in India is basically a labor intensive small scale industry where most of the operations are performed manually. Very little information is currently available regarding dust emissions from these units, associated occupational exposures, and the baseline respiratory health status of workers. During the stone crushing operation large size stone, mined from quarries in the size range of 200-300 mm, is crushed to smaller usable sizes, generally 6,12,25 mm. many crushed stone operations tend to be located relatively near populated areas or on the highways to avoid high transportation costs. This can result in dust associated health problems along the highways. The risks of accidents are increased when the crushers are located near the highway. In the absence of proper control devices these units, the work place can become highly polluted.(cpcb,1984)

As per NEERI's 1998 estimate, there are 1191 units with low capital investment in the state of Tamil Nadu, of which only 16 are reported to be located in industrial areas and 190 units are located along the national or state highways and the remaining 985 units are located in the residential area. The large number of stone crushers distributed all over the Tamil Nadu state in India, pose the problems of dust concentrations in the form of a heavy siliceous dust cloud produced during the various operations of crushing, impaired visibility, and potential harm to human health and the surrounding vegetation.

The occupational environment at the stone crushing sites poses a potential health hazard to the workers, since inhalation of particles rich in free silica for long periods of time may cause silicosis. Exposure to heavy dust concentration from stone crushers, may produce several diseases, chief among them being pneumoconiosis. Silicosis, caused by inhalation of dust containing silica, is an important form of this disease. Respiratory damage resulting from such exposures can range from reversible functional changes to irreversible damage to the lungs, and in, some extreme exposures, causes lung cancer. The human respiratory system can remove large particles, and the present ambient air quality standard based on the mass concentration of the suspended particulate matter, is poorly related to the actual pollutant burden on exposed individuals. Hence, particle size is the most important factor in determining the rate of deposition and its potential for adverse effects on health and visibility.

This sector employs rural, migrant, and unskilled workers and often provides only seasonal employment. High turnover, exploitative managements, and low socio-economic status with limited access to health, education, and housing have resulted in lack of programs to address workers health and safety in this sector. Since workers also reside close to these units, environmental and occupational exposures coexist and increase vulnerability of all members of the community to health impacts. Although a few earlier studies have recognized the potential for environmental health impacts in this sector, little is known about the baseline situation with respect to exposures and respiratory health status in this cluster.

The primary objective of this study was to assess the dust concentration and its fallout in and around the workplace and assess pulmonary function of workers in this cluster of stone crushing units so as to understand their environmental health profile. For this purpose an extensive air pollution survey was carried out in the study area.

The dust generated from stone crushing activities contains a significant amount of tiny inhalable matter. The effect of fine particulate matter can be disproportionately large even though it constitutes only a small fraction of the total suspended particulate matter. The presence of a high percentage of silica in the dust and the particle size distribution further suggest that the occupational environment of the workers and surrounding areas may be hazardous to human health. Air quality and health survey conducted at the site indicate that the observed dust may be producing significant damage to respiratory health. The study through a combination of extensive air quality assessment and a limited set of health assessment has pointed out the imminent need for a comprehensive occupational and environmental health management strategy for this type of essential small scale industries and it is hoped that the information presented here will be used to provide additional impetus to environmental policy measures for this sector. The results of the study have provided a detailed baseline assessment of dust exposures prevalent in this sector and an imminent need for implementing environmental controls in this important occupational sector.

When the total amount of particulates in the atmosphere increases, particulates may absorb incoming solar radiation, causing an increase in the atmospheric and land surface temperature.

Particulate air pollution is a heterogeneous classification of liquid and solid aerosols which includes anthropogenic emissions from fuel combustion and high temperature industrial processes. Smaller particles include viruses and some bacteria, but mostly come from anthropogenic sources, including sulfate and nitrate aerosols and other combustion derived atmospheric reaction products. Whereas larger particles include pollen, spores, crustal dusts, and other Mechanically Generated Dusts. Size is a critical determinant of deposition site, with larger particles tending to deposit in the nasal and tracheobronchial regions, the smaller particles penetrating deeper into the lungs. Regional air pollution exacerbations may be due to intermediate and long range troposheric transport in addition to local influences such strong emission sources, proximity to heavily used roadways, stagnant air masses, and local weather temperature inversions. Effects such as smog, climate change are a few of known consequences through air emissions.

Air constitutes about eighty percent of the man's daily intake by weight. We breathe about 2200 times a day, inhaling around 16kg. of air. It is therefore essential that we know more about the atmosphere and the ways in which it is polluted. Increasing industrialization and urbanization have created growing demands to use the atmosphere as a waste disposal medium. Thus the accumulation of waste gases and particles from economic activities exceeds the natural dispersion capacity of the atmosphere. When air movements are unable to disperse wastes as the rate they enter the atmosphere, air quality deteriorates and the seemingly infinite supply of clean air diminishes. Thus air is polluted.

Particulate mater suspended in the air is one of the most noticeable of air pollutants and consists of chemically stable substances such as dust. These pollutants are classified as primary pollutants because they do not change their form after entering the atmosphere. Besides industrial fuels, building materials also disperse articulates into the atmosphere.

It has been found that accumulation of dust particles has the opposite effect of carbon dioxide, rather then warming the earth, an increase in dustiness, reduces the amount of solar energy that reaches the earth's surface, thus resulting in a cooling of the atmosphere. It is estimated that a rise of 3.6 degree centigrade in earth's temperature would make ice caps in the Antarctica and the arctic melt. On the other hand there are others who think that the cooling brought about by increasing dust particles will create another ice age. This needs a temperature drop of 4 degree centigrade only. In sum, we can say that an increase in the carbon dioxide content of the atmosphere, an increase in the amount of aerosols i.e., dust thermal pollution and other activities of this highly urbanized world, could disturb the earth's heat balanced climate.

With the deposition of aerosols on materials, especially buildings, although little damage is caused to the materials, the effect is expensive to remove deposited particulates which damages vegetation by preventing them from photosynthesis. An assessment of the biological characteristics of some plant species in and around quarrying and crushing areas of Bangalore District was carried out. Chlorophyll concentration differed significantly with control in most cases and a few samples possessed high proline content. A reduction in leaf area was also observed. These changes are mainly attributed to the accumulation of dust as per the study made on *impact of granaite mining on some plant species around quarries and crushers of bangalore district.*

An interesting study conducted by *nalanda college, biharishariff. envfor.nic.in.* The study area was confined to the maize crop situated in the prevailing wind direction of stone crusher, Karwandiya, Rohtas, Bihar to know the impact of dust on the biomass and chlorophyll content. The biomass was found to be higher at each sampling date of the control maize plant than the polluted ones.

Dust affects visibility too and causes road accidents it since most of these stone crusher clusters are set up along the national highways. *It is dark even at midnoon* on the Mukerian-Pathankot national highway due to dust from stone crushing units situated along the highway. Dust that emanates from stone crushing units along the highway at times is so thick that it becomes difficult to negotiate the path. Besides stone crushers clouds of dust also hover on the road due to trucks carrying material from the stone crushers.

According to Punjab pollution control board guidelines the roads leading to the stone crushing units should be metalled. The crushing units are also directed to spray water around the premises to minimize the dust emanating there. However, due to lax attitude of the Punjab Pollution Control Board (ppcb) authorities none of the stone crushing units has been following the norms. The result is high level of pollution right along the highway. A year ago Himachal High Court ordered the closure of all stone crushing units located in the Damtal area on the said road till the units adhered to the ppcb norms. Following the high court's order the Himachal government ordered closure of some units that were not following the pollution guidelines.

The authorities were not taking action against the units functioning illegally. The units functioning in the Punjab territory were more blatant in violating the norms, as the ppcb had turned a blind eye toward their illegal functioning. According to the ppcb norms the Suspended Particulate Matter (spm) emitted by a stone crushing unit should exceed 600ug/ m3. Keeping in view dust clouds it seems the said maximum norm for spm was being violated blatantly. The sources told that the high-level of pollution around the stone crushing units was affecting health of the workers. Workers and people residing in the areas surrounding units were suffering from respiratory problems. According to practice stone crushing units should get health of their workers monitored regularly. However, due to lack of supervising authority no such check up was being conducted.

The units have been prohibited from dumping waste material near the road. However, the waste material can be seen lying along the national highway. The waste material adds to pollution as it spreads in the air with the passing vehicles.

PREVALENT ENVIRONMENTAL MANAGEMENT SCENARIO IN STONE CRUSHERS

Though environmental legislation for stone crushers for control of emissions exist, the existing environmental management scenario is far from satisfactory. This could be primarily due to factors such as lack of availability of low cost and appropriate dust control system, lack of pressure from the regulatory authorities, lack of willingness and awareness in unit owners, and lack of awareness in the affected general public living in surrounding areas. However, some units have taken steps to improve environmental scenario by way of providing containments, water sprays, developing green belts, etc., The types of measures adopted predominantly are briefly described below:

DUST CONTAINMENT MEASURES

Some units provide partial enclosures for the vibratory screen area. These enclosures are partial sheets or used gunny bag clothes. Window door type openings are provided for accommodating conveyor belts and for maintenance purposes. Some units have enclosures only for housing the screen while some units have enclosures covering even the bottom discharge ends.

Some units provide partial enclosures covering conveyor belts form the top and sides, which also act as protection from sunrays and rain.

Some units have installed storage hoppers for the storage of products and direct loading in trucks. This reduces secondary dust emissions which occur from open area stockpile.

REASONS FOR INADEQUACY OF DUST CONTAINMENT MEASURES

In general, most of the units have provided partial enclosures, leaving open various openings. The dust escapes through these openings. In the absence of water sprays prior to screening, only the enclosure is not expected to control dust emissions adequately.

DUST SUPPRESSION MEASURES

Many stone crushers have one or other type of water spray arrangements, but due to reasons like choking of spray holes, inadequate water pressure, lack of water or too much consumption of water etc., majority of the stone crushers are unable to operate the water sprays. The water generally drawn from bore wells dug within the premises.

REASONS FOR INADEQUACY OF PREVALNT WATER SPRAY SYSTEMS

Most of the water tanks do not have covered surface and as a result fine dust keeps entering the water tank. There is no filter arrangement to clean the water of dust. Over a period of time this dust gets into the pipes and blocks the holes thereby blocking the spray formation. As a result excessive water is put on the stone . This increases moisture content in the stone which adversely affects product quality. The gravity head provided by the elevated water tank is not sufficient enough to enable spray formation, as the pressure head is not sufficient. Also, due to the absence of appropriate spray nozzles, the spray formation is not fine but coarse. For suppressing airborne dust very fine water droplets are required which can suppress the fine dust. The manual spraying of water on stone though suppresses dust during unloading excessive water gets added to the stones without desirable effect. The water sprinklers are hardly effective for suppressing dust because by the time the dust emissions reach the boundary of the unit the dust gets sprayed in wider area, beyond the capture limit of any sprinkler sprays. It only wets the ground area and excessive operation of sprinklers may even create muddy ground conditions. Also, the water sprinklers consume large quantity of water.

WIND BREAKING MEASURES

Green Belt

Most of the permanently located units have planted trees along the periphery of the premises which forms a green belt. However, the width of the green belt, leafiness and density of the trees, etc., varies widely from place to place. In most places, trees are planted and then left solely to the nature. Some units do provide proper fertilizers and water etc.,

Wind Breaking Walls

Some of the units have wind breaking walls erected in a V-shape alongside the stockpiles. Some units have wind breaking walls made of corrugated GI sheets along the boundary of the premises in the predominant wind direction. Most units do not have adequate wind breaking wall arrangement.

Ambient Air Quality Scenario

Based on ambient air quality monitoring studies carried out in many units for generating information on the existing level of emissions from uncontrolled or partially controlled stone crushing operations, the following ambient air quality scenario has emerged. The suspended particulate matter in the ambient air at the crusher sites range from 2340 to 24000ug/-. Which is substantially higher than the desirable limits.

CLEANER PRODUCTION POSSIBILITIES IN STONE CRUSHING UNITS

Keeping in view of the economic and social importance of this unorganized sector and the gravity of environmental problems associated, it is urgently required to take large-scale iniatives to achieve cleaner production. Various state governments have already initiated such initiatives by way of demonstrating cleaner production in few stone crushers. It is likely that after visualizing the improvements other stone crushers may adopt such cleaner production practices. Typically to achieve cleaner production following things need to be done:

- Modification of existing layout and material flow to reduce dust generation.
- Improvements in crushers and screens to increase their efficiency.
- Provision of adequate dust containment enclosures.
- Provision of appropriate dust suppression system.
- Provision of metalled roads within the unit premises.
- Development of green belt around the periphery of the unit.

The details of the above proposed modifications are briefly described below:

DUST CONTAINMENT ENCLOSURE

Dust containment enclosures are required for the purpose of containing the emissions within an enclosure and to prevent wind currents, which can spread the dust to larger areas. Such enclosures are recommended for the following locations.

Primary crusher discharge area, Vibratory Screen, Product storage hoppers, conveyor belts

The enclosures should be complete from all the four sides and roof. There should not be an open windows, openings etc. Any opening should be kept closed during operation. The gap should be sealed using gaskets or wool type packing etc.,

ADEQUATE DUST SUPPRESSION SYSTEM

The dust suppression system should comprises a covered water storage tank, a pump, an online water filter, connecting GI pipes, spray nozzles each fitted with flow regulating valves etc., The storage water tank should be cover from top, with a manhole type provision with cover for maintenance provision. Atmospheric dust should not enter into the tank. The tank should be located at the ground level. Water from bore well could be pumped to fill the tank periodically. The pump should be a centrifugal monobloc type self-priming pump. Pump should be installed on the water tank. The water filter unit should have two parallel cells so that while one cell is in operation, the other cell could be under backwash cleaning. Subsequently, the connections can be reversed such that the choked filter could be put in for backwash cleaning and the clean filter is put online. The filters should not be opened frequently for cleaning purposes and only online backwash cleaning should be adhered to. The filter may have about 100 stainless steel mesh for adequate filtration. Only the filtered water should be supplied to the spray nozzles. The filter is essential otherwise the dirt in the water may choke the nozzles, which would affect the spray and thereby affecting the efficiency of the dust suppression system.

The spray nozzles should be appropriated selected as per the requirement of spray such as coverage, fineness, installation limitations and space etc. Mainly, two types of nozzles could be used., namely full cone type nozzle or impingement type nozzle. The sprays should be located as close to the points of missions as possible such that the dust is suppressed at the source itself, before it spreads into larger area. The recommended locations where sprays could be located are:

- On the stones while unloading from the truck dumper
- At the primary crusher feeder chut
- At the secondary/tertiary crusher inlet chut and hoppers
- At the transfer points from one conveyor belt to another
- At crusher discharge points, if necessary

It may be noted that, water is not required to be sprayed at the vibratory screen area. The water gets automatically evaporated over a period of time due to atmospheric heat.

CLEANER PRODUCTION SCHEMES AND RESULTS

It has been measured that implementation of cleaner production schemes in stone crusher units could lead to substantial reduction in ambient SPM levels by about 88% and more. A few of the benefits achieved through implementation of cleaner production schemes are highlighted below:

- Significant reduction in dust emission
- Significant reduction in adverse impacts on human health
- Reduced breakdowns of rotating equipment
- Reduced accident hazards
- improved morale among the work force and thereby increase in productivity and reduction in down time of the maintenance of the stone crushing unit Motivation to the unit to go for expansion of the existing plant.
- Happy work fore due to reduced health hazards
- Improved environmentally friendly image of the unit in the local region.

CONCLUSIONS

Most of the stone crushers in the country have inadequate dust control system. Smaller units mostly have neither enclosures nor water spaying arrangements. As a result, the dust emissions are substantial which leads to adverse impacts on workers as well as the surrounding environment. The dust emissions from the stone crushers are measured to be in the range of 2300 to 36000ug. The existing control measures such as dust containment enclosures, water spray arrangements etc., are generally found to be inadequate, largely due to reasons like inadequate availability. The cleaner production schemes are low cost ones and therefore, should be adopted by all stone crusher units. Environmental management scenario in the stone crusher industry sector can be substantially improved through adoption of cleaner production schemes. This would also increase the productivity of these units by way of reduced dust generation, reduced energy consumption, lesser breakdowns leading to increased plant availability.

REFERENCES

Aigbedion, I and Iyasi, S.E. (2005), "Environmental Effect of Mineral Exploitation in Nigeria" Ambrose Alli University, Ekpoma-Nigeria.

Book on "Integration of Endogenous Cultural dimension into Development "(1997), IGNCA and DK Print world Pvt Ltd.- compilation of 17 presentations of a UNESCO sponsored workshop 19-23 april, 1995 at IGNCA, New Delhi, "Voluntary Action and Alternative Developmnet in Tribal Areas" by Sachchidananda.

M.A. Patil (2001), National Productivity Council,New Delhi,(2001) " Environmental Management Scenario in Stone Crusher Industry Sector and Cleaner Production Possibilities", TERI,VOL.6, No.2, Dec.

M.N. Samdani, (21st Nov, 2002), "Stone Crushing Industries Flout Pollution Norms", Times of India.

Naik DP, Ushamalini, Somashekar R.K. (2005), Jnana Bharathi, Bangalore University, Bangalore) "Reduction of Protein and Chlorophyll Contents in Some Plant Species due to Some Stone Quarrying Activity" Environ Polln Contl J,8(2) (2005),42-44

Nick, Kevin E. (2004), "Crushed Stone Industries and Respirable Dust in Southern India", Geological Society of America Abstracts with Programs, Vol. 36, No. 5, p.126

R. Sivacoumar, R. Jayabalou, S. Swarnalatha, K. Balakrishnan (March,2006), "Particulate Matter from Stone Crushing Industry: Size Distribution and Health Effects" J. Envir.engg., Vol.132, Issue 3, pp.405-414

Ruchika M. Khanna (March, 30th, 2005), "Stone Crushers Violate Pollution Control Norms", Tribune News Service.

V.B. Ghotkar, B.R. Maldhure, S.P. Zodpey (1995), "Involvement of Lung and Lung Function Tests in Stone quarry Workers", Indian J. Tub., 42,155.

World Bank Project, "Stone Crushing Industry in Gujarat".

SECTION - IV

Law & Government Policy and Environment

41

ENVIRONMENTAL CRISIS: GLOBAL PROBLEMS AND LOCAL SOLUTIONS

Sudhakar Panda

United Nation's "World Summit on "Sustainable Development" held at Johannesburg in August 2002 was attended by as many as 21,000 delegates from all over the world. Presidents, Ministers, Political dignitaries, Environmental activities, business representatives from energy companies, bank, aluminium company, oil and mining companies and non-governmental groups participated in deliberations to design policies and restructure international production, trade, and aid-packages from the rich countries to the poor nations to create a better, healthier, secure and beautiful world with less (if not totally free) of poverty, pollution ecological degradation and less of diseases and human misery. To make the world safe enough for sustainable development.

In fact ".....the great race between development and degradation ...." And our efforts to achieve a harmonious blending of growth with ecological balance, economic policies with environmental protection, and reconcile the greens with business interests and the growing demands of mankind with sustainable development have come to occupy the center stage of world agenda on future development and ecological change. The Stockholm Conference (1972) made an effort to create a world-wide public awareness of the need to harmonize development and environment and create a framework for sustainable development. The UNEP Report (The State of the Environment, 1972-82) focused mankind's attention on environmental crisis and ecological degradation in the developing countries. The Brandt Commission (1983) Report "Common Crisis" urged that prevention of destruction of environment as something of "Common Interest" for the countries in the North and South. It expressed the concern "Growing pressure on the available land, increasing use of chemicals, desert expansion and deforestation are diminishing the productivity of soil in many parts of the world. The clearance of forests, incautious use of chemicals and fertilizers and erosion destroy the soil and the agricultural potential of scarce land and serious damage to environment. We therefore emphasize the need for means with the help of which these processes of ecological decay which in the meanwhile reached emergency proportions must be stopped and reversed". What the Brandt Commission says in its report about development and degradation and loss of environment is very much visible in India, and in any of the regions in South or North India.

The Brundtland Report "Our Common Future" called for institutional approach to find solutions to the problem. In its words, "Governments must begin now to make the key national economic and sectoral agencies directly responsible and fully accountable for ensuring that their policies, programmes and budgets support development that is ecologically as well as economically sustainable. The regional organizations in particular need to do more to integrate environment fully in their goals and activities. All major international bodies and agencies should ensure that their programmes and budgets encourage and support sustainable development".

The message is clear. All international bodies, national governments, regional authorities and even local councils have to work for sustainable development and ecological balance.

"Global 2000" Report (1980) on aspects of pollution, "Economic and Ecological Interdependence" Report (1982) on the "Interrelationship between economies and ecology", "The Global Possible" Report (1964) on future resources of the World, UN Conference "Earth Summit" in Rio Janerio (1992) on environment, the Kyoto Protocol (1998) on global warming and the Summit on Sustainable Development" at Johannesburg (2002) have addressed themselves to economic, environmental, and ecological problems in the developed and more particularly in the developing nations.

Economists may, however, look at these problems of poverty, hunger, health hazards, pollution, land degradation and miserable living of people in the developing nations as the result of under development and population explosion. Their emphasis therefore would be on population planning and accelerated development that would bring relief to the poor and enhance their standard of living. Development and higher development may provide the panacea to poverty and environmental hazards. The strength of this approach lies in the evidence available in the developed countries where the levels of pollution and green house effects get reduced with growing affluence. Development and environment are inversely related. Poverty and environmental hazards are positively inter linked. This is well expressed by late Julian Simon, "One of the greatest trend of the past 100 years has been the astonishing rate of progress in reducing every form of pollution" (It is Getting Better All the Time - Economist, 6th- 12 July 2002). It gives the message that with growth the developing countries will grow greener.

Bjorn Lombarg, a statistician by profession, gave rise to a bitter controversy about development and ecology with the publication of his book "The Skeptical Environmentalist" (2002). Lombarg, on the basis of evidence argues that (I) known reserves of fossil fuels and metals have increased, (II) agricultural production per head has grown appreciable, (III) The threat to loss of bio-diversity and tropical forests though real is exaggerated and (IV) Pollution level declines with higher development. (Economist; February 2, 2002). Remedy for environmental problems lies in higher and faster development.

Not with standing what Lombarg says, the world to-day suffers from a declining environmental quality, lifestyles, consumption standards and material well-being enjoyed by the people in the West cannot be made available for the people in Asia, Latin America and Africa. The planet earth does not have unlimited resources to provide American lifestyle to every Asian, Latin American or African. Viewed against the "U.S. consumption as a percentage of world total: aluminium, 42 percent; chromium, 19 percent; coal, 44 percent; cobalt, 32 percent; copper, 33 percent; gold, 22 percent; iron, 28 percent; lead, 25 percent; manganese, 14 percent; mercury, 24 percent; molybdenum, 40 percent; natural gas, 63 percent; nickel, 38 percent; petroleum, 33 percent; platinum group, 31 percent, silver, 26 percent; tin, 24 percent; tungsten, 22 percent, zinc, 22 percent." Can the developing nations afford to compete with the United States to acquire these resources for their use? What Mahatma Gandhi said more than half a century ago should come as words of caution to all developing countries? "God forbid that India should ever take to industrialize after the manner of the West. It took Britain half the resources of the planet to achieve this prosperity. How many planets will a country like India require"? What Lombarg say may be true of the rich and affluent countries but should not misguide the poor nations to destroy their resources to achieve the American quality of life.

Where does the solution lie? In imitating of the West blindly? In living a simple life? Or in following the middle path: a reasonable good quality life? (Which again is difficult to define?) There is perhaps no universal answer to these questions. We can hardly reach a consensus on these sensitive issues; particularly in the context of ever increasing consumerism at the individual level. Globalization of the Indian economy makes it all the more difficult.

But then how do we look at environmental problems in our regions in our towns and in out villages? I look at some of the following problems in Orissa;

INFRASTRUCTURE, HOUSING AND GREENERIES

Construction of a four-way national highway (parts completed and open to traffic) will be of great help to people and automobile industry. Travel time will be reduced. New generation cars will play. This, however, has resulted in cutting down thousands of old, huge and living trees, many of who were 200 years old. We need high-speed roads. We also need Greeneries. In fact we need both.

Expansion of housing schemes in Orissan cities has also led to rapid disappearance of greeneries. Lush green areas have been converted to housing plots.

WATER POLLUTION

Major rivers in Orissa carry polluted water. Brahmani is the worst polluted river in the State. Release of chemical wastes, industrial pollutants, sewerage water and wastage's in to Mahanandi, Brahmani and other rivers have been causing health hazards and depletion of fish stock. Even the large tanks in the holy city of Puri are highly polluted.

WATER BORNE DISEASES

People in rural areas, particularly in tribal regions like Mayurbanj suffer from water borne diseases. Non-availability of safe drinking water and the use of stagnant and polluted water for domestic purpose contribute to such ailments. It begins with slow fever, ends with death. Such deaths are still attributed to supernatural deaths.

HIGH INCIDENCE OF AIR POLLUTION (CO2)

Cities and towns in Orissa have been witnessing a phenomenal growth in the number of vehicles. Old and polluting vehicles from the neighboring states and eve from Delhi and Haryana find a market in Orissa. Old cars, buses, trucks and three-wheelers, because of inefficient burning of fossil fuels contribute to air pollution. Loss of trees, increased transport along with the growth of high rise buildings may partly explain the rise in temperature in Bhuvaneswar.

LOSS OF FORESTS

There is a steady loss of dense forest area in the state. Area under forest cover declined from 38 percent in 1981 to 37.3 percent in 1991. Even during 1991-2001 there is a great fall in the size of forests. Similar trends can be observed even during 2001-2009. Along with the loss of forest area, many of the important genetic species found earlier in the Gandhamardhan range of hills are also lost. Not only that this also causes a loss of sources of livelihood for the tribals.

LOSS OF BIO-DIVERSITY IN RURAL AREAS

Ever increasing use of fertilizers, chemicals and pesticides in agriculture though gives higher output causes great damage to land, water, bio-diversity and atmosphere. There is land degradation, water pollution and loss of living organisms like worms, fish, crabs, birds and animals. Added to conversion of land to prawn cultivation causes loss of bio-diversity and ecological harm. This may ultimately affect "the foundations essential for sustainable food security, such as land, water, bio-diversity, forests and the atmosphere".

These are some of the environment problems Orissa faces today; similar problems may also exist in other states. Do we have solutions to the loss of trees, loss greeneries, increased water pollution, air pollution, deforestation and loss of bio-diversity? Can we think of an institutional cum legal approach to tackle these problems? Will it be feasible for the State Pollution Boards, urban bodies like the Municipalities, corporations to have strict enforcement of existing rules and regulations about industrial pollution, housing development, sewerage disposal and development of greeneries? Can there be regular checks on vehicles to measure their emissions? Can we entrust the Panchayats in villages with development of social forestry, protection of standing trees in government land and protection of species? An Indian villager will not understand the global threat to environment, but he will immediately react to the loss of trees and pollution of village tank water. Can we launch a campaign to make the villagers conscious of the long-term sustainability of agriculture? NGOs and the rural youth can play a role to safeguard our environment. It may therefore be necessary to have joint participation between the government private sector and the NGOs to preserve, protect and promote our environment.

REFERENCES

The Economist, January 18th–24th, 2003, September 7th–13th 2002, August 31st–Sept 6th, 2002, July 6th–12th 2002, May 11th–17th 2002, February 2nd–8th 2002.

Government of Orissa (2001), Economic Survey, 2000-01.

Hartje, Volkmar J. (1987), Environmental Problems in the Third World. What can the North do"? Economics, Vol. 35 pp.67-86.

Pearce, Joseph (2001), Small is Still Beautiful, Harper Collins, London.

Samulson, Paul A. Noardhaus, William D. (1995), Economics, Mc.Graw-Hill, New York.

Saxena, N.C. (2002), "Forests in India: People and Trees" Survey of the Environment, The Hindu.

Simonis, Udo Ernst (1984), "Environmental Crisis–The Missing Dimension in the North-South Dialogue". Economic Vol.39 pp.39-53.

Swaminathan, M.S. (2002), "Agriculture" Survey of the Environment, pp. 33-41, The Hindu.

42

THE ENVIRONMENTAL SECURITY THREATS AND THE RESPONSIBILITY OF THE NATIONS

N. Namasivayam, S.P. Kanaga Anubuselvam

In this paper an attempt has been made to study on about the need for environmental security, and the current threats to the environmental security and the policies and responsibilities of the nations to issue such security.

THREE MAIN DIAMENSIONS

- The need of Environmental Security.
- The threats to the security.
- The policies and responsibilities to issue the security.

The gradual deteoriation of the environment lends compelling weight to the need to find balance between human development and exploitation of natural resources. Department of environmentally efficient technologies, participation of the individual, and a change in a thinking and behavior should help guide us to a sustainable path of ecological stability, bearing in mind the equity and justice ought to prevail within and between human generations.

Environmental Degradation' and 'Environmental Refugees' are found in Third World Nations. Some examples are as follows:

- Only half of the worlds population breathes healthy air;
- Less than half of the worlds rural population has clean water;
- The annual increase in the world's food production is only half the world's population growth.
- Millions of tones of hazardous waste flood the environment every year.
- And about a hundred species of plants and animals are predicted to disappear every year.

The Need for Environmental Security

Environmental security is an increasing issue in world affairs. The definition of security centers around two central concepts and about a hundred species of plants and animals are predicted to disappear every year.

Environmental security is the relative safety from environmental damages caused by natural or human processes due to ignorance, accident, mismanagement or design and originating within or across national boarders. It also refers to the state of human - environment dynamics that includes restoration of the environment damaged by military actions, and amelioration of resource scarcities, environmental degradation and biological threats that could lead to social disorder and conflict.

The Three General Categories Of Environmental Threat Are As Follows.

(i) Concerns about the direct and indirect efforts of various forms of environmental change, which may be natural or human-generated on national and regional security.

(ii) Concern about the adverse impact of human activities on the environment.

(iii) Concerns about the insecurity individuals and groups experience due to environmental change such as

- Water Scarcity
- Air Pollution

- Global Warming
- Ozone Depletion
- Nuclear Safety Issues
- Ground Water Contamination
- Deforestation
- Environmental Refugees

POLICIES OF LEADERSHIP RESPONCIBILITY TO MAINTAIN ENVIRONMENTAL SECURITY

1. UN agencies should lead but the implementation requires all levels and all divisions within national bureaucracies to instigate reform. It has to be an integral part of nation's foreign policy. It cannot be pursued in isolation by lower level organizations. Therefore national governments should lead in policy development.
2. Most MNEs in Africa sponsor numerous conservation projects or game parks.
3. NGO's can play useful roles as stakeholders and lobbying groups.
4. Research by academic institutes with findings spread by mass media will help people understand the mechanisms and responsibilities associated with environment security, and mobilize the masses to form ideologies to take care of the environment.
5. Sustainable development is a key aspect of the condition of environment security, and
6. Should be promoted through a variety of mechanisms including education, steering national economics with tax and subsidy programs, promoting green technology innovation, diffusion and implementation and strengthening Multilateral Environmental Agreements (MEAs).
7. All the organizations should set internal policies on how to deal with a variety of these situations. In the case of militaries and the Governmental intelligence communities,

their policies should be reflecting the boarder policy direction set-forth by the political leadership and in co-ordination with civilian agency policies.

8. Environmental security should be part of all ministries and organizations, although during the initial steps the existence of a dedicated organization would be beneficial to act like on "engine" for the implementation of environmental security. Government should assume the responsibility of protection of public resources and environments.
9. At national level, the Ministry of Environment should be given more importance for environment and sustainable development.

Environmental information and education should be founded by advanced states. UNEP play a key role in upgrading data standards, making information available and supporting environmental education. New electronic media, such as Internet will play increasingly important roles in terms of promoting awareness and communication.

STRATEGIES SUGGESTED FOR IMPROVING ENVIRONMENTAL SECURITY IN DEVELOPING NATIONS

1. To conclude, one of the biggest contributions the developed world can make towards environmental security at all levels is through strengthened commitment to foreign assistance and technology transfer to the development world.
2. Countries with weaker capacities to participate in international agreements need to be technically strengthened so that they are equal players at the fable. In particular, the countries need technical and about a hundred species of plants and animals are predicted to disappear every year capacity to monitor the deal with environmental change more proactively should be substituted for resorting to conflict.

Table 1
The Environmental Threats can be given in a Table Form

By Ignorance/ or Mismanagement	*By Intention*	*Mix of National and Human Activities*			
Within a Country 1. Oil spills in Ogoniland Nigeria.	1. Sarin gas attack in Tokyo subway	1. Flood	Transborder 1. Rain forest depletion	1. Boiling oil fields in Kuwait	1. Solar ration change
2. Aral Sea Depletion in Russia	2. Chemical attacks in Iraq	2. Famines	2. River usage (Jordan, Nile, Tigris Euphrates)	2. Biological weapons	2. AIDS and other diseases
3. Indonesian fires	3. Poisoning or diversion or misuse of water resource	3. Stalinization	3. Chernobyl nuclear accident		3. Global warming
4. Ground water contamination and fresh ware scarcity		4. Earthquakes	4. Ozone depletion		4. Population Growth
5. Soil erosion			5. Acid Rain and ir Pollution		
6. Human settlement and development patterns			6. Radio active waste		

REFERENCES

Project Report.

American Council for the United Nations University, The Millennium Project 2001, State of the Future, Jerome C. Glenn and Theodore J. Gordon, Volume I & II.

Books

Environment Managemet (2000), R. Narayan, A.P.H. Publishing Corporation, New Delhi.

43

A STUDY ON THE ROLE OF GOVERNMENT TO MAINTAIN ENVIRONMENTAL ETHICS AN ANALYSIS

S. Vijaya Kumar

INTRODUCTION

I wonder whether the term "ethics" has any place or relevance to the modern world. Does is enjoy any respect today? Does it have meaning? Is it out dated? We do not know our goals. In fact the concept of goal itself is something unheard of in the present ties. Is prosperity or pleasant living the ultimate goal? Can we sacrifice morality, values and ethics for prosperity? This is the question that has been prevailing for several centuries. There has always been a conflict between good and bad, just and unjust, self and sacrifice, profit and legitimate earning. Even in today's fast life it looks as though all are concerned with money, more money and only money.

IMPORTANCE OF THE STUDY

In this paper an attempt is made by the author to analyse the environmental ethics in detail in different heads such as in business and society. And also an attempt is made to analyse the role played by the government to maintain environmental ethics in different situation. The dictionary meaning of ethics is science of moral values. It also means the correct knowledge of practical wisdom. Similarly environment means surroundings.

Ethics in life should start from the cradle. Mother is the first and greatest teacher to a child. The saying is "the hand that rocks the cradle rules the world". Much of the misery of the world can be attributed to our ignorance of the saying. More so to our indifference to its content. The society around us comes second. The teacher's design decides the shape of an individual and nation. Do we have any course of ethics and value based education in schools and colleges? Should not we pay more attention to this issue either in Assembly or in Parliament?

The era in which we live is coupled with unbalanced expansion of science and technology manifested in unlimited business application–science and technology have opened new doors higher to unknown, with the disregards of science and technology to environment ethics in society.

With the multiplication of the TV channels, "Ads" which are not only provocative but also display vulgarity of the third rate with no aesthetic and ethical sense, only aim at selling a product, without considering the environmental ethics. Again they only bother to catch the market and never think of the impact they are going to create on our society. Science and technology in the hands of MNC have completely reversed the value systems, ethical standards and social values.

I am shocked to see the telecast of cricket matches at different intervals. It is certainly to promote business, without considering the environmental ethics. I feel ashamed and disturbed to watch the match with children and family members when liquor advertisements glorify the habits of drinking. Liquor, condoms and Carefree may not be the right advertisements for the youth. But we have no sense of justice (or) shame in introducing these products at the wrong timeslot.

These things are developed through media. The entire environmental ethics will be spoiled in society. We need to care for our mind and for out surrounding. The former may be difficult for us. But we should do our best to keep our surrounding free from pollution.

The surroundings are important to us. Clean surroundings keep us in good health, whereas today the people pollute the surroundings in the following ways:

– Many people throw the garbage on the street. In turn it pollutes the land, air and water.
– the municipal drainage is let into the river and lakes. This pollutes our drinking water and agricultural lands.
– The factories let their wastes into the river; lakes (or) open land. This pollutes the rivers, lakes and wells.
– Factory smoke and the smoke from the vehicles on the roads pollute air.
– Spitting in public places also causes some diseases.

REMEDIAL MEASURES TO MAINTAIN IN ENVIRONMENTAL ETHICS CLEAN

1. We must put all garbage in the dustbin. The municipal staff should clear the dustbin daily.
2. The municipal drainage water should be taken to a place far away from the town. There it should be cleaned and used to grow trees, grass etc.
3. Factories should recycle the waste.
4. Factories should remove the dust from the smoke. Motor vehicles should be kept in good condition. This will reduce pollution.
5. Adequate spittoons should be provided invariable at all public places. If any one fails to use spittoons he she should be severely punished.
6. Separate law should be enforced to maintain environmental ethics in business. If any one acts against the rules and regulations imposed by the government he/ she should be punished.

Apart from these, sometimes-environmental ethics may be spoiled in out society due to some grievances. In democratic country every citizen must be given the opportunity to ventilate their grievances against the officials and policies.

GRIEVANCES AND ENVIRONMENTAL ETHICS

Grievances may be divided into three categories, they are

Grievances Against Polices: Citizens may have grievances against certain Government policies, adversely affecting the interests of some organised groups of people. This provides them with grounds to complain about the Government policies. To get the policies modified, citizens pressure the Government with the help of certain pressure and interest groups. For this purpose, they make use of various techniques. To avoid any confrontation, policies should appropriate serving the general interests of all sections of the society.

At the time of framing policies, the policy makers should adhere to the policy of protecting the common interest of the citizens. Whenever any grievances arised, it should be death with by the authorities with utmost integrity and they should be impartial. In turn we can maintain a very good environmental ethics in society.

Grievances Against Misadministration: It is widely expected that the policies ought to be implemented efficiency but cumbersome procedures and inadequate administrative processes may cause resentment between the recipient and beneficiaries. Many grievances also rise because of the inefficiency or delays caused by the workload of the officials. Moreover, the nature of public complaint is found to be closely linked with the nature of duties that the officials have been assigned. The official should have the mind and interest in settling the grievances of the citizens, without misusing their powers and expecting any thing from the public. Then only the environmental ethics in society may consider as good.

Grievances Against Corruption: It has been observed that honesty and integrity in both policies and administration are deteriorating. Generally, it is felt that nothing can be achieved through straightforward and honest ways and means; this may result in lack of confidence in the administration. Every Government department has become a den of corruption. It has increased to such an extent that people have started losing faith in the integrity of the administration. In this way, the prevalence of corruption also became an important factor responsible for providing grounds for complaint. Every Government employee should discharge their duties efficiently, because they are the servants of the citizens of the country.

ENVIRONMENTAL ETHICS IN FUNDAMENTAL RIGHTS

In Part III the Constitution grounds to the citizens of India certain fundamental rights. These rights are necessary for the development of the individual and for the promotion of his/her dignity and welfare. The rights are justifiable and can be enforced through the courts. However, Government can impose reasonable restrictions on the rights; the courts can decide the reasonableness of the restrictions.

CLASSIFICATION OF RIGHTS

The original constitution granted seven categories of fundamental rights; however, in 1979, the 44th Amendment removed the right to property from this list, making it merely a legal right. Hence, at present there are only six categories of rights, which are as follows:

- *Right to Equality (Articles 14-18):* Equality of opportunity in matters of public employment is also ensured. However, the State has the right to make special provisions for women, and backward classes, most backward classes, SC and ST. The selection for employment must be fair and honest. But, now a day, the process of selection is being made with money, political pressure. Favouritism and nepotism are process of selection is being made with money, political pressure. Favouritism and nepotism are exercised while filling up vacancies in the public sector undertaking even in the private sectors too.
- *Right to Freedom (Article 19-22):* Freedom of speech and expression had a past, it has a present and no doubt, it will have a future, but with the passage of time, through several amendments a number of restrictions

have been paced on the exercise f these rights, which have narrowed, down their scope considerably.

Even though freedom of expression is a fundamental right, people in this democratic country are not able to express anything; otherwise they may be punished with TADA (or) POTA.

- *Right against Exploitation (Article 23-34):* It prohibits employment of children below 14 years of age in hazardous occupations. Even though provisions warne the employer, still most of the undertakings particularly in private sectors, employing child labour, without offerings adequate wage and facilities.
- *Right to Freedom of Religion (Article 25-28):* Guarantees the freedom of every citizen to progress, practice and propagate any religion. But in practice, the citizens are threatened while propagating any religious matters among the society.
- *Cultural and Educational Rights (Article 29-30):* Confer rights on every community to protect its language, script or culture; gives minorities the right to establish and administer their own educational institutions. The State does not discriminate on these issues.
- *Right to Constitutional Remedy (Article 32):* Every citizen has the right to approach the Supreme Court for the enforcement of his fundamental rights. The Supreme Court should be fair while giving verdict on complaint made by the citizens.

MACHINERY FOR THE REDRESS OF GRIEVANCES

Through Court

To redress the grievances of citizens is not an easy task. These are redressed at judicial, legislative and administrative levels. Whenever there is an attack on the fundamental rights of the citizens, they seek redressal in courts of law either through writs and injuctions or by filling some suits against the administration for violating certain rules. In this way, an aggrieved party knocks at the door of the court for the redressel of its grievances. The judicial remedies against the administration may include suits against the Government for quashing of its orders, reinstatement of employees, arrears of salaries and other damages, etc. Whenever aggrieved citizen approaches the court for verdict, the judgment given by the judge should be fair without bias.

Through Elected Representatives

Sometimes, the elected representatives, having been persuaded by the citizens, ask questions in Parliament to draw the attention of the House to a particular matter. As a result, the administration may be moved into taking action so that the grievances may be redressed. Here, the elected representatives role is most important since represent she problem of citizens in the Parliament.

Through Committees

There is another committee known as Committee on Government assurance to watch the implementation of certain promises and assurances, which are given by ministers. In addition, there has been a committee on petitioners to serve as a link between the aggrieved citizens, administration and Parliament for the purpose of examining the petitions addressed to Parliament by the citizens, either directly or through some Member of Parliament. The committee must be free from favouritism and nepotism.

Complaint Cells

Separate complaint cells have been created in various Government organizations for speedy disposal of public complaints. The specially designated officers head these cells. The State Governments also appoint high-powered senior officers at different levels to deal with complaints of corruption, lack of integrity and abuse of power on the part of their officials.

But the appointment of grievance officers within the administrative units has, by large, failed to achieve reduction in the area of citizens' grievances, with their primary obligation to their own colleagues or superior and not to the citizen. The grievance officers have been reluctant or otherwise unable to penetrate the defenses that the bureaucracy tends to generate for its own protection. Here the grievance officers should take stringent action against the person who is reluctant in their duties.

Agency for SC and ST

There is also another agency for redressel of grievances of the SC/ST. Under the Constitution, the commissioner is appointed by the government to evaluate the implementation of safeguards provided for this Section. The Commissioner should see, whether the facilities given by the Government have finally reached these sections. Effective follow up action is very important to redress the grievances of these citizens.

CONCLUSION

In the concluding observation, we may say that several steps have been taken by the Governments to redress the grievances of the citizens and also to maintain environmental ethics in society. But success in this ultimately depends on the sincere efforts, proper and adequate support, effective implementation of remedial steps and follow-up action. The need of the hour is to revamp the activities of the institutions and agencies engaged in the redressing citizens grievances. The sincere and full involvement of citizens is also required, they should avoid creating false implications and should come forward only with genuine complaints/grievances.

REFERENCES

D. Veerendra Heggade (1998), "Etics in Business and Management", Forum of Free Enterprise, Mumbai.

S.N. Chaturved (1966), "Machinery for Redress of Citizen's Grievances", Indian Journal of Public Administration, Vol.XII, No.1, July-September, p.36.

R. Dhillon (1993), "Foundation Course in General Studies", Dhillon Group of Publication, New Delhi.

44

POSITIVE ROLE OF ENVIRONMENTAL POLICIES IN SUSTAINABLE DEVLOPMENT: A NOTE

C. Basavaiah, P. Kodandarami Reddy

INTRODUCTION

The World Commission on Environment and Development (WCED) foresaw the possibility for a new era of Economic growth, based on policies that sustain and expand the environmental resource base. The Commission was chaired by Mrs. Gro Harlem Brundtland of Norway, who defined that environment as "Where we all live" and development as "What we all do" in attempting to improve our lot within that abode. After nearly three years of analysis by experts, an exhaustive review of documents, public hearings at eight sites throughout the world, and careful consideration of the evidence, the Brundtland Commission called for action to break out past patterns, seek security through change, reduce risks to survival and put future development on paths that are sustainable. In 1987 the United Nations General Assembly endorsed the Commission Report, Our Common Future, and requested all Organisations affiliated with the United Nations to follow up its recommendations.

DEVELOPMENT OF ENVIRONMENTAL ECONOMICS

Environmental stress and strains are now ubiquitous phenomena appearing in all economic systems, regardless of political ideology, from the very poorest to the very rich. Despite the impression given in some of the environmental literature, environmental degradation is not the unique attribute of advanced Western Industrial Capitalism. Eastern bloc economies face acute water and air pollution threats, notable examples being river water pollution in many industrial areas of Poland and declining urban air quality levels in industrial Zechoslovakia. The Soviet environment has suffered from a catalogue of pollution abuses over a long period of heavy industrialization. Pollution there now threatens even the most precious of bio-spherical assets such as Lake Baikal. Among the developing economies, air pollution in cities such as Caracas, Mexico city and Sao Paulo is extremely severe and poses a significant health hazard. For the group of Thirty six (the poorest countries of the earth) their very poverty is a major cause and effect of environmental problems. Poverty which denies poor people the means to act in their own long term interest, creates environmental stress (Such as overgrazing of rangeland, soil erosion and eventual desertification) leading to resource degradation.

ECONOMIC AND ENVIRONMENTAL VALUES

The environmental literature has identified three basic value relationships which seem to underlie the policy and ethics adopted in society. Values expressed via individual preferences, public preference value which finds expression via social norms, and functional physical ecosystem value. Some writers argue that economic value measures are context specific assigned values and may therefore be inappropriate as the sole value measures for public resource allocation. Eco-centric ideologies seek to base policy on social norms that individuals accept as members of a community (public preferences) and that are operationalized via social legislation. Deep ecology advocates place primary emphasis on a distinction between instrumental value (expressed via human held values) and intrinsic, non-preference related value. They lay particular stress on the argument-that functions and potentials of ecosystems themselves are rich source of intrinsic value. This value would, it is argued, exist even if humans and their experiences were extinct. Human may capture part of the intrinsic value in their preferences, eg. Valuing on behalf of other species. Economists use the term existence value to encompass these notions.

Economic research into the monetary valuation of environmental commodities is still in a state of flux, although considerable progress has been made. In the absence of a demand curve and market price for many environmental commodities a number of non-market methods for estimating value has been devised. For value data collection techniques - Travel cost method, participation/unit-day value method, hedonic pricing and contingent valuation have been extensively tested. A growing literature has suggested that non-use values (bequest and existence values) and option value should be counted as part of the total economic value of the natural resource.

LINKAGE BETWEEN POVERTY AND ENVIRONMENT

It is clear that low levels of income by themselves do not lead inexorably to degradation of the environment. For centuries population in many parts of the world lived in harmony with their natural environment. Environmental degradation and the disinterpretation of traditional social systems have generally occurred in response to outside pressures of different kinds. For example in recent decades rapid declines in mortality rates occurred which were not accompanied by declining fertility rates. This imbalance created pressures on the natural resource base which were not immediately matched by the expansion of production capabilities through new technology, investment, or efficiency through specialization and reorganization.

Poverty as such can not be said to cause environmental degradation, however, often the two are associated with each other. It is the failure of policies to adapt to new circumstances that is a common cause of these two. As change occurs, it leaves behind winners and loosers; typically the loosers have few choices available and are forced to adopt short term survival strategies under which longer term resource management considerations appear to be an unaffordable luxury.

DECENTRALIZATION OF ADMINISTRATION AND PLANNING

It is becoming more and more evident that poverty eradication and resource conservation measures are location specific activities. Pressures on natural resources are strongly interlinked with local production systems. Poverty eradication requires a clear understanding of local environmental and socio economic characteristics and local opportunities. Problems of implementation have been quite apparent even in well-designed programmes handled by otherwise competent central level institutions. The Integrated Rural Development Programme in Nepal is a case in point. Obviously, there are serious limitations in the technical capacities of local organizations also, many so called local institutions are only agents of central level institutions. The important point being emphasized in that programmes designed at the centre and implemented by the centre have not succeeded in the fields of poverty eradication and resource conservation. What is needed is to provide greater opportunities for local people to organize their own management systems. Outside support should be provided selectively in full awareness of the limited extent to which it can be sustained without becoming outside interference.

THE NEED FOR NEW APPROACHES TO INTEGRATED PLANNING

The WCED Report has emphasized the need for the new approaches to environment and development. A selection of quotations serves to illustrate WCED recommendations on this issue. "Environment and development are not separate challenges; They are inexorably linked... in a complex system of cause and effect". "Environmental stresses and patterns of economic development are linked one to another ... agricultural policies ... energy policies... Thus economic policies and ecology must be completely integrated in decision making and law making not just to protect the environment but also to protect and promote.

"In the past responsibility for environmental matters has been placed in environmental ministries and institutions that often have had little or no control over destruction caused by agricultural, industrial, Urban development, Forestry and transportation policies and practices.

Society has failed to give the responsibility for preventing environmental damage to the "Sectoral" ministries and agencies whose policies cause it. Thus our environmental management practices have focused largely upon after-the-fact repair of damage: reforestation, reclaiming desert lands, rebuilding urban environments, restoring natural habitats and rehabilitating wild lands. The ability to anticipate and prevent environmental damage will require that the ecological dimensions of policy be considered at the same time as the economic, trade, energy, agricultural and other dimensions".

CONCLUSION

"What is required is a new approach in which all nations aim at a type of development that integrates production with resource conservation and enhancement, and that links both the provision for all of an adequate livelihood and equitable access to resources. Physical sustainability can not be secured. Unless development policies pay attention to such considerations as changes in access to resources and in the distribution of costs and benefits".

REFERENCES

David W. Pearce and R. Kerry Turner (1990), "Economics of Natural Resources and the Environment", Harvester Wheatsheaf, New York.

Asian Development Bank (1990), "Economic Policies for Sustainable Development", Manila.

World Bank (1992), "World Development Report", Oxford University Press, New York, Washington, D.C. U.S.A.

45

LAW AND ENVIRONMENT

M. Rajasekhara Babu

One of the banes of the modern civilization and industrialisation has been the imbalance in the ecological and natural environment of the earth. This imbalance has been aggravated by the explosion in population. This environment pollution problem is in fact a world wide one and questions are being asked every where about the future of man kind if such hazards are not checked without delay. It has posed the highest threat to human existence at present, though the problem of solution of environment is as old as the emergence of "homo sapiens" on the planet and it was realized in the times of plato 2500 years ago[1]. The introduction of man into any part of the environment of waste matter or surplus energy, which so changes the environment as directly or indirectly adversely to effect the opportunity of men to use or enjoy it[2]. The problem though, is not new but it is more relevant now than ever before in view of the imperative need for urgent solution.

The advancement in the field of science and technology, apart from urban industrialization, has been responsible for the present crisis of environmental pollution. There are various ways in which environment gets polluted. Water source is one of the hazards, which has a direct bearing on public health.

The instinct of self-preservation is inherent in men and it motivates them to lay down certain rules and to take corresponding measures in an attempt to protect public health.

This paper attempts to study

- The legislation preventing pollution
- The Water (Prevention and Control of Pollution) Act, 1974.

LEGISLATION PREVENTING POLLUTION

In recent years, the law relating to environmental pollution and human environment has come to be called conceptually as a separate system of "Environmental Law". However, in truth laws have been in existence for a long time, which cover a wide range of subjects like protection of public health, allocation of natural resources, resource management and conservation of resources. The 42nd Amendment Act clearly spelt out in the amendment to the preamble the concept of socialism. In the socialism pattern of society, the bestows place more attention on the social problems, than any individual problem, and the pollution is one of them.

Directive Principle

One of the directive principles added by the 42nd Amendment Act provides for the protection and improvement of environment. Article 47 provides for the improvement of public health as one of the primary duties of the State. Article 48 says "the State shall endeavour to protect and improve the environment. It uses the word "environment" which means the aggregate of all the external conditions and influences effecting life and development of organs of human beings, animals and plants. Article 51(g) specially deals with the fundamental duty with respect to environment.

State Control and Regulation of Pollution

- IPC-1872 section 277 of the code says who ever voluntarily corrupts or fouls the water of any spring or reservoir, so as to render it less fit for the purpose for which it is ordinarily used shall be punished with imprisonment of either description for a term which may extend to three months or with fine which extend to 500 rupees or with both. Pollution of water other than springs and reservoirs will be covered by section 290 of the code since pollution of public stream is a public nuisance which can be punished under the section 268. Section 426 which deals with mischief, which means destruction of any property.

- The factories act 1948: There is a provision in the Factories Act with regard to disposal of waters and effluents by factories. Section 12 provides
  - Effective arrangements shall be made in every factory for the disposal of the wastes and effluents due to the manufacturing process carried there in.
  - The state government may make rules prescribing the arrangements to be made under sub section (1). The punishments for the violation of the above provisions and the rules made there-under is imprisonment for a term which may extend to three months or fine which may extend to Rs.500 or both.

THE WATER (PREVENTION AND CONTROL OF POLLUTION ACT), 1974

The object of the Act is to prevent and control water pollution. It states that the central government has the responsibility of regulation and development of interstate rivers and valleys to the extent to which such regulation and development is declared by the parliament to be expedient in the public interest.

The Act has been passed in pursuance of clauses (1) of article 252 of the Indian Constitution. In consequence with the resolutions passed by all the houses of legislatures of the states of Assam, Bihar, Gujarat, Haryana, Karnataka, Kerala, M.P. and West Bengal. Section 4 of the Act makes a provision for the constitution of the Boards for prevention and control of water pollution both at the center and in the states. The following are the important functions, which have been entrusted under section 17 of the act to the boards.

- To plan comprehensive programme for the prevention, control or abatement of pollution of streams and wells in the state and to secure the execution there of:
- To collect and disseminate information relating this matter.
- To evolve methods, utilization of sewage and suitable trade effluents in agriculture.
- To encourage, conduct and participate in investigations and research relating to this problem.

CONCLUSION

The common law, as we have seen is inadequate and too difficult to operate in modern conditions. It may not be an exaggeration to say that in a modern society riparian rights are not practicable and therefore need to be curbed. Perhaps some amount of control is necessary to limit pollution. Our criminal laws contain provisions, which are not adequate to deal with the environmental pollutions. We may examine the feasibility of criminal sanction in addition to damages and administrative sanctions in an increasing manner to take action against massive pollution of land, water and air whether by industrial waste and effluents or by chemicals etc. It is essential that there should be effective cooperation between authorities so that a better control can be evolved for the prevention and pollution of environment. The administrators, scientists and economists etc., should make concentrated efforts to channelise their energies to meet the challenges posed by the pollution.

SUGGESTIONS

The following are the suggestions in the matter of making the pollution control program-a practical success.

1. As the success largely depends upon the proper functioning of the boards, the government should attract the best ecologists and experts as members of the boards. The work of the boards should not be handicaped for lack of financial resources.

2. The grant and renewal of industrial licenses should be made conditional on the industries satisfying the required standards in the matter of pollution control.
3. Effective pollution control demands devoted and genuine appreciation on the parts of all concerned to promote a clear environment.

REFERENCES

Hambro. E. (1974), The Human Environment- Stockholm and After, year book of world affairs 204, 206.

J. Mc Loughlin (1972), The Law Relating to Pollution.

Entry 56, List 1, Seventh Schedule of the Constitution.

Sunil Rai Chowdary (1962), Social Security in India and Bhutan.

Ramesh Chandran (1977), The World is Running Out of Water, illustrated weekly of India, April 24, page 11.

Liptak, Environmental Engineers (1974), II Handbook, Water Pollution 1956-57.

XIV Encyclopedia Britannica 750 (1974).

46

ENVIRONMENT PROTECTION MEASURES IN X PLAN

K. Vydehi

Water, Soil, Air, Biological, Forest and Fisheries resources are collectively called as environment which provider the basic life support system to us. Intensive utilization of natural resources, energy intensive industrial technology resulted in environmental degradation over the years in our country. The issue of environmental sustainability has formally entered the international agenda only after the earth summit, which was held in Rio de Janeiro in 1992. It has been ant integral part of Indian Planning and Policy making for at least two decades prior to that. The fourth five-year plan, which was launched in 1969, clearly articulated the need to harmonies our development plans with preservation of environment. Subsequent plans have reformed and given concrete shape to strategies for addressing this concern.

Environmental equality is essential for quality of life. So there is a need to improve the state of our environment for present and future generations. The concept of sustainable development has emerged as a prescription for human survival and for the maintenance of eco-system health.

ENVIRONMENTAL PROTECTION ISSUE IN X PLAN

Environmental strategies in X plan are having the following issue.

- Encouraging multi stakeholder participatory process in involving effective and efficient exchange of information.
- Supplementing command and control regime with market based economic instruments and evolving environmental markets on experimental basis within the country.
- Evolving methodology and instruments for indicators of sustainability, evolving system of incentives and accountability.
- Promote sustainable consumption levels and pattern through effective dissemination and awareness programmes, environmental consciousness, eco-labeling and packaging.
- Promote sustainable production, transportation packaging and distribution.
- Institutionalizing cross- scrotal and inter-disciplinary research and transparency in decision making to bring abroad a convergence of presently fragmental responsibility.
- Infusing cutting edge scientific and technological inputs into the sector.
- Streamlining environment and forestry clearance systems.
- Present environmental laws should be revamped with a view to make them productive, pre-people, pro-poor, pro-gender, pro-caste, pro-tribal, pro-handicapped and pro-rural and the marginalized.
- Professionalizing pollution control boarder with built in accountability.
- Evolve long-term vision and perspective on sustainable development.
- Evolve an early warming and rapid response system through strengthened meaningful comprehensive and integrated surveillance system on sustainable

development by linking health, safety and environmental and forestry monitoring networks.

ENVIRONMENTAL PROGRAMMES OF X PLAN

1. *Central Pollution Control Board (CPCB):* This board puts its focus on a few issues which govern environmental protection in view of increasing diversity of pollutants emitted from vehicular and industrial resources. Environment managerial plan would abode prepared for about 30 urban cities. Small and medium towns with tourist or religious importance should be developed as eco-cities. Other major focus areas for CPCB should be pollution control enforcement in the areas vehicular pollution, bio-medical waste management noise labeling of appliances, plastic waste management, industrial pollution control, management of municipal solid waste and mapping regional air quality.
2. *Common Effluent Treatment Plants (CETP):* Under this scheme effluent emanating from the cluster of compatible small scale industries is treated for removal of polyvalent at common effluent treatment plants which are set up by involving financial participation of promoters, central and state governments and loan if any from financial institutions waste water management and water conservation are the prime objective of CETP.

ENVIRONMENTAL MANAGEMENT IN HERITAGE AND TOURIST CENTRES

So far there are many schemes and programmes for the protection of Tajmahal. It is now proposed to select some additional heritage pilgrimage and tourist centers other than Taj and implement detailed environmental management plan at these places.

ENVIRONMENTAL HEALTH

It is scheme putting its focus on development of a National Environmental Epidemiological Studies and investigation with respect to heavily polluted areas specific pollutant, water pollution, air pollution, indoor pollution and environmental toxics, industrial accidents and urban planning and waste disposal based on these profiler, National environment health plan should be developed to mitigate effects of above.

PROMOTION OF CLEANER TECHNOLOGY

The new projects proposed under the scheme during the 10th plan for resource conservation energy efficiency and waste minimization one life cycle assessment studies for steel coal and other sectors.

- Natural resource accounting studies on the pattern of earlier studies undertaken for upper Yamuna basin.
- Inter rational policies harmonization for industry, health, tourism, transport and agriculture sectors.
- Demonstration projects like development of bamboo based composites panels in North Eastern Region.
- Setting up center of excellence for fostering the identification, verification, adoption and development of cleaner technology.

IMPACT ASSESSMENT

The new Environmental Impact Assessment (EIA) a component of World Bank has set of an environmental Information Centre (EIC), which shall cover A.P., M.P., Gujarath, Tamilnadu, Karnataka and entire country during the 10th plan there after. During the 10th plan this scheme should put its focus on chemical safety sound management of hazard our wastes.

BOTANICAL SURVEY OF INDIA (BSI)

During the 10th plan new botanical gardens would also be set up with the help of organizations coming up with suitable land for the purpose with free of cost. The thrust areas of zoological survey of India during 10th plan should be exploration survey of conservation areas including tiger reserves, taxonomic studios of faunal components, status survey of endangered species, chromosome mapping and DNA finger printing etc.,

BIOSPHERE RESERVES

This scheme puts focus on alternative livelihood options for local communicative to reduce pressure on core zone. During X plan 14 additional sites identified in different biogeography zones should be taken up for designation as additional biosphere reserves.

CONSERVATION AND MANAGEMENT OF MANGROVES CORAL REEF AND WET LANDS

During the X plan 30 identified mangroves and 4 coral reef areas are proposed to be covered for intensive conservation and management. The activities proposed are afforest ration, regeneration, community participation, promoting alternative livelihood options training and capacity building etc., conservation and management of wetland is on going scheme and shall be strengthened in the X plan by conservation and management through catchments area treatment water management and bio-diversity conservation and community participation.

BIO-DIVERSITY CONSERVATION

Thrust area during X plan should be conservation of medicinal plants, conservation and management of scared groves, conservation of costal and marine bio-diversity.

The twenty-one, thrust areas have been identified, which would guide the selection of research projects during the X plan. Stronger R&D would be encouraged on adoption of cleaner technologies for sustainable development. Efforts would be made to conserve, project and enhance. Bio-diversity in two hot areas namely eastern Himalayas. R&D would also be encouraged in other emerging and frontier area such as Persistent Organic Pollutants (POP), Climate change, Management of Hazard our waste and rehabilitation of degraded and mined eco systems including safe disposal of tailing.

ENVIRONMENTAL EDUCATION

Some of the major schemes during the 10th five year plan for imparting environmental education and creation of awareness among the general public are environment education and training, seminar, symposia, workshops and center of excellence and training involves programme like National Environment Awareness Campaign setting up of eco-clubs in schools professional management courser being offered by AICTE recognized management institution. So far eight centers of excellence have been setup supported on various area of environmental science and management.

INTERNATIONAL NETWORKING

International co-operation activities on a continuous basis to be undertaken through various bilateral and multilateral environmental efforts during the X plan. India continues to activity participate in various international meetings, conferences, relating to environment climate change biodiversity and mono trial protocol commission on sustainable development etc.,

STATE OF ENVIRONMENT REPORTS

The central aim of the scheme is assessment and introduction of corrective measure in main streaming environmental concern. With a view to improve the sustainability of the river and lake-cleaning programmer a number of institutions are proposed with an integrated and holistic approach.

NATIONAL LAKE CONSERVATION PLAN (NLCP)

Under the NLCP ten polluted urban takes have been identified for conservation and management.

GREENING INDIA

In order to achieve the national goal of 33% of land under forest tree cover it is impressive to involve the public in tree planning activities outside forest areas certainly sponsored scheme of Greening India with 100% funding is proposed to be implemented during the X plan period.

CONCLUSION

The X plan has taken the due note of the concern interim of threat to food security due to degradation of land, forest and over exploitation of ground water, lake of access of the community to basic services particularly energy, drinking water, sanitation facilities, low level of socio-economic development high incidence of unemployment, stagnant infant mortality, under nourishment and deterioration in quality of life this assumes significant importance in the participative of the growing and increasing realization for sustainable economic growth. The environmental concerns have to be integrated with poverty alleviation and economic development strategy. The X plan therefore marks a paradigm shift as it visualize that economic growth also is not alone the objective of national planning but it recognize the centrally of the enhancement of the human welfare as the determinant fact of development strategy.

REFERENCES

Draft of the X Plan, Govt. of India, New Delhi.

Article by Environment Division of Planning Commission (2003), Yojana, Jan.

Indian Survey. (Various Issues)

Kurukshetra, Govt. of India, New Delhi. (Various Issues)

Text book of Academy for Intermediate. (Various Issues)

47

GLOBAL ENVIRONMENTAL POLLUTION AND SECTORAL PLANNING

I. Annapurna

INTRODUCTION

If the development destroys the future of mankind it is meaningless to say it is an Economic Development so while considering the modernization and industrialization for luxurious living standards we must simultaneously calculate the after effects from a 1000 coming years while planning. And the industry and planners should always be ready to convert the whole infrastructure if necessary if it is harmful to nature and future of mankind. Today the global communication system has made the globe just like a village i.e., any small incidence is immediately exposed by the media and the communication network to every citizen of this world in the very next minute. The statistical data of environmental degradation, pollution and the relevant analysis is reaching every one every day. So I don't want to repeat the same. And here I want to deal only with the economic aspects of technological reformations related to the improvement of the standards of nature and life.

In the name of agricultural development we have introduced farm mechanization, chemical fertilizer, chemical pesticides and synthetic pesticides, Nuclear gene mutative technology and finally bio technological methods of disturbing and restructuring of the bio-cell. Surely every scientist knows the truth, every technique the list given above definitely destroy the ecological and biological balance of the nature and the environment. And lot of debate is going on to avert the scientific destruction of mankind and so keep the health of human being as in the past.

Another serous sector of pollution generator is the petroleum sector. It is multi fanged and multi winged. It starts polluting the places of production, transportation, refinement synthesisation and finally the consumption. At every stage minimum negligence and installing of this producer is always creating hazardous, anti human in nature results. So if we can totally replace this type of energy with other types of resources the global pollution can be reduce to its lowest level.

For Example:

- Use of hydrogen as fuel cell for motor vehicles, energization.
- Solar and Thermo Nuclear Energy for the production of electricity.
- Agricultural products like sugar cane by producer and other resin extracts of plants for production of synthetic fiber's and other materials.
- Replacing CFC's with other types of organic gases for refrigeration purpose.

Here I want to give few examples of hazardous nature of petro-chemicals. Generally the bore wells of petroleum are drilled to a depth of 2000 to 6000 meters at the time of drilling if any thing goes wrong with the locking systems of the wells there happens the most notorious blow outs which will cause destruction by fire, heat and poisonous gases destroy human, animal and vegetative structures totally around few kilometers. If it is a density inhabitant area just like coastal areas of Andhra Pradesh. The losses are enormous. There are so many blowout incidents in the history of Krishna, Godavari basin, petroleum exploration. At the time of transportation on the high seas we know that there are very large spill over from the accidents of oil tankers and thereby spooling the entire nature balance of the oceans by destroying the birds, the fish, water animals and the flora and fauna of the oceans.

At the time of refining there is very dark history of blaze outs and explosions of refineries. Ex: The Hindustan Petroleum Refinery at Vizag recently gutted away causing billions of rupees damage to the national wealth and nature.

At the time of utilization the petrol and diesel it is known fact they creates tones and tones of dangerous and pumps poisonous gases by carbon dioxide and Sulpher dioxide particularly in the metro-politan cities causing total destruction of public health.

There are hundreds of examples of catastrophe play to the nature by human beings through industrialization. The only alternate to control the pollution and destruction of nature is to change our pattern of life which we have developed from industrial revolution onwards. The industrial nations like USA and others should voluntarily came forward to invest fresh capitals on new and environmental friendly technologies fro energy productions like solar and utilization of hydrogen. Another most important sector where the developing and developed nations have to take care is waste disposal, though they are systematic waste disposal points in some places of the world, major countries are not observing any norms to dispose industrial, domestic, nuclear, thermal electrical plant waste, chemical industry waste etc. are to be dealt reminenses do not escape into the earth layers or the atmosphere.

As an economics students if we think and calculate the after effects of pollution and destruction of nature, for generations together caused by the dangerous chemical, biological and radio active disturbances. The amount of money and loss of development, loss of human element, the beauty of nature, the expenditures on medical care are inhospitable conditions of earth, amounts to more than the gains which we are estimating as profits by present day destructive activities.

Human being is a part of the beautiful and blossoming nature. The crippled inadequacies of human psychology began to destroy the warmth character of the nature into a hazardous environment in the name of development and necessity of existence. But we don't have any right to degrade and destroy the inheritance. Our prime responsibility is to transfer the peace and gay of the nature to our tomorrows generations with original condition. Though we have to keep the nature forever at its original condition living in a 21st century we cannot plan and think of our life without a single modern amenity. So we have to arrange things so that the scientific and technological development should be given priority simultaneously reconstructing the industry with appropriate modern technologies so that, we can protect and improve quality of nature, "To keep our modern happy life in a permanent rosy future".

REFERENCES

Khoshoo, T.N.(1984), "Environmental Concerns and Strategies", Indian Environmental Society.

Hutchinson, G.E. (1978), "An Introduction to Population Ecology", Yale Univ. Press, New Haven.

Strakler, A.N. and Strakler A.H. (1974), "Introduction to Environmental Science", Hamilton Publishing Co., Barbara, California, USA.

48

LAW AND ENVIRONMENTAL SAFETY

D. Nageswara Rao

INTRODUCTION

A country's environmental problems are affected by the level of its economic development, the availability of natural resources, and the life-style of its population. Poverty presents special problems for a heavily-populated country with limited resources. Environmental problems have become serious in many parts of the country, and can no longer be neglected. The main environmental problems in India relate to air pollution, water pollution etc. Particularly in the metropolitan and industrial zones, degradation of common property resources which affect the poor adversely due to a degeneration of their life support system, threat to biodiversity and inadequate system of solid waste disposal and sanitation with consequent adverse impact on health, infant mortality and birth rate. These problems impose a serious cost on society, but we do not have a satisfactory system of accounting for costs of degradation of environment and natural resources. Thus, we know the environmental legal procedure and the various laws to control the environment pollution. Against, this background an attempt has been made in the present paper to highlight the environmental laws and its implications in the society.

ENVIRONMENT

According to section 2(a) of the environmental protection Act - 1986 'environment' includes

- water, air and land and
- the inter-relationship which exists among and between.
- water, air and land and
- human beings, other living creatures, plants, micro-organisms and property.

The different statutes/legislations enacted in India exclusively for environment protection are :

- The water (prevention and control of pollution) Act 1974.
- The Air (prevention and control of pollution) Act 1981
- The environment protect Act, 1986
- The Forest conservation Act, 1980
- The wildlife protection Act, 1972
- The Public Liability Insurance Act, 1991, etc.

LAWS ENACTED BEFORE AND AFTER INDEPENDENCE

There are about two hundred laws dealing with environmental protection both before and after independence in India. However, the pre-independence laws have not dealt with environmental protection exclusively. For example, the Indian Penal Code (IPC) 1860 had a chapter (Chapter XIV) which deals with offences affecting the public health, safety and convenience, which covered aspects like water, air, and noise pollution whereas some of the post-independence laws like those mentioned above deal exclusively with environmental protection.

THE INDIAN PENAL CODE FOR ENVIRONMENTAL PROTECTION

The Indian Penal Code has a chapter on offences affecting the public health, safety, convenience (Chapter XIV). Sec. 268 provides that "a person is guily of a public nuisance who does any act or is quality of an illegal omission which causes any common injury, danger or annoyance to the public or to the people in general who dwell or occupy property in the vicinity, or which must necessarily cause injury, obstruction, danger or annoyance to persons who may have occasion to use any public right. In case of public nuisance the penal code provides fine upto Rs.200/- by way of punishment (sec. 290 IPC) and for making the atmosphere noxious to health Rs.500/- only (Sec. 78 IPC). The punishment is too meagre to meet the objectives. With these Penal provisions it is not possible to check environmental pollution. Therefore, it is an inadequate measure.

RESPONSIBILITY OF GOVERNMENT TOWARDS ENVIRONMENTAL PROTECTION

The states responsibility with regard to environmental protection has been laid down under article 48-A of our constitution as "the State shall endeavor to protect and improve the environment and to safeguard the forests and wildlife of the country.

CITIZENS RESPONSIBILITIES

Environmental protection has been made a fundamental duty of every citizen of this country under article 51A(g) of our constitution "It shall be the duty of every citizen of India to protect and improve the natural environment including forests, lakes, rivers and wildlife and to have compassion for living creatures.

IMPORTANCE OF THE 42ND AMENDMENT OF INDIAN CONSTITUTION

The importance of 42nd Amendment to the Constitution brought about in the year 1974 is that it has inserted two new articles namely Act 48A and Act 51A(g) the former under Directive principles of state policy making it the responsibility of the state governments to protect and improve the environment and to safeguard the forests and wild life of the country and making it the fundamental duty of every citizen to protect and improve the natural environment including forests, lakes, rivers and wildlife.

WATER PREVENTION AND CONTROL OF POLLUTION ACT 1974

"Pollution" means such contamination of water or such alteration of the physical, chemical or biological properties of water or such discharge of any sewage or trade effluent of any other liquid, gaseous or solid substance into water.

IMPORTANCE OF SECTION 24 OF THE WATER ACT 1974

According to section 24 of the water act, 1974 no person should knowingly cause or permit any poisonous, noxious or polluting matter determined in accordance with such standards as may be laid down by the state board to enter (whether directly or indirectly) into any stream or well or sewer or on land or no person shall knowingly cause or permit to enter into any stream any other matter which may tend, either directly or on combination with similar matters, to impede the proper flow of the water of the stream in a manner leading or likely to lead a substantial aggrieved of pollution due to other causes or of its consequence.

PENALTY FOR CONTRAVENTION OF PROVISIONS OF SEC. 24

Contravenes of the provisions of sec.24 shall be punishable with imprisonment for a term which shall not be less than one year and six months but which may extend to six years and with fine (After amendment Act of 1977)

AIR PREVENTION AND CONTROL OF POLLUTION ACT 1981

"Air Pollution" means the presence in the atmosphere of any air pollutant. It means any solid, liquid or gaseous substance (including noise) present in the atmosphere in such concentration as may be or tend to be injurious to human beings or other living creatures or plants or property or environment. The objective of this act is to provide for the prevention, control and abatement of air pollution, for the establishment, with a view to carrying out the aforesaid purposes.

PENALTIES FOR VIOLATION OF THE AIR ACT-1981

Whoever fails to comply with the provisions of section 21 or section 22 or directions issued under section 31-A, shall, in respect of each such failure, be punishable with imprisonment for a term which shall not be less than one year and six months but which may extend to six years and with fine, and in case the failure continues, with an additional fine which may extend to five thousand rupees for every day during which such failure continues after conviction for the first such failure. And also government departments, companies be also prosecuted under the Air Act secs. 40,41.

AUTOMOBILE POLLUTION UNDER THE MOTOR VEHICLES ACT, 1988

"Automobile" means any vehicle powered either by any method or generating power to drive such vehicle by brining fuel. As regards power to give instructions for ensuring standards for emission from automobiles, section 20 of the Act lays down that with a view to ensuring that the standards for emission of air pollutants from automobiles laid down by the State Board under clause (f) of subsection (1) of section 17 are complied with, the State Board, give such instruction as may be deemed necessary to the concerned authority in-charge of registration of motor vehicles under the 'Motor Vehicles Act' 1988, and such authority shall not withstanding anything contained in that act or the rules made there under be found to comply with such instructions.

FOREST CONSERVATION ACT-1980

It is well known that breaking up of the soil on the clearing of the forest land seriously affects regeneration of forest and, therefore, such breaking up of the soil can only be permitted after taking into consideration all aspects of the question, such as, the overall advantages and disadvantages to the economy of the country, environmental conditions, ecological imbalance, that is, likely to occur, its effects on the flora and fauna in the area etc. It was, therefore, thought that the entire control of forest areas should vest in the central government. With that end in view Sec. 2 provided that prior approval of the Central Government should be obtained before permitting the use of the forest land for non-forest purpose.

SECTION 29 PROTECTED FORESTS

The State Government may, by notification in the official Gazette declare the provisions of this chapter applicable to any forest-land or waste-land which is not included in a reserved forest, but which is the property of the government or over which the government has proprietary rights, or to the whole or any part of the forest produce of which the government is entitled. The forest-land and waste-land comprised in any such notification shall be called a "protected forest".

THE WILDLIFE PROTECTION ACT-1972

According to the Wildlife protection Act-1972 "Wild Life" includes any animal, bees, butterflies, crustaceans, fish and moths; and aquatic or land vegetation which forms part of any habitat. The Wild Life Protection Act was passed by the Indian Parliament in the year 1972 to protect India's Wildlife. The growing consumer society and the increasing emphasis on luxury and vanity items has also caused the exploitation of wildlife in the name of industrial progress.

The major task of protecting the wildlife cannot be handled by the government machinery alone through its limited officials, but should be the duty of every individual. This was one of the reasons why a new provision, Article 51A(g), was inserted into our constitution.

CONCLUSION

There are about two hundred laws dealing with environmental protection both before and after independence in India. The Environmental Protection Movement should be strengthened as it improves the country's economic and industrial development. The duty of every citizen of India to protect and improve the natural environment including forests, lakes, rivers and wildlife and to have compassion for living creatures.

Further, a fundamental principle of law is that every person ought to know the law and that is why it is said, "Ignorance of Law is Not Excusable".

REFERENCES

Desh Bandhu Ekalavya Chouhan (1979), "Current Trends in Indian Environment", Today and Tomorrow Printers and Publishers, New Delhi.

Karpagam M. (2002), "Environmental Economics", Sterling Publishers.

Planning Commission, Government of India, Economic Survey 2000-01 to 2001-02.

Timmy Katyal and M. Satrake (1990), "Environmental Pollution", Annual Publications, New Delhi.

49

ENVIRONMENT AND DEVELOPMENT – SOME ISSUES

B. Saaranga Paani

Over the years, India has become a home to one of the most degraded environments in the World. About half of India's land i.e., 130 millions hectares is affected by soil erosion. The drought prone areas have gone up from 55.3 million hectares in 1974 to 74.6 million hectares in 2005. This means 29 percent of India's land, which is used for biomass production, is degraded in just two decades. Deforestation is drying up water sources and is threatening the livelihoods of people. Non-forest timber produce provides upto 50 percent of income to about 30 percent of rural people. Due to Deforestation, nearly 400 millions are losing their primary sources of livelihood. The Common Property Resources (CRPs) on which people depend for survival are fast depleting. In 1900, the CRPs comprised about 44 percent of the geographical area. Today they comprise just 15 percent of the area. The CPRs are declining by 1.9 percent every year bringing half of the rural households in the country close to starvation.

Industrial pollution is threatening the country. A million people die each year due to water pollution. One lakh people are estimated to die each year due to air pollution. Tens of millions of people are suffering from high rates of illness and poor quality of life because of various forms of pollutions. Tens of thousands of marginalized people are losing their sources of livelihood every year due to environmental degradation and displacement from their traditional habitats due to construction of big dams, industrialization, indiscriminate mining etc.

APPROACHES TO THE PROBLEM

Some have tried to explain environmental degradation in terms of a neo-Malthusian framework. In the neo-Malthusian framework, environmental degradation is the net result of population explosion. The sheer increase in the numbers would become a burden on the scarce natural resources and hence degradation. However the neo-Malthusian approach ignores the aspects of structural inequality and political economy origins of environmental degradation.

According to some others, the very model of growth, which we have adopted, results in environmental degradation. The western model of economic growth is both resource and capital intensive. The resource intensity of the model results in the mobilization and use of natural and energy resources on a massive scale. This in turn leads to enormous amounts of pollution and degradation of natural resources. As more matter is extracted by the production process, more waste is generated which must eventually be returned to the environment since the matter and energy content of extracted matter cannot be destroyed. In other words economic growth, which results in increased extraction of material and energy resources, must produce an equivalent increase in residuals output.

According to some economists, the current rates of pollution and environmental degradation can be traced to the peculiar character of dominant social order–capitalism. Capitalism, propelled by the dictates of capital accumulation, attempts a qualitative transformation of nature. The complexity of nature and its innumerable linkages are broken down in the process of capital accumulation and the environmental goods, which are free gifts of nature are transformed into economic goods.

For example, with the penetration of capital into plant breeding industry, the unity between seed as grain and means of production has been broken with the help of science of hybridization. Terminator seeds are a classical example of the signature of capital on the gene. Terminator seeds dispossess the primary producer from the ownership and control over seeds. The seed now becomes an input regulated by the laws of market and ultimately the accumulation imperative. Thus the capitalist expansion results in disarticulation - in the form of disruption to the integration of ecological processes and in the form of disruption to the livelihoods of millions of people dependent on nature.

Disarticulation, however, is not peculiar to the capitalism alone. Different social forms bring in different rates of disarticulation to their ecological contexts. With capitalism, disarticulation will be on a global scale and unprecedented. Attempts have to be made both at the global and national levels to contain the rates of disarticulation for a sustained development.

RESPONSE OF THE GOVERNMENT

However the response of the Governments in India to the problems of environmental conservation and pollution control is weak and lopsided. In the initial years of planned development, nature was treated as given, a resource to be managed through application of science and technology. It was only after the publication of Rachel Carson's Classic Silent Spring (1962) and the club of Rome Report - Limits to Growth (1972), our Policy makers have realized the importance of limits to intervention in nature.

The institutional and legal framework created over the years in the country for protecting environment was built on the western paradigm of exclusion and protectionism. The state was made responsible for every thing - protection of bio-diversity, forests, and water use, control of pollution etc. A number of legislations were made and rules and regulations were formulated as response to the enlightened public opinion and often consequent to judicial intervention. But environment administration in the country has been dismal because of the nexus between the politicians, bureaucrats and big polluters. With the result, the pollution control laws and conservation strategies largely remained on paper. The Supreme Court of India in a recent Judgment commented on the sorry state of environmental administration in India. It says "If mere enactment of laws relating to protection of environment was to ensure a clean and pollution free environment, then India would perhaps be the least polluted country in the world. But that was not so".

The governments both at the center and state levels seem to be unprepared to face the emerging challenges of ecological globalization. Ecological globalization is based on global rules that are dominated by the interest of the developed countries. Fighting unjust ecological globalization requires substantial financial and intellectual resources. We have yet to realize the gravity of the situation.

INDIAN ENVIRONMENTAL ETHIC

The major issues in our tropical, agrarian and densely populated country are around the use of renewable resources such as land, water, forest, air and seas and their conservation, than around non-renewable resources like hydrocarbons. The Indian Environmental movements have successfully highlighted the above issues. They have also highlighted the immiserisation of marginalized communities because of alienation of their livelihood resources. The environmental ethic in India is different from that of the developed countries. It is a pro-poor, human centered environmental ethic compared to the nature centered environmental ethic espoused by the Greens of the West. Thus the Indian environmental movements have been built on the concept of 'Utilitarian Conservatism' in contrast to the 'Protectionist Conservatism'. Utilitarianism with respect to environment emphasizes the well being people attain from environment, whether it be materialistic or spiritual, instrumental or intrinsic.

Millions of people in India are dependent on nature and denial of access to the products of nature threatens the sources of livelihoods of these people. Hence the issues of equity and social justice play a crucial role in Indian ecological imagination.

The popular environmental struggles in India such as Chipko Movement against deforestation in Himalayas, Narmada Bachavo Andolan, Tehri and Koel Karo – resistance movements against big dams, Chilka Andolan against shrimp farming by the Tatas in the Chilka lake are all about protecting the livelihood interests of the Adivasis and other marginalized communities.

ENVIRONMENTAL SUSTAINABILITY

Environmental Sustainability has been defined by the World Commission on Environment and Development (1987) as "development that meets the needs of the present generation with out compromising the ability of future generations to meet their owns". Achieving sustainability involves achieving equity both within generations and across generations. According to the Commission equity between generations and across generations are equally important.

The debate on sustainability has focused on two key aspects

1. The degree to which natural capital can be replaced by human capital and
2. The obligations the present generation owes to future generations.

Natural capital can be exploited by man but cannot be created by man. Natural capital and man made capital in most cases are compliments rather than substitutes. Prof. Christensen terms the various elements of natural capital stock 'primary inputs' and man made capital and labor as 'agents of transformation'. While substitution possibilities are high within each of these two groups, substitution possibilities between the two are very low. The degree of substitutability between inputs derived from environment, man made capital and the human capital is considered very limited and hence growth has 'limits'.

In view of the above, four operation principles for sustainable development have been suggested by Prof. Daly. These are –

1. Setting all harvest levels at less or equal to the population growth for some predetermined size in the case of renewable resources.
2. Establishing assimilative capacities for eco-systems and maintain waste discharges below these levels and setting the cumulative pollutants close to zero.
3. Dividing the receipts from non-renewable resource extraction into an income stream and an investment stream. The investment stream has to be invested in renewable substitutes and only the income stream should be available for consumption.
4. Minimizing the matter energy used in the economy. Such controls must be quantitative and aimed at population levels and resource use.

Besides in the Indian context, the environmental sustainability demands creation of a political order in which the control of natural resources rests with the local community. A typical Indian village is built around gross nature product. The Indian villages share a complex, yet fragile ecological equation with both private and common resources. The decline of common resources is bringing misery to millions of people in the country.

Both the central and State Governments are currently spending Rs.40,000 crores annually on poverty alleviation programs. It is now well established that environmental degradation results in poverty. Yet the anti poverty programs fail to understand the crucial linkages between ecology and poverty.

They are not providing ecological security. With the result, the poor are now totally dependent on Government Programs. In view critical linkages between ecology and poverty, efforts should be made to create and build ecological capital in the villages. It solves the twin problems of poverty and environmental degradation.

For this purpose the current legal and institutional framework will have to be changed to give people access and control over their immediate resources. The environment is not about planting trees or protecting tigers. But it is about deepening democracy. The long term economic and ecological interests of the country will be served better by the involvement and participation of the community in the conservation and management of environment.